MULTICULTURAL EDUCATION SERIES

James A. Banks, *Series Editor*

(continued)

Race Frameworks

A Multidimensional Theory of Racism and Education

ZEUS LEONARDO

TEACHERS COLLEGE PRESS

TEACHERS COLLEGE | COLUMBIA UNIVERSITY

NEW YORK AND LONDON

A earlier version of the second half of Chapter 1 first appeared as Leonardo, Z. (2012). The race for class: Reflections on a critical raceclass theory of education. *Educational Studies, 48*(5), 427–499. Reprinted by permission of Taylor and Francis.

An earlier version of Chapter 5 first appeared in Leonardo, Z. (2011). After the glow: Race ambivalence and other educational progrnoses. *Educational Philosophy and Theory, 43*(6), 675–698. Reprinted by permission of Taylor and Francis.

Published by Teachers College Press, 1234 Amsterdam Avenue, New York, NY 10027

Library of Congress Cataloging-in-Publication Data

Leonardo, Zeus, 1968–
    Race frameworks : a multidimensional theory of racism and education / Zeus Leonardo.
        pages cm
    Includes bibliographical references and index.
    ISBN 978-0-8077-5462-7 (pbk. : alk. paper)
    ISBN 978-0-8077-5463-4 (hardcover : alk. paper)
        1. Racism in education–United States. 2. United States–Race relations.
    3. Critical theory. I. Title. II. Series: Multicultural Education Series.
    LC212.2.L48 2013
    371.82900973–dc23   2013015700

ISBN 978-0-8077-5462-7 (paper)
ISBN 978-0-8077-5463-4 (hardcover)

Printed on acid-free paper
Manufactured in the United States of America

For my Tatay,
Jesus F. Leonardo

Contents

Series Foreword

Race still casts a long, formidable, and intricate shadow on U.S. society writ large and on its schools, colleges, and universities. In the two elections of the nation's first African American president in 2008 and 2012–which many commentators interpreted as the beginning of a post-racial period in the United States–the manifestations of race were explicit, cogent, and strident. In the 2012 election, 93% of African Americans, 71% of Hispanics, and 73% of Asian Americans voted for Obama, while 59% of Whites voted for Romney (Roper Center, 2012). The large percentage of Jewish people who voted for Obama in 2012 (69%) (Stone, 2013) indicates how race intersects with many other factors when people vote. While President Obama was presenting a major speech on health care on September 9, 2009, Congressman Joe Wilson, a Republican from South Carolina, yelled out "You Lie!" Some observers viewed Wilson's behavior as a racialized response to the nation's first African American president.

This astute and skillfully crafted book is timely and significant because of the persistence and complexity of race in American society and in other nations around the world (Banks, 2009). Most books on race describe one theory or framework for understanding race, such as Critical Race Theory or Cultural Studies. In this book, Zeus Leonardo makes an original, unique, and needed contribution to the literature on education and race by providing a sophisticated analysis and critique of four frameworks for understanding and studying race: Critical Race Theory, Marxism, Whiteness Studies, and Cultural Studies. In the concluding chapter, Leonardo describes a multidimensional theory of race, which he derives from his synthesis and critique of the four theoretical frameworks discussed in the previous chapters.

This erudite, incisive, and rigorously researched book will help teachers and other educational practitioners to examine and to better understand the structural factors in American society that result in racialization and racial hierarchies, and to use their enhanced comprehensions to implement actions that can help make their schools, colleges, and universities less racialized and more empowering for students from diverse racial, cultural, ethnic, and language groups. In less racialized and more culturally responsive educational environments (Au, 2011; Gay, 2010), students from diverse groups are more likely to attain cultural recognition (Gutmann, 2004) and empowerment, and to increase their academic skills. Reforming the structure of schools to make them less racialized and more culturally empowering will greatly benefit students from diverse groups, which are rapidly growing in our nation's schools.

American classrooms are experiencing the largest influx of immigrant students since the beginning of the 20th century. Almost 14 million new immigrants–both documented and undocumented–settled in the United States between 2000 and 2010. Less than 10% came from nations in Europe. Most came from Mexico and nations in Asia, Latin America, the Caribbean, and Central America (Camarota, 2011). A large but undetermined number of undocumented immigrants enter the United States each year. The U.S. Department of Homeland Security (2010) estimated that in January 2010, 10.8 million undocumented immigrants were living in the United States–a decrease from the January 2007 estimate of 11.8 million. In 2007, approximately 3.2 million children and young adults were among the 11.8 million undocumented immigrants living in the United States, most of whom grew up in the this country (Perez, 2011). The influence of an increasingly ethnically diverse population on U.S. schools, colleges, and universities is and will continue to be enormous.

Schools in the United States are more diverse today than they have been since the early 1900s when a multitude of immigrants entered the United States from Southern, Central, and Eastern Europe. In the 20-year period between 1989 and 2009, the percentage of students of color in U.S. public schools increased from 32% to 45% (Aud, Hussar, Kena et al., 2011). If current trends continue, within 1 or 2 decades students of color will equal or exceed the percentage of White students in U.S. public schools. In 2010–2011, students of color exceeded the number of White students in the District of Columbia and in 13 states (listed in descending order of the percentage of ethnic minority students therein): Hawaii, California, New Mexico, Texas, Nevada, Arizona, Florida, Maryland, Mississippi, Georgia, Louisiana, Delaware, and New York (Aud, Hussar, Johnson et al., 2012). In 2009, children of undocumented immigrants made up 6.8% of students in grades kindergarten through 12 (Perez, 2011).

Language and religious diversity is also increasing in the U.S. student population. The 2010 American Community Survey indicates that approximately 19.8% of the school-age population spoke a language at home other than English (U.S. Census Bureau, 2010). The Progressive Policy Institute (2008) estimated that 50 million Americans (out of 300 million) spoke a language at home other than English in 2008. Harvard professor Diana L. Eck (2001) calls the United States the "most religiously diverse nation on earth"

(p. 4). Islam is now the fastest-growing religion in the United State, as well as in several European nations such as France, the United Kingdom, and The Netherlands (Banks, 2009; Cesari, 2004). Most teachers currently in the classroom and in teacher education programs are likely to have students from diverse ethnic, racial, linguistic, and religious groups in their classrooms during their careers. This is true for both inner-city and suburban teachers in the United States, as well as for those in many other Western nations, such as Canada, Australia, and the United Kingdom (Banks, 2009).

The major purpose of the Multicultural Education Series is to provide preservice educators, practicing educators, graduate students, scholars, and policymakers with an interrelated and comprehensive set of books that summarizes and analyzes important research, theory, and practice related to the education of ethnic, racial, cultural, and linguistic groups in the United States and the education of mainstream students about diversity. The dimensions of multicultural education, developed by Banks (2004) and described in the *Handbook of Research on Multicultural Education* and in the *Encyclopedia of Diversity in Education* (Banks, 2012), provide the conceptual framework for the development of the publications in the Series. They are content integration, the knowledge construction process, prejudice reduction, an equity pedagogy, and an empowering institutional culture and social structure.

The books in the Series provide research, theoretical, and practical knowledge about the behaviors and learning characteristics of students of color, language minority students, and low-income students. They also provide knowledge about ways to improve academic achievement and race relations in educational settings. Multicultural education is consequently as important for middle-class White suburban students as it is for students of color who live in the inner city. Multicultural education fosters the public good and the overarching goals of the commonwealth.

This book nicely complements the book by Gary R. Howard (2006) in the Multicultural Education Series, *We Can't Teach What We Don't Know: White Teachers, Multiracial Schools*. Howard's book describes ways in which teachers can experience personal transformations in order to become effective teachers in multicultural classrooms and schools. Leonardo's book provides its readers with a comprehensive description of the structural factors that cause racialization and racial hierarchies. The need for personal transformation described by Howard and the deep understanding of the structural factors illuminated by this adept and creative book provide educational practitioners with a tool kit that will help them to create just, democratic, and culturally empowering schools for all of our nation's youth.

–James A. Banks

REFERENCES

Au, K. H. (2011). *Literacy achievement and diversity: Keys to success for students, teachers, and schools.* New York: Teachers College Press.

Aud, S., Hussar, W., Johnson, F., Kena, G., Roth, E., Manning, E., Wang, X., & Zhang, J. (2012). *The condition of education 2012* (NCES 2012-045). Washington, DC: U.S. Department of Education, National Center for Education Statistics. Available at http://nces.ed.gov/pubsearch

Aud, S., Hussar, W., Kena, G., Bianco, K., Frohlich, L., Kemp, J., & Tahan, K. (2011). *The condition of education 2011* (NCES 2011-033). Washington, DC: U.S. Department of Education, National Center for Education Statistics. Available at www.nces.ed.gov/programs/coe/pdf/coe_1er.pdf

Banks, J. A. (2004). Multicultural education: Historical development, dimensions, and practice. In J. A. Banks & C. A. M. Banks (Eds.), *Handbook of research on multicultural education* (2nd ed., pp. 3–29). San Francisco: Jossey-Bass.

Banks, J. A. (Ed.). (2009). *The Routledge international companion to multicultural education.* New York and London: Routledge.

Banks, J. A. (2012). Multicultural education: Dimensions of. In J. A. Banks (Ed.), *Encyclopedia of diversity in education* (vol. 3, pp. 1538–1547). Thousand Oaks, CA: Sage Publications.

Camarota, S. A. (2011, October). A record-setting decade of immigration: 2000 to 2010. Washington, DC: Center for Immigration Studies. Available at www.cis.org/2000-2010-record-setting-decade-of-immigration

Cesari, J. (2004). *When Islam and democracy meet: Muslims in Europe and the United States.* New York: Pelgrave Macmillan.

Eck, D. L. (2001). *A new religious America: How a "Christian country" has become the world's most religiously diverse nation.* New York: HarperSanFrancisco.

Gay, G. (2010). *Culturally responsive teaching: Theory, research, and practice.* New York: Teachers College Press.

Gutmann, A. (2004). Unity and diversity in democratic multicultural education: Creative and destructive tensions. In J. A. Banks (Ed.), *Diversity and citizenship education: Global perspectives* (pp. 71–98). San Francisco: Jossey-Bass.

Howard, G. R. (2006). *We can't teach what we don't know: White teachers, multicultural schools* (2nd ed.). New York: Teachers College Press.

Perez, W. (2011). *Americans by heart: Undocumented Latino students and the promise of higher education.* New York: Teachers College Press.

Progressive Policy Institute. (2008). 50 million Americans speak languages other than English at home. Available at www.ppionline.org/ppi_ci.cfm?knlgAreaID=108&subsecID=900003&contentID=254619

Roberts, S. (2008, August 14). A generation away, minorities may become the majority in U.S. *The New York Times,* CLVII [175](no. 54,402), pp. A1 & A18.

Roper Center. (2012). US elections: How groups voted in 2012. Available at www.ropercenter.uconn.edu/elections/how_groups_voted/voted_12.html

Stone, A. (2013, May 19). Jewish vote goes 69 percent for Barack Obama: Exit polls. *Huffington Post.* Available at www.huffingtonpost.com/2012/11/07/jewish-voter-exit-polls_n_2084008.html

U.S. Census Bureau. (2008, August 14). Statistical abstract of the United States. Available at www.census.gov/prod/2006pubs/07statab/pop.pdf

U.S. Census Bureau. (2010). 2010 American community survey. Available at www.factfinder2.census.gov/faces/tableservices/jsf/pages/productview.xhtml?pid=ACS_10_1YR_S1603&prodType=table

U.S. Department of Homeland Security. (2010, February). Estimates of the unauthorized immigrant population residing in the United States: January 2010. Available at www.dhs.gov/files/statistics/immigration.shtm

Acknowledgments

I wrote this book in order to be helpful. Concerning scholars of race, and the courses we teach, I feel a strong conviction that the topic we take up is one of the most difficult of our time. Race thought is never easy—it is full of tension, ripe with contradictions, and needs all the help it can recruit. The analysis should be as complex as the topic itself.

I chose the title for this book deliberately, having been influenced by Jaggar and Rothenberg's use of multiple frames to explain gender relations in *Feminist Frameworks* (1993). As you will soon recognize, I associate myself with all four frameworks appraised here; they represent my intellectual homes. So my criticisms are internal and come from my experience of having lived in the four intellectual seasons every year. Because of this, I also have never felt quite at home with any paradigmatic study of race, preferring instead to travel among them, setting up roots for the meantime but never putting up my feet to relax long enough to remove my shoes. It has enabled me to appreciate a sense of belonging in a community without the possessiveness that may accompany this process. Perhaps I have always been like this.

Along the way, I have discovered similarly concerned people, who are comrades in the struggle to put critical education and thought at the top of the national agenda. To Michael Apple, Seehwa Cho, Henry Giroux, Gloria Ladson-Billings, Donaldo Macedo, and Peter McLaren, the way I think about education and social relations, such as race and class, would not be the same without your influence. To Eduardo Bonilla-Silva, Joe Feagin, Charles Mills, Pedro Noguera, David Roediger, and Howie Winant, thank you for your intellectual fearlessness and clarity. Having confronted your scholarship, race work became more complex for me . . . and infinitely more interesting.

The friendships I have cultivated with critical scholars convince me that we do this work to feel connected, even when geography is not convenient for us. Close to home, Ricky Lee Allen, Alicia Broderick, Kristen Buras, Roland Coloma, Ezekiel Dixon-Román, Michael Dumas, Kris Gutierrez, Sherick Hughes, Korina Jocson, Jackson Katz, Joyce King, Cheryl Matias, and

Jonathan Warren remind me that I am sane and even likeable on occasion. Across two "ponds," my brothers and sisters include Kalwant Bhopal, Dave Gillborn, Kal Gulson, Rasoul Nejadmehr, Michael Peters, John Preston, Paul Warmington, Deborah Youdell, and Michalinos Zembylas. They welcomed me into their circles as if I had been there all along.

At UC Berkeley, my students are as sharp as they come. Erica Boas, Patrick Johnson, Ellen Lin, Nicole Rangel, Jocyl Sacramento, Hoang Tran, and Mali Vafai do their best not to embarrass me in public with their smarts. My colleagues in Social and Cultural Studies in Education—Patricia Baqueda-no-López, Lisa García Bedolla, Na'ilah Nasir, and Dan Perlstein—have been my co-conspirators and consistent lunch mates. Thanks for being down the hall from me. To my colleague and elder, Michael Omi, thank you for the conversations and guidance. To my colleagues in the Critical Theory DE at UC Berkeley, particularly Marty Jay, Judith Butler, Wendy Brown, and Rob Kaufman: thanks for keeping me critical.

A special thanks goes out to my friend and mentor, Jim Banks, whose faith in my work runs as deep as his academic reputation. I owe you a debt that cannot be repaid. To my editor, Brian Ellerbeck, and his team at Teachers College Press: a huge thanks.

Finally, this book is for Maggie, Max, and Zoë, whose zest for life never puts me to sleep at night but for whom I wake up every morning.

–Z. M. L., March 2013

Introduction
Critical Frameworks on Race

This book is intended to introduce and appraise the insights gained from critical studies of race from four frameworks: Critical Race Theory, Marxism, Whiteness Studies, and Cultural Studies. It enters the mode of criticism that is central to any critical research project on education and race. By *criticism*, I mean something quite specific. Criticism exists in everyday parlance and usually is considered a negative mode of appraising an idea or proposal. In daily circles, being critical is often not welcomed. To be critical may mean:

1. urgent: as in, critical condition
2. central: critical point or idea
3. scrutinizing, discerning: criticism of a movie, art, or a book

Although criticism in the educational sense includes these common iterations, the tradition of intellectual criticism deployed here examines the limits of social thought. Educational criticism accomplishes this move by going through an interpretive exercise of a hermeneutics of suspicion as well as empathy (Leonardo, 2003; Ricoeur, 1986).

TWO ASPECTS OF CRITICISM: SUSPICION AND EMPATHY

A hermeneutics of suspicion is a project of negation insofar as it represents interpreting the distortions contained within a thought experiment. Of this mode of criticism, Marx, Freud, and Nietzsche were exemplars, even masters. However, the ultimate goal is not simply mastery but emancipation from falsehoods. The objective is less to exalt the critic or refute a set of texts, but in this book to affirm critical thought that is central to any race project. As such, I assess and appraise critical race frameworks for their ability to explain as well as incompletely capture racial phenomena. This form of criticism assumes that because race is contradictory, even critical race thought contains double binds that need to be fully worked out. This negative appraisal does not signal limitations at the level of the personal or the authorial, but rather at the social. That is, racial contradictions at the social level enter scholars' attempts to apprehend the very phenomenon they endeavor to understand. So it is arguably a commentary less on any individual thinker as on the collective project put forth, of how it may be limited by its own precepts. This is a large, if not unreasonable, claim. The collective project of race is diverse and multifaceted, and therefore resists simplification. However, in order to assess any framework's strengths as well as limitations, a reduction is unavoidable and becomes a risk in any project of criticism. Just as a chef produces a reduction to allow a flavor to infuse a dish, a critic reduces a theory to its basic components in order to objectify it for study. For the intellectual as opposed to the chef, this is a risky process but necessary in order to begin a conversation whose end is not determined.

On the other hand, a hermeneutics of empathy is an appraisal of a perspective's ability to transcend current limitations in racial understanding. Contrary to the ability of a hermeneutics of suspicion to expose the "true nature" of reality *behind* the veil, a hermeneutics of empathy unfolds the project *in front* of it. This second form of interpretation asks to what extent an intellectual project extends our understanding, even shatters and breaks through conventions to offer a new vision of the racial predicament. In this sense, the critic enters a new world through the word, hoping for a glimpse of a new word/world order. A framework is critical not only because it exposes lies and myths but equally because it makes possible a new regime of truth (Foucault, 1980). Ricoeur (1986) is instructive when he pairs a hermeneutics of suspicion with ideology critique and a hermeneutics of empathy with utopic thinking. The first is a distortion of reality as worse than exists, whereas the second represents reality as better than exists. Critical race hermeneutics is the capacity to maintain the intimate dance between social commentary marred by the effects of ideology (in its classical sense as distortion) and utopia, without which a society—or an intellectual framework—lacks direction as it flails about in search of a better condition or explanation. Both moments misrepresent race reality as it exists before human interpretation. Appraising their presence in race frameworks is part of any criticism whose goal is to shed light on what is hidden behind an explanation, as well as shining it in front for a way forward.

OVERVIEW OF THIS BOOK

Each of Chapters 1–4 in this book focuses on one of four frameworks regarding the uptake of race: Critical Race Theory (CRT), Marxism, Whiteness Studies, and Cultural Studies, in that order. The first part of each chapter introduces the framework, and the second part assesses the framework for what it illuminates about race (hermeneutics of empathy), as well as what it covers up (hermeneutics of suspicion). This organization is intended to be useful for readers who desire, in one volume, an integrated discussion of race from several theoretical traditions. It is more common for scholars to present a study of race driven from a singular theoretical perspective. This tradition has much to recommend it, not the least of which is its cohesion, but this book offers a global look at race, like a probe that makes a pass at the eight planets. In this manner, it is able to assess the larger collection of race theories, their orbits, and how they behave as a system of thought through mutual gravity and repulsion. In addition, the book problematizes theories in order to forge some critical distance from them and, in so doing, to recognize gaps and holes in the frameworks, which need to be filled through reflection.

Finally, in Chapter 5, I synthesize the four frameworks to promote what I call a Multidimensional Theory of Race, which argues nominally for integrating them into a syncretic framework for studying race, racism, and education. The chapter concludes by promoting a "race ambivalent" analysis, which affirms what may be conveniently labeled as real about race while scrutinizing what is invented about it.

Critical Race Theory

Chapter 1 begins with an introduction followed by an appraisal of Critical Race Theory in Education. As an intellectual movement, CRT was inspired by innovations in legal studies that were partly a reaction to Critical Legal Studies, a Marxist-inspired orientation, and Liberal Legal Studies. In education, CRT began in earnest when Gloria Ladson-Billings and William Tate published their article "Toward a Critical Race Theory of Education" in the *Teachers College Record* in 1995. Since then, many essays, books, and hundreds of conference presentations on CRT have streamed into the discipline of education. CRT in education is thus largely an American original, although with the publication of Gillborn's book *Racism and Education* (2008), CRT has reached across the Atlantic to the United Kingdom. The main focus of this chapter is inspired by CRT's insistence regarding the complete racialization of the educational enterprise such that race is no longer only a variable to be plugged into a research study but rather a dynamic that saturates the entire schooling process. Whereas educators commonly think of race as attached only to issues of curricular transformation led by multiculturalism, CRT argues that race and racism are implicated in every aspect of education. It is an ethos captured by Omi and Winant's (1994) phrase "racial formation," Bonilla-Silva's "racialized social system," (2005), or Mills's (1997) "racial contract." In short, Chapter 1 examines CRT's suggestion that education is itself a racial project, which cannot be easily parsed out in domain studies, such as school disciplinary policies, tracking, or curriculum transformation (although there are many good studies that attempt this).

It is worth explaining what Ladson-Billings and Tate (1995) had in mind when they wrote the essay that launched a thousand publications. To Ladson-Billings and Tate, CRT is not so much incompatible with its predecessor, multiculturalism, but represents its militant form. After a 2-decade head start, multiculturalism might be perceived as having laid the groundwork based on which CRT would start its intervention. Having been a fledgling discourse in education in the 1970s, multiculturalism challenged Eurocentrism, arguing first for a more inclusive curriculum that incorporated the achievements and contributions of non-European and non-White groups. This was considered an incendiary and unwelcomed act by pro-establishment scholars and educators, reaching the apex of its debate during the "cultural wars" of the 1990s (Symcox, 2002).

By the end of the 1990s, it seemed we had a winner and the question was no longer whether or not schools should accommodate the Multiculturalists, such as James Banks, Sonia Nieto, Carl Grant, and Christine Sleeter. The question centered on *the kind* and *amount* of multiculturalism that schools should practice (Buras, 2010). Even Eurocentrists on the Right, who argued for the centrality of "Dead White Men" in the official curriculum, did so *through* the language of diversity—that is, by including White authors as part of the overall respect for difference. Although this is not a statement about absolute victory for multiculturalism, it speaks to a new stage in the struggle for race and representation in education, particularly the moment when multicultural thought reaches common sense. The possibility of co-optation becomes real as diversity and difference are accepted as the mantra of education. One might even go as far as suggesting that multiculturalism has become hegemonic insofar as it is the dominant frame in education. Even conservatives have launched their bid for a "Rightist Multiculturalism" (Buras, 2008).

As multiculturalism shifted from a rebellious discourse in education in the 1970s, to a threatening movement in the 1980s and 1990s, and then an accepted educational agenda by the 2000s, it also gave birth to a reaction on the educational Left. Seen in this light, Critical Race Theory does not represent a break from multiculturalism but rather its extension and intensification within a color-blind era, in which CRT in legal studies was well-prepared to intervene (e.g., see Gotanda, 1995; Lopez, 2006). One of the founders of multiculturalism, James Banks, was sensitive to this development and included a chapter on CRT by Gloria Ladson-Billings (2004b) in the second edition of the *Handbook of Research on Multicultural Education.* From the other direction, the collection *Critical Pedagogy and Race*, a dialogue between

Critical Pedagogy and CRT, included a chapter by Banks on multicultural education (Leonardo, 2005a). In addition, the *Handbook* contains a chapter by Sleeter and Bernal (2004) on anti-racism, critical multiculturalism, and CRT. In particular, Sleeter has been a key figure who bridges multiculturalism with CRT. In this light, the difference between multiculturalism and CRT is not insurmountable, and each perspective developed in its specific historical context: the first as a response to Eurocentrism (J. Banks, 2005), intercultural education (C. M. Banks, 2004), and ethnic studies traditions (J. Banks, 2008); the second on the limitations of liberal and Marxist perspectives on the law (Crenshaw et al., 1995) and education (Ladson-Billings & Tate, 1995; Tate, 1997; E. Taylor, 1998). That established, there are specific discursive features that define a CRT program, as explained in the first part of Chapter 1.

The second part of the chapter performs an appraisal of CRT as a framework in education scholarship. The main points of appraisal fall within two areas. First, CRT includes a study of class disparities as part of its uptake of general inequality in education. However, it falls short of engaging the Marxist literature on the causes and effects of economic disparities. In effect, CRT grafts racial analysis onto class inequality wherein class "achieves a color" and becomes a variant of race. There are good, historical reasons why CRT avoids a deeper engagement with Marxism, such as its suspicions about the limitations of White Marxism. But it also may forsake certain insights that could help it explain racism. This portion of the chapter will determine to what extent a Black or "endarkened" Marxism, or labor-informed CRT, is possible. Second, while CRT provides a deep critique of racism, it does not do the same for the concept of "race." It leaves race largely undertheorized, which comes with two consequences: one, it may end up reifying it as natural and perpetual; and two, it does not problematize the dependency between racism and a racially organized society.

Marxism

Chapter 2 takes up the Marxist framework on race. Unlike CRT, a Marxist interpretation of education finds its inspiration in European philosophy, such as the Frankfurt School. Some Marxist theorists of racism offer fundamental challenges to race thought, arguing that "race" is unavoidably caught in a reification of what is at heart an ideological concept. In short, within this framework a critical study of race is not a study of race at all, but an analysis of class antagonism found within capitalism, which gives rise to the reality of racial division that is not caused by racial structures per se. A Marxist-inspired version of race scholarship is not a racial analysis of race but a class analysis of racialization. The first part of this chapter introduces

Marxism's contention that a theory oriented to the study of an ideological concept, such as race, cannot pass the litmus test of "critical." Instead, only a class-based analysis of race earns that title. Racism, then, is really a variant of class disparity.

Although Marxism generally is known for its critique of capitalism and priority for class struggle, it is a paradigm that includes the critical uptake of race. Because it argues for a materialist analysis of social processes, Marxism conceives of race as a social relation within a general study of economic stratification. However, because race is itself an idea, even an invention, it retains an ideological status within Marxism. That is, although race matters centrally in nations like the United States, it is not made of matter but represents an idea. Far from being dismissive, this framing of race attests to its power, even as an ideological relation and concept. But far from accepting its reification, Marxism incorporates racialization as a function of development within the general political economy. Much of this is traceable to the beginnings of race relations as a way for the capitalist elite to convince working-class Whites to embrace their Whiteness, thereby dividing them from workers of color through racial affiliation, creating what Bonacich (1972) calls a "split labor" between traditional, White workers and immigrant, largely minority workers. The process of workers' racial affiliation strengthens the capitalists' ability to dominate the productive system by increasing competition for labor and driving down workers' wages, not to mention subverting their objective interests in solidarity by fracturing their group cohesion.

The second part of Chapter 2 is an appraisal of the Marxist framework for studying race. In education, Marxism's influence means that race has to be bracketed as a dependent concept and does not explain a primary relation, a status that belongs to class. In writing and conversation, race is set off in quotation marks to designate its ideological status. Racism, on the other hand, merits critical study because it is a real process within the intellectual division of labor found in schooling. The main appraisal here is whether Marxism is another color-blind attempt at evading analysis of race relations, which makes it compatible with the continuation of racism, rather than an intervention. Marxism fails to analyze racism with a specifically meaningful framework that makes sense to the lived lives of people of color, and, while racism certainly is complicated by class struggle, it is neither reducible nor explainable by appealing to Marxism.

Whiteness Studies

Chapter 3 delves into the more recent, arguably 2-decade old, intervention called Whiteness Studies. Within the framework of Critical Whiteness Studies, Whiteness and Whites come to the center of analysis in an unprecedented and unforeseen way. This is different from the centering that Whiteness usually is afforded in Eurocentric curricula and writing. Indeed it would be problematic for civilization, progress, and rationality to recenter Whiteness as a point of reference in order once again to relegate people of color to the margins. In Whiteness Studies, *Whiteness becomes the center of critique and transformation.* It represents the much-neglected anxiety around race that is now receiving attention. Conceptually, Whiteness Studies poses critical questions about the history and status of Whiteness (a process not to be equated with Blackness or Otherness). Whiteness is not coterminous with the notion that some people have lighter skin tone than others; rather, Whiteness, along with race, is the structural valuation of skin color, which invests it with meaning regarding the overall organization of education and society. In this sense, Whiteness conceptually had to be invented and now has to be maintained.

There are two significant camps regarding the uptake of Whiteness: White reconstruction and White abolition. In the first, reconstructionists offer discourses—as forms of social practice—that transform or rehabilitate Whiteness, and therefore White people, into something other than an oppressive identity and ideology. On the other hand, White abolitionism is guided by Roediger's (1994) announcement that "Whiteness is not only false and oppressive, it is *nothing but* false and oppressive" (p. 13; emphasis in original). In general, there is a preference in the literature for a reconstructionist approach to Whiteness.

The framework of Whiteness Studies has certain strengths that recommend it. First, it focuses on the deepest investment in raciology, without which race relations would not exist as a form of domination. Second, Whiteness Studies provides an avenue for progressive White educators to enter race struggle *as* Whites without the usual suspicions that they are either hovering as universal humans in a racial struggle or enfleshing Blackness in order to blend in. Third, in education the emphasis on Whiteness reminds us that White children and adults relearn how to be White on a consistent basis, if not daily.

The challenges to the framework of Whiteness Studies fall within two unresolved tensions:

1. What does it mean to center Whiteness in education, even while critiquing it, when White-as-center was the original problem to begin with? This effectively remarginalizes people of color and becomes another excuse for White scholars to ignore the concrete lives of minorities.
2. Or worse, it sanctions White self-indulgence in the name of racial progress, which may end up being disingenuous.

Although there is much to recommend the conceptual uptake of Whiteness within Whiteness Studies, there are practical challenges to either reconstructing or abolishing Whiteness, which I take up in the second part of Chapter 3.

Cultural Studies

The last race framework to round out the book is Cultural Studies, discussed in Chapter 4. As we turn to issues of representation, language, and meaning, race takes on a properly symbolic status. As an invention, race becomes real through discourses and regimes of meaning (see Foucault, 1980) through which racialized subjects make sense of their lived conditions, act on them, and then place limitations on them.

In education, a Cultural Studies framework has made the politics of representation central to understanding the relationship between meaning and power. With respect to race, whose meaning is always contested and contextual, representation constitutes the racial themes of our time. We speak of race by representing it, but it also speaks through us as a corporeal, if not also material, experience. As a somatic relation, race is signified as an embodied meaning system wherein our flesh and blood are implicated in its circuits. We represent race intersubjectively through complex chains of meanings via the educative functions of the state, such as schools and the media, but we also represent it intercorporeally by regulating what student bodies can and cannot do. School segregation, discipline, and access to knowledge constrain what otherwise would be a freedom of movement, but they also expose the limits of social movements around education.

As for assessing the challenges for Cultural Studies, the turn to culture as a material, rather than idealist, practice was a necessary intervention in social theory with respect to the impasse within Marxism regarding the role of ideology. Following Althusser's elevation of ideology studies, its replacement is found in studies of discourse, specifically through engagement of Foucault's work. After affirming the role of analyses of representations, I assess some of the challenges of a Cultural Studies framework of race and representation.

As powerful as it is power-centric, Cultural Studies sometimes suffers from a flattening out of such relations, particularly as it relates to institutional forms and their counterpart in resistance movements. It is ultimately not clear how race representations, while certainly forceful, do their work in limiting actual living conditions, particularly for people of color. For this, the necessary link between representations, whether their literary or social science varieties (cf. Said's, 1979, point about European versus American orientalism), and social policies provides a possible accounting for the manner whereby significations are ideologically made to stick (J. Thompson, 1984). This segues into a discussion of whether cultural representations themselves are material, even if they recruit concrete apparatuses, such as schools, to accomplish their purposes. The "real" is a stubborn concept in social theory, and Cultural Studies has not succeeded in arguing for its obsolescence. Chapter 4 inserts itself into this debate.

A Multidimensional Theory of Race:
Or, the Era of Race Ambivalence

Having argued for the strengths and weaknesses of the four aforementioned frameworks, this book ends with thoughts about future directions for a critical study of race. Chapter 5 introduces the main contours of a post-race, or race ambivalent, framework as a form of aspiration rather than a description of society as it exists today. There are many confusions and conflations involving the "post" in post-race, and two trends are worth mentioning upfront. Whereas conservative thought uses post-raciality as a *fait accompli*, progressives have the opportunity to consider it as a futuristic goal and in effect wrestle the concept away from its commonsense use. It is important to note that color-blindness is different from post-race thinking as presented here, where the former denies the importance of race relations and the latter performs a critical analysis of it. This chapter synthesizes the literature about the possibility of a "post-racial project." First, it asks whether race is worthwhile sustaining *in perpetuity* as a form of socio-educational organization. Second, it analyzes the theoretical space of post-race as a source of possible insights when race theory becomes aware and reflective about its own conceptual apparatus. Third, it shows that post-race perspectives *go through* race in order to ponder transcending it as opposed to dismissing it merely as an ideological illusion. While questioning the creation and maintenance of race, post-race thought treats it seriously as a social relation.

Taken less to mean a period "after" race and more a fundamental ambivalence toward it, in this chapter post-race theory is defined as a new stage of intellectual production with respect to race. Just as modern thought, according to Lyotard (1984), emerges from the other end only after it reckons with the postmodern condition, race thought becomes itself after it confronts post-race critique. To be clear, this condition does not exist outside of the language used to apprehend it. The post-race predicament is a discourse as much as it is a material condition. The former provides its conditions of necessity, and the latter its conditions of eligibility.

Engaging post-race discourse is driven less by the need to pronounce that race is walking out the door, that it is an interpellation that is getting increasingly harder to hear, and more by the future status of race–or better yet, its future standing. Racial hailing still occurs, and many of its subjects still turn around when their subjectivity is called upon to answer (Leonardo,

2009a). Race is, as Warmington (2009) argues, still a powerful mediating tool, and "we live race as if it has meaning and we live within a society in which those raced meanings have innumerable consequences. We live with race as a social fact" (p. 284). Although racism involves a whole range of social processes, it never excludes language, which is always in play. It is not language *qua* language, but language as a form of social practice. This establishes the fact that in order to know racism, we must know language intimately.

In this concluding chapter, I also have another curiosity regarding racism: that is, whether or not (1) the discourse of race, or race language in practice, is itself intimately tied to racism and (2) any hopes of ending racism may have to pose the end of racial signification. Particularly in the United States, racialized language is still the dominant public discourse and represents the nation's anxiety with difference. Whether this fact alone recommends its perpetuity is another question.

This chapter serves as the culminating appraisal for the book insofar as it attempts to introduce a new framework for the study of race and education. Synthesizing the insights from the previous paradigms, I argue for a Multidimensional Theory of Race and Education, at the heart of which is an appeal for *race ambivalence*. This means that far from an attempt at being eclectic, the chapter attempts to build a dialogical framework that is least possessive and invested in a particular line of thought about intervening into the problems of race and racism. Tying it all together in a multidimensional theory of race and education, and faithful to the design of the book, the argument confirms the reflexivity that has been central to a "critical program" in education as well as the dominant concern with inequality and liberation from it that are so emphasized in any study of race worth mentioning.

CHAPTER 1

Critical Race Theory in Education
On Racial State Apparatuses

Beginning this book with a chapter on Critical Race Theory in Education is arguably the most appropriate way to set the stage for what a critical analysis of race and education looks like. In the United States, Critical Race Theory is the dominant framework for a critical study of race and education, judging by the frequency of journal articles, special issues, edited collections and anthologies, and authored books on the topic. Even a cursory look at the program for the American Educational Research Association's (AERA) annual meeting of any year after 2000 provides ample justification for the claim that CRT is the most visible framework for critically studying and researching race. Often, the CRT presentations are well-attended and draw huge followings, spawning preconference workshops. Every year since 2007, the Critical Race Studies in Education Association (CRSEA) has held its annual conference. Its official sponsoring journal is *Race Ethnicity & Education*, whose chief and founding editor, David Gillborn, holds the title of Professor of Critical Race Studies and Director of the Centre for Research in Race and Education at the University of Birmingham in England. In fact, the acronym's popularity may suggest that CRT is no longer a curiosity in education but a household name, much like Coke became a synonym for soda. CRT may even be here to stay. Or it has reached the level of common sense whereby even non-CRT-oriented research on race has appropriated the label. This may be cause for some concern, lest CRT lose its "critical" edge. Either way, these trends speak to CRT's growing influence in education.

As I explained in the Introduction, there is also very little debate as to the beginnings of a program in Critical Race Theory in Education, which dates from the 1995 publication of Ladson-Billings and Tate's inaugural essay on the movement. The intellectual effects were felt immediately. Within a few years, articles and book contributions bearing CRT in their title began to appear, and a scholarly intervention was born. A little over 15 years later, the field has only become more visible, organized, and influential. It covers topics as diverse as curriculum, research methodology, leadership, attitudes and aspirations, funding, higher education, sports and athletics, and teacher education. Marvin Lynn and Adrienne Dixson (2013), both former presidents of the CRSEA, are the editors the *Handbook of Critical Race Theory in Education*. Although drawing much of its inspiration from original writings in legal studies, such as those by Derrick Bell, Kimberlé Crenshaw, and Richard Delgado, and then importing them into education, CRT is interdisciplinary and appropriates insights from the philosophy of Charles Mills, draws from the sociological thought of W. E. B. Du Bois and Eduardo Bonilla-Silva, and engages cultural studies from Stuart Hall to Paul Gilroy, and social theory from Althusser to Žižek. As resourceful as it is trenchant in its critique, CRT leaves no intellectual stone unturned. Because racism in education and society is multifaceted, so must its analysis attest to the complexity of the problem, and CRT recruits allies from across the aisle as well as university departments.

For our purposes, it suffices to say that race and racism are endemic to U.S. society. This does not suggest that racism is pandemic or out of control and cannot be ameliorated. CRT in education is precisely the intervention that aims to halt racism by highlighting its pedagogical dimensions and affirming an equally pedagogical solution rooted in anti-racism. In this, CRT displays some *chutzpah* or at least a "theory with an attitude." That said, CRT in education is a paradigmatic study of race in which the problem of the color line is made to speak within a particular discourse, community, and postulates. For instance, the appropriation of Bell's (1992) well-known, defiant injunction regarding the "permanence of racism" is understood within the particular context and constraints (in the Foucauldian sense) of a CRT understanding of education.

To some, CRT is unnecessarily pessimistic. However, it is possibly less an announcement of defeatism and more about being vigilant about racism. As Gillborn (2005) observes, "This process of radical critique should not be confused with a prophecy of doom. To identify the complex and deep-rooted nature of racism is not to assume that it is inevitable nor insurmountable" (p. 497). CRT focuses its attention more on conceptual and practical strategies to end racism and less on ending race as an organizing principle. It does not so much focus on agents' intentions, which are rarely transparent to individuals. According to Gillborn (2006a), "This approach moves away from endless debates about intent by insisting upon a focus on the outcomes of actions and processes" (p. 21). Although intent is integral to the volition of individual subjects, it does not explain the inner workings of an entire racial system, which is judged by its effects.

FRAMEWORK OF CRITICAL RACE THEORY

Critical Race Theory has at least three components based on its moniker. First, in this section I trace the specificities of what criticality might mean in the context of a study of race, including its premium on the politics of naming. Second, I synthesize the various analyses of the status of race, its conceptual meaning, and its pervasiveness in social life, particularly in the United States. Third, I end with the role of theory in understanding the nature of race contestation as well as a form of intellectual intervention into racial oppression.

The "Critical" in CRT

Just as Kant's critique of reason generally is acknowledged as the moment when philosophy first became critical, CRT is credited with inaugurating the break when race research in education first became critical. Of course, being critical is always a relative honor, and scholars may find the line of separation shifting, where one's criticality is, for another, nothing more than an ideology. Calling a scholar "critical" sometimes is perceived as a slight if by using that word the instigator intends to draw attention to the other's politics and apparent lack of objectivity. *Critical* becomes a code word for an ideologue, a politicized educator. For their detractors, Derrick Bell and Richard Delgado are critical because they lack neutrality, which is enough to derogate them. In these instances, "critical" is not considered an honor but something to be hurled, like an insult.

However, to Eagleton (1996), neutrality is different from objectivity. Objectivity is the ability to analyze social processes as they actually transpire, often recruiting science to explain them, whereas lack of neutrality is the capacity to take a stand on them. Accomplishing the first does not prevent an educator from taking a position on these dynamics. For example, many CRT-inspired scholars are able to capture the inner workings of racism but are committed to the next step of denouncing it and offering ways to counteract it. It is in this sense that they may achieve objectivity but lack neutrality, thus warranting the label "critical." But the label "uncritical" is rarely, if ever, appreciated, and even less often self-generated. Just as few people claim to espouse an ideology, let alone write a treatise on one of their own (Ricoeur, 1986), fewer still would embrace being called uncritical. It becomes the ultimate insult in the academic world because most educated people pride themselves on being critical thinkers.

For the progressive Left, being critical has become the norm. In a word: hegemonic. This is a good trend, if not a tradition, but, as I will show, criticality needs also to be delineated in specific terms lest it be stripped of its edgy and meaningful deployment, particularly for the study of race. Otherwise, the well-intended use of "critical" becomes meaningless—and therefore uncritical. If, in studying race matters, all treatises wave the flag of critical, then critical loses its differential status as something set off from commonsense thinking. Critical thinking suggests that schooling ought to distinguish between the surface and substance of learning in an unequal, if not also racialized, context.

Of course, there is an older sense of critical, traceable to Plato, which is synonymous with analytical thinking that cuts to the heart of the matter through criticism (McPeck, 1992). Although the critical tradition in education accepts and adopts this stance, it ultimately does not suffice for CRTheorists when it fails to speak to the problem of structural oppression, in particular racism, which is central to the critical project. Or, in Kincheloe's (1993) doubling words, we need an enhanced form of "critical critical thinking." In this useful repetition, critical takes on the meaning of both analysis and a politics. As critical descends into common sense, it is in danger of becoming nonsense, of adopting an uncritically critical stance. Educators would do well to guard against this development.

This chapter, indeed this book, uses "critical" in a specific way and should not be thought of as a general preference for analytical thinking about race, over which CRT does not have a monopoly. It is not meant to berate scholars who are not considered critical but to set some parameters on its usage for the sake of clarity. It is an analytical point, not unlike distinguishing land from sea. There is soft ground between shore and sand where they mix, but as travelers, most scholars find it helpful to map out the intellectual terrain before they are stuck in mud. Without this contrast, critical does not retain its uniqueness and CRTheorists, most of whom are not ready to throw in the towel, would have to abdicate its meaning. In terms particular to race, this is important because with the spreading popularity of CRT, the risk of stripping its critical edge has been flagged (Ladson-Billings, 2004a, 2005). We might even imagine Nathan Glazer, author of *We Are All Multiculturalists Now* (1997), writing his sardonic follow-up, *We Are All Critical Race Theorists Now*. In other words, not all scholarship on race and racism warrants the title of "critical," just as not all critical work is concerned with race. CRT may claim that scholarship is better when it is critical, but this seems beside the point because it does not explain how deploying criticality produces political effects. This is my focus on the "critical" within CRT.

Naming Racial Oppression. Critical within a CRT framework begins from the premise that structured racial oppression is an educational reality. Certainly race is a social construction, but its consequences are as real as gravity. Western society may have dreamed up race but now lives with its

nightmares. This is not an unfortunate consequence of uneven group development and the natural disparity it produces. It is even less the fault of the
limitations of people of color, of which they have many, but enforcing racism
does not seem to be one of them. Racial inequality and its vestiges in education are products of historical events, not the least of which are the examples
of slavery, cultural and physical genocide, and labor exploitation. These
injuries would have been enough, but their reach and influence into daily
practices should not be underestimated. In this sense, being critical requires
that a link between national, even global, and personal/group histories be
established in order to set the record straight with respect to the challenges
faced by people of color. In fact, CRT proponents prefer to name the process
in the most direct way possible. With Macedo (2000b), CRTheorists believe
that a critical sensibility begins with a language of demystification and prefer
to call it "racial oppression," rather than arguably more acceptable terms,
such as inequality, disparity, or the achievement gap. I am not suggesting
that it is inappropriate to use these terms or that CRTheorists avoid them.
However, their limitations become apparent when the more emotive and arguably philosophical term *oppression* is criticized for being overly politicized
or jargonistic. The ability to name this process in the deepest way possible is
part of demystifying racism.

Racial oppression names the injury in the most dialectical and critical
manner possible. Speaking against a politics of clarity without clarity about
politics, in his Introduction to the 30th-Year Anniversary of Freire's *Pedagogy
of the Oppressed*, Macedo (2000b) writes:

> Freire's language was the only means through which he could have done jus-
> tice to the complexity of the various concepts dealing with oppression. For one
> thing, I reminded her [a student], "Imagine that instead of writing *Pedagogy of
> the Oppressed* Freire had written "*Pedagogy of the Disenfranchised.*" The first title
> utilizes a discourse that names the oppressor, whereas the second fails to do
> so. If you have an "oppressed," you must have an "oppressor." What would be
> the counterpart of disenfranchised? "*Pedagogy of the Disenfranchised*" dislodges
> the agent of the action while leaving in doubt who bears the responsibility for
> such action. This leaves the ground wide open for blaming the victim of disen-
> franchisement for his or her own disenfranchisement. This example is a clear
> case in which the object of oppression can also be understood as the subject of
> oppression. Language like this distorts reality. (p. 21)

Like Derrick Bell's (1992) harsh prognosis that racism is likely to be permanent, which makes even a thick-skinned CRTheorist cringe at the thought,
using "oppression" as the preferred descriptor for the racial state of affairs
makes the seriousness of racism intelligible through a critical frame.

Unlike disenfranchisement (an awkward mouthful), which has no counterpart to the disenfranchised (disenfranchiser?), oppression recalls the fundamental link between the oppressed and oppressor *as a relation.* In other words, a racialized society cannot have the racially oppressed without the racial oppressor, two dialectical poles where each owes its existence to the other. Just like the exploiter and exploited (Marx & Engels, 1964) and colonizer and colonized (Memmi, 1965), the oppressor–oppressed dialectic reminds us that oppression is neither the masochistic drive of the first nor the inadequate properties of the second, but *the resulting dynamics of a social relationship* that favors Whites and dispossesses people of color. Therefore, race scholars are *critical* insofar as they are able to name this predicament characterized by an intimate, concrete relationship.

Recognizing Racial Realism. Ricky Lee Allen (2005) suggests that a "pedagogy of the oppressor" is necessary if educators deserve a complete picture of racialization. I will have more to say about Whiteness Studies in Chapter 3, but here I will take up Allen's point that a pedagogy of the oppressed exists because a pedagogy of the oppressor is hidden from our view. Critical Race Theorists are not satisfied with the complacent narrative of racial progress and prefer racial realism. The United States no longer functions within the era of legal enslavement, but Blacks are enslaved by new regimes of unequal treatment, not the least of which is ghettoization. Physical genocide of Native Americans has turned cultural, giving rise to a different kind of death. Land takeover for Mexicans has been replaced with the miseducation of Mexican youth and policing of the border. And Coolies may be a thing of the past but it is not cool to be Asian in American society, despite the recent visibility of Asian hip hop in popular shows like "America's Best Dance Crew," the relative success of Asian American singers on "American Idol," and the rise of singing groups like Far East Movement, or that K-pop phenom, Psy, of the song "Gangnam Style." These trends speak to the ebb and flow of race relations.

The transparency of racial power is arguably more opaque in the era of color-blindness or post-Civil Rights race relations. Unlike the overt forms of White supremacy, the softened and coded/coated expressions, like normative knowledge and unequal funding in schools, are either harder to transfix on race or confounded by class issues. However, the resulting relationship is consistent: White reigns supreme. Although many Whites rightfully would now admit Jim Crow and other transparent forms of racism as evidence of a tilted playing field, when polled, the majority of White Americans claim that the problem of race inequality is largely a thing of the past (Hartmann, Gerteis, & Croll, 2009). Against this, the majority of African Americans record much less optimistic attitudes toward racial progress.

Racism in education does not require a White conspiracy. Just as each driver on the freeway does not consent to group spectator slowing, the concerted curiosity that ensues after an accident is enough to halt traffic to a stop. Similarly, White educators do not need to collude with one another in order for racism to become a formidable force in the lives of people of color. In fact, Gillborn (2008) argues that because racial oppression is already a structural problem, conducting schooling as usual ensures that race-based inequality will continue. That is, doing nothing affirmative against racism is a default action contributing to its survival, just as a moving object in space moves in the same direction without a deliberate force to counter it. As surely as spectator slowing does not result from conscious collusion, the traffic to which it gives rise becomes a problem for every motorist behind it. As long as each driver behaves in predictable ways, traffic is the logical outcome; as long as Whites follow their inclinations, the continuation of racist outcomes comes as no surprise and is regarded as an unremarkable consequence of a system over which no individual exercises much control.

Racism does not require willful acts of hatred, although this would have been enough. It does not always necessitate overt forms of racism, despite their debilitating effect. And it does not suggest that people of color are not unwitting participants in their own oppression. Far from it. They are not dupes of a system mysterious to their comprehension, albeit imperfectly. As Pierre Orelus (2011b) notes:

> Despite the empty rhetoric of many American politicians, including politicians of color, we have yet to see a significant shift in the racial paradigm. Even though we now have a Black president, Barack Obama, after centuries of political domination and control by privileged heterosexual, Christian, and able-bodied White males, the United States remains racially divided and segregated. The symbolic and historical presidency of Barack Obama does not necessarily mean we are living in, or approaching, a post-racial era. Race mattered during slavery and colonization in terms of how the slaves and the colonized peoples were treated. It continues to matter today and will most likely continue to matter for centuries to come unless there is a profound transformation of the unequally race-based political and economic system. (p. 1)

Orelus's point (see also Orelus, 2011a), and Gillborn's before him, is that because the racialized social system is embedded in all decisions that educators make, nothing short of a concerted, self-conscious intervention would alter the state of affairs.

Like a fast-moving, heavy train maintains its trajectory without the application of force to the contrary, racism in education becomes indomitable unless it meets with active resistance. We note what others may consider as excessive pessimism in Orelus's tone, established earlier by Derrick Bell's (1992) racial realism. To counter the impression that CRTheorists are wont to exaggerate racism's magnitude, Bell's Afro-pessimism is explained as a form of defiance in the face of diminishing odds that racism will end. It is the ability to question despite hopelessness, helped along by the evidence of 500 years of racial oppression that is empirically on your side. Anything less would be cast as cynical, anything more as simply surplus hopefulness. Racial realism is a perspective that attempts to apprehend actual race relations, while avoiding the negativity of ideology critique and the positivity of utopian thinking. In colloquial terms, it is what it is.

Although CRT is known as activist-oriented, it does not reduce such ambitions to their commonsense forms, what Freire (1970/1993) once called "mere activism," or a misinformed and anti-intellectual action plan. For CRT, intellectual production is one of those areas where the conceptual understanding of race and racism helps to clarify the problem at hand. It does not promote action as a good in itself, preferring instead its critical form, one informed by careful and thoughtful analyses of the racial formation. Its shorthand is known as critical race thought, or the assemblage of discourses that recruits interdisciplinary frameworks that resist the temptation to act, and by merely acting reproduce the set of problems that it labors to transcend, such as authoritarianism, essentialism, or a politics of inevitability. Critical Race Theory in education proceeds without guarantees (Hall, 1996b), taking apart some of the most intimately held belief systems that define the educational enterprise. Meritocracy, naturalized canons of knowledge, historical facticity, and inevitability of racial equality become targets of educational criticism. It is this spirit of demystification that sets CRT apart as "critical." Nothing is taken for granted, everything is open for scrutiny. As we will see, it shares an affinity with other critical discourses, such as Marxism, in affirming demystification as a methodology against falsehood. More important, in search of an authentic existence, demystification is a move against racial domination.

The Centrality of Race

Critical Race Theory insists on the centrality of race within U.S. social development. It acknowledges what many educators already understand: that the nation was created as a racial project. Recognition of slavery, dispossession of Indian land, and other race events in history is not the hallmark of critical race thought. It is a perspective shared by most people who understand U.S. history with at least one eye open. Reading history with two eyes extends the analysis to include current racializations, not the least of which are consequences of slavery and genocide, but many of which are new forms. To the CRTheorist, race is indicative of not just U.S. creation but its continuation, a contract that is rewritten over and again (Mills, 1997), a formation reworked to fit current cultural understandings and material arrangements (Omi & Winant, 1994).

Unmasking Race. Race plays a central role in determining what the United States looks like. The nation is segregated into racialized neighborhoods and networks, which give rise to differential schooling experiences for Whites and students of color. This is well documented and hardly mysterious (see Noguera, 2003; Oakes, 2005). From which schools children attend (T. Howard, 2010), to the inequitable funding that shortchanges ghetto and barrio schools populated by Black and Latino children (Darling-Hammond, 2010), and the curriculum that occasionally challenges Whites and underwhelms minorities, race relations becomes a powerful and compelling explanation. Furthermore, because race policies, from immigration to naturalization laws, influence who can become a citizen of the United States or enter its national borders, race literally affects what the country looks like because of the gene pool that exists within its population (Lopez, 2006).

Like CRT in Legal Studies, CRT in Education proceeds by unmasking apparently nonracial phenomena as precisely racial in their nature. Just as Crenshaw et al. (1995) argue that race is found not only in the criminal justice system but equally in tax, property, and inheritance laws, Parker and Stovall (2005) find that race explains the uneven and harsh treatment of students of color when it comes to discipline in schools. They corroborate Ferguson's (2001) findings that Black students, particularly Black males, are targets of a certain racial panopticon in schools, which disciplines them harshly for behaviors that would be overlooked for White students. Solórzano (1998) uses the concept of "racial microaggression" to explain processes whereby apparently nonracial interactions are racial in nature when power relations are made explicit. In other words, the racial dimensions of daily, even mundane, exchanges become significant if we consider their compound effect of demoralizing and psychologically breaking down people of color in institutional settings.

The upshot is that, without disregarding the importance of well-acknowledged areas of structural racism in schools, such as tracking (Oakes, 2005), funding (Darling-Hammond, 2010), or curriculum development (J. Banks, 2006), CRT provides clear and compelling evidence of the pervasiveness of race and racism within education. Not unlike Fanon's (1952/1967) sociogenic approach to the psychology of colonial interactions, CRTheorists expose a world of violence in what otherwise are touted as "safe spaces," like race dialogue in the classroom (Leonardo & Porter, 2010; see also Yancy, 2009). In this, CRT succeeds in developing a perspective that frames the everydayness of race and removes the otherwise unhelpful argument that racism is understood only through extreme and aberrant examples, such as slavery, genocide, or the Klan. Race is central to the inner workings of schools and society, woven into the common sense that drives decisions as formal as policy making and as quotidian as where kids sit together in the cafeteria (Tatum, 1997).

Race as Narrative. If race is a social construction, then it takes the form of a narrative. Long-held beliefs about the inherent inferiority of people of color and White superiority are examined for their storytelling origins. Insofar as social life is structured in narrative form, this does not necessarily represent a position on truth or falsehood, but a critical appreciation for the power of myths and their consequences. Here, myth is less a synonym for falsehood and more about the tales that bind together a society and its people (Richardson, 1994). CRTheorists, like Richard Delgado (2011), suggest that stories do not devolve the debate into a relativistic matter of opinions and affirm the power of storytelling as a mechanism that binds our understanding of social phenomena, like race. Storytelling is not valued so much for its *truth content* as its *truth effects*, its ability to affect our actions and orientation to the Other. Narrating race then becomes a political choice, such as when educators perceive families of color to be obstacles to school governance because of their low rates of participation in official events, like Open House. In addition, the longevity of the narrative that constructs Latino and Black families as valuing education less than do White families is questioned for its deficit thinking about their uncounted involvements with learning that schools do not readily recognize (see Moll & Gonzalez, 2004; Yosso, 2006). In all, by conceiving of race as a story, CRT breaks down its apparent objectivity.

Critical Race Theory does not go so far as to deny that differences exist between Whites and people of color in terms of social patterns and cultural make-up. For example, there are serious challenges that haunt communities of color, from the achievement gap to graduation rates. Also, CRT does not disconfirm differences between mainstream and marginalized cultures, which are readily apparent. That said, CRTheorists are committed to renarrating the dominant racial frame that writes people of color into the story through consistently negative images at best and pathological histories at worst. Convinced that these racial perceptions are anointed as facts, CRT uses counterstorytelling (Jocson, 2008; Matias, 2012; Solórzano & Yosso, 2002; Yosso, 2006) to reframe the tale, to flip the script. Questioning that race is a fact and favoring a social-constructionist perspective, counterstorytelling becomes an antidote to the majority's line of thinking and a way to speak back in emotive, often firsthand, recountings of how race affects minority lives. Offering a counterstory does not make pretenses about truth value but begins the discussion from the lived experience of the people most affected by race.

Starting our understanding of racial oppression from the epistemological standpoint of the oppressed is not particular to CRT. Feminist researchers, such as Nancy Hartsock (1987), Sandra Harding (1991), Dorothy Smith (1989), Carol Gilligan (1993), and Patricia Hill Collins (2000), informed insurgent scholars that although social analysis may begin from the perspective of those most affected by subordination, it does not end there. They are clear in avoiding the misimpression that the oppressed "have it right" by virtue of their social position. Instead, they affirm the political soundness of starting *there* in order to arrive *here*. Paulo Freire (1970/1993) says as much when he argues for a "pedagogy of the oppressed," where the objective experience of the oppressed, rather than their subjective self-understandings, guides educators' apprehension of both domination and possibilities for change. Likewise, CRT believes it is important to determine whence the plot begins and the importance of the narrator, which affects the story's development and eventual resolution. Even a casual understanding of fiction or a favorite television show confirms this insight.

Racial-Formation Analysis. To the CRT observer, U.S. society and its institutions are continuations of the racial project. In other words, institutions are racialized because they are embedded in a racial predicament, which they reinforce and help reproduce. Agents in this arrangement are limited by their condition, which makes it difficult to imagine acting independently from it. In turn, they instantiate the structure and invest in it, shape it, or change it (Bourdieu & Wacquant, 1992; Craib, 1992; Giddens, 1986; Shilling, 1992). It is in this sense that the racial agent and race structure are involved in a complicated dance of mutual constitution. Using a spoonful of Gramsci and a pinch of Althusser, Omi and Winant (1994) argue that a racial formation shifts and morphs according to the current material and representational arrangement between Whites and people of color. Race has no essence, and race contestation is the result of political movements on one side and compromises on the other. It may be reformed, deformed, or transformed. In fact, if race has an essence at all, it is the seemingly endless pulsation of racist constriction on one end and liberatory impulses on the other. The racial formation may reconfigure the nature of this power relationship and rewrite the racial narrative, but Omi and Winant are clear that race is always in play, never irrelevant.

Using a racial-formation analysis of education allows CRT to argue that race is the dominant trope of modern schooling, without the convenient criticism that it is being essentialist or reductive. This has much to recommend it because Omi and Winant's historicism breaks from the more or less transcendental argument that fails to explain why race looks this way in this era and that way in a different era. Like labor, race does not assume a consistent form but serves the needs of a particular relationship between Whites and people of color within a historically determined juncture (on labor and historicism, see Lukács, 1971; Willis, 1977). It allows Bobo and Smith (1998), for instance, to argue that the transition from Jim Crow to laissez-faire racism is explainable less by a growing sentiment among Whites with moral turpitude that de jure segregation was indefensible. Rather, the authors place this racial upheaval within its proper historical condition wherein the United States found itself defending its global image as a democratic nation, compromised by the media images of Whites hosing down Blacks and arresting them for engaging in peaceful protest during the Civil Rights Movement. Said another way, the institution of Jim Crow had to change if White America wished to maintain both its public image and favorable relations with allies across the globe.

This contextual understanding confirms the concept of "interest convergence," an analytical concept (as opposed to a political strategy) dear to CRT, whereby Black progress is bound up with upholding White interests (see Bell, 1995). Racism did not end with the dissolution of slavery, which morphed into 100 years of Jim Crow. In fact, one might argue that the American Civil War was not meant to end White supremacy but a *particular form* of it. Likewise, when Jim Crow suffered from ill repute, it was replaced by a more underground expression of racism. Of course, not many people of color would argue for a return to slavery or Jim Crow, so this is prima facie proof of racial progress. Meanwhile, the standard of living for people of color lags woefully behind that for Whites. In the end, the racial organization of society changes over time but maintains its axiomatic status in determining people's life chances.

The Role of Theory

Within CRT, the role of theory means that racism is not only a practical problem but an intellectual one. This requires the recruitment of perspectives that make critical theory sensitive to race as well as making race theory itself critical (Goldberg & Essed, 2002). This means that the explanatory frameworks that scholars have at their disposal affect their ability to perform a symptomatic reading of racism. Like "critical," theory maintains a specific and special sense. In order to be critical, theory must make oppression and liberation from it a central preoccupation. In order to have theoretical import, critical race thought must muck through the distortions that threaten either to compromise its ability to cut to the heart of the matter or become easily co-optable. Because it represents a relatively militant position on the problem of racism, CRT is not in any danger of being co-opted anytime soon. But as its discourse increases in popularity (which it arguably desires) and becomes organized as a movement (which it arguably already has), CRT, like other movements that the mainstream contends with, faces possibilities of convergence with White interests.

Development of CRT in Education. Critical Race Theory in education developed out of two responses to current theorizing. First, as mentioned in the Introduction, Ladson-Billings and Tate (1995) observed that multiculturalism was the mainline race critique. They contended that a more militant race theory was necessary in order to unseat the pervasive racism in schools and unsettle the field of education. Most race scholars in education are familiar with this intervention.

Second and less well known, like CRT in law (A. Harris, 2008), CRT in education was taken up as a response to the limitations of a class-focused analysis of education in confronting the problem of racism, specifically White supremacy. Critical Pedagogy ascended as a favored theoretical framework for critical work in education. Since Paulo Freire's *Pedagogy of the Oppressed* (1970/1993) appeared on the intellectual scene, a generation of scholars found a compelling theory for understanding the nature of oppression in education. It gave them the language they were looking for. This development was flanked by Paul Willis's *Learning to Labor* (1977) on one side and Bowles and Gintis's *Schooling in Capitalist America* (1976) on the other. The latter's correspondence theory traced in magnificent fashion the reproduction of the relations of production through education (see also Althusser, 1971). It hails from the Structural Marxist arm of economic analysis of schooling. In his work, Willis provided a theory of resistance by retelling the fate of the lads who disqualified themselves from the credential race but not before getting a "laff" out of school. It was considered an uptake of the excessive determinism in correspondence theory and has since become the inspiration for a Cultural Marxist study of education (see McGrew, 2011).

Despite the differences among Freire, Willis, and Bowles and Gintis, they share a family resemblance in their commitment to class analysis in education. Freire's favored historical revolutionary subject is a member of the working class. Although Freire's participants in Recife, Brazil, were predominantly Black, Freire's text, at least by U.S. standards, does not contain an overtly racial analysis (one can add gender as well), giving the nod to a universalist theory of oppression (see Freire & Macedo, 1995; see also Apple, 2003). Willis takes up the question of race as well as gender with the lads' interactions with their Pakistani and West Indian counterparts, but it is quite clear that the lads were the story's protagonists (McCarthy & Logue, 2010). A certain White ethnocentrism was at work in Willis's choice for "partial penetration" into capitalist social relations, while others served as foils for the lads. Finally, Bowles and Gintis are quite clear that race relations are secondary to class relations, and do not perform a synthesis of the racialized political economy. At the level of theory, race receives short shrift within a critical study of education. It is important but not central, dominant but not determining, and ideological rather than real. That race becomes the stepchild of class may be considered a conceptual form of White supremacy at the level of theory. It is not insignificant that race is theorized out of centrality.

Struggle over Voice. Theory production is not just a hypothesis put forth to explain social life or, in CRT's terms, to tell a story about it. Theory is also part of race relations because it speaks to questions of legitimacy and the right to matter. If critical educational studies do not give proper weight to race, it is consequential because it speaks to making a people and their concerns visible or invisible.

Because theory is not disembodied, dominant theorizing determines whose voice is privileged in education. By voice, CRT means something more than who has the right to speak, although this would have been enough. Voice is the striving to exist in a condition wherein people of color struggle for human status. For example, Charles Mills (2003a) takes the discipline of philosophy to task when he cites its failure to take up race in philosophical discourse (see also Peters, 2012). In addition, Black philosophers are found few and far between, which makes mentoring aspiring Black philosophers that much more difficult. Within the discipline, race becomes *conceptua non grata*, left up to the few who carry the philosophical burden of speaking to the color line. It is not surprising, then, that theories of the human in philosophical discourse are overwhelmingly about European humanity (Maldonado-Torres, 2007; Porter, 2012). This is not the case in other disciplines, where scholars of color who study race in education, sociology, and social work are not a mere curiosity. That said, they represent the margins of their disciplines and fight for legitimacy. Philosophy may be an extreme example, but it points to the fact that the struggle over voice and theory defines the intellectual terrain, whose experiences count, and, plainly speaking, who exists. Theory has always been part of the battle, what Althusser (1976) once called politics in philosophical form. In race scholarship, it is no different, and theory allows educators to see or not see racism, to regard or not regard people of color as concrete beings.

More Than an Abstraction. For CRT, theory is not a matter of abstraction but a way to make intelligible the lived dimensions of race. With Althusser (1976), CRT guards against theoreticism or what Leonardo and Porter (2010) call intellectualism. While not anti-intellectual, CRTheorists reject an intellectualist approach that reduces racism to an idea and prefer to testify to its brutal reality. In this sense, although racism includes an attitudinal component, which is still central to daily interactions between Whites and people of color, the turn toward structural explanations of racism is a relatively recent innovation in education.

By structural, CRTheorists do not mean simply that racism is pervasive, but that it is *built into* a social system, brick by brick (Bonilla-Silva, 2005; Leonardo, 2009b; Mills, 2003b; Omi & Winant, 1994). Whites' racial attitudes may be an expression of racism, but a focus on racial attitudes does not go far enough in explaining why students of color, particularly Blacks and Latinos, confront the materiality of racism in the form of lower funding and absence of basic educational material. In this interaction, White attitudes are not dismissed as insignificant because they have the ability to institutionalize a color-blind orientation that must be taken seriously.

Attitudes make up the cognitive component of material racism, its psychological horizon. In a fundamental way, attitudes are inseparable from the structural apparatus that supports and sanctions them, and that gives attitudes their force. While giving the nod to structural analysis, CRT integrates the psychosocial levels to arrive at the psychological plane of structural racism. Without a psychological component, CRT fails to capture the personal assaults against which people of color defend daily; without a structural component, CRT forgoes analysis of the extra-mental process that is institutionalized in policies, laws, and state governance. In effect, CRT integrates the two levels of racism: the individual and institutional.

Rich Tapestry of Perspectives. With respect to the economy, Critical Race Theory does not jettison class analysis but integrates it, for CRTheorists in education—many of whom are scholars of color—are well aware of the partnership between racism and capitalism. The plight of people of color is always implicated in the economy, but *reducing* it to the economy is another matter altogether and has not been well received by CRTheorists (Allen, 2002a; Bonilla-Silva, 2011). Rather than choose between race or class analysis, CRT relies instead on Crenshaw's (1991) intersectional analysis, which shares a theoretical affinity with King's (1993) notion of multiple jeopardy, bell hooks's (1984) contention that forms of oppression interlock and "one system cannot be eradicated while the others remain intact" (p. 35), and Patricia Hill Collins's (2000) idea of "matrix of oppression." Intersectional analysis does not center race as much as it weaves together a theory of co-implication among factors, such as race, gender, class, and culture. This means that each social system is shot through with the others, best captured by hooks's phrase, "White supremacist capitalist patriarchy" (Jhally, 1997). In educational analysis, this suggests that the race project is at the same time a gender project, which is a class and cultural politics.

In terms of perspectives, CRT becomes a rich tapestry of theories. For example, Ann Ferguson's (2001) school ethnography recruits Foucault to unearth the disciplining of Black boys, speaking to their specific experience with a racialized masculinity. Dolores Delgado Bernal (1998) argues for a Chicana feminist epistemology to extend Black feminism by adding issues specific to Chicanas and Latinas, like immigration and language discrimination. Sofia Villenas's (2010) work on Chicana Cultural Studies in Education takes its cue from Anzaldua's border writings and Saldivar's trans-frontera provocations to push the limits on Latino/a social thought. Marvin Lynn's (1999) well-known phrase, "critical race pedagogy," elevates the role of Black teachers, and his synthesis between Afrocentricity and CRT represents a creative appropriation of two previously separate perspectives. Bryan Brayboy's (2005) TribalCrit brings issues particular to indigenous peoples into CRT discussions. Finally, queering CRT introduces an ambiguity to race analysis, arguably long before postmodernism walked into the room (Lorde, 1984).

In all, theory in CRT represents the conceptual front in combating racial oppression. It is theory in the critical sense of bringing clarity to the racial predicament, even as it deposes race from the center on occasion. This sensibility for complexity does not take away from race analysis but reminds educators that "race" is not an empty box but contains gender, class, and culture within it. As a homegrown American intervention, where race is the public language, CRT may have begun as more or less a racial analysis, but it has since evolved into an elegant architecture to explain the nature of oppression. It may privilege racial analysis by virtue of its moniker, but by and large CRT does not argue for the elimination of racism, by definition, as the liberation of society, but for the total emancipation of society as the liberation from racism and other forms of oppression. It is a theory of a new society.

APPRAISAL OF CRT, RACE, AND EDUCATION

In the mid-1990s, CRT quickly became a well-known discourse. By this, I mean that a way of making sense of a phenomenon, of rendering it intelligible, became possible through a family of terms. Critical Race Theory gave educational scholars an arsenal of concepts, such as knowledge apartheid (Bernal & Villalpando, 2005), microaggressions (Solórzano, 1998), and critical race pedagogy (Lynn, 1999; see also Lynn & Jennings, 2009). As an intellectual practice, CRT legitimated a critical study of race and education, which does not stop at the obvious iterations of racial contestation that many educators are aware of, such as tracking, unequal funding, and the valorization of Eurocentric curriculum (see Dixson & Rousseau, 2005). Critical race theorists in education argue that race and racism permeate the entire educational enterprise, from aspirations (Yosso, 2006), to spatial configurations

(Allen, 1999), to teacher education itself (Sleeter, 1993, 2011). As such, CRT in education is a thorough examination of schooling as a racial state apparatus (Leonardo, 2005b). Through CRT we learn that education is, in essence, a racial project and race consists of an educational project.

I am particularly interested in CRT's relationship with Marxist discourse. Although there are equally interesting angles to pursue, such as CRT methodology (Solórzano & Yosso, 2002), its stance on particular topics, like NCLB (Leonardo, 2007) or the curriculum (Solórzano & Yosso, 2002), or the law as it affects education (Chapman, 2005), CRT's proximity to or distance from Marxism provides a productive beginning to determine the possibilities of a *raceclass* analysis of education, two intimately related points on one axis, or an elliptical discourse. Because the United States is unarguably one of the most advanced nations with respect to race and class relations, it is possible to find here examples of mature contradictions related to their dynamics. As a result, the likelihood of their resolution also may be posed. The coordinated but awkward dance between race and class represents the dilemma around which educators and students twirl and spin. Breaking up that dance then requires understanding what each partner contributes to racial oppression in schools.

The Concept of Race

Within the framework of CRT, the concept of race is centered. Even when an intersectional analysis (Crenshaw, 1991) is deployed, race analysis in education is arguably foregrounded. Just as Raymond Williams (1977) once argued that a Marxism without determinisms is hardly recognizable, CRT in education sans race determinism would belie itself. In other words, despite its capacity to speak to other social identities and systems, CRT is perceived by most scholars as first and foremost a racial intervention. It is a bit like looking to the side of a dim star in order actually to see it more clearly because looking directly at it fails to register the faint light. Or in the case of looking directly at the sun, it is overwhelmingly bright and one is forced to look indirectly at it in order to see it. Williams also brings up the point that Marxism's current set of determinisms cripples its politics and effectivity, but I will return to the problem of race determinism later in Chapter 5. For now, I want to recognize the centrality of the race concept within CRT's intellectual borders. This preference has a lot to recommend it, one of which is the clarity of the project regarding the problematic it sets in motion, mainly the awesome burden and influence of racialization in schools and society.

In addition, not unlike Marxism, CRT lays down the gauntlet that other social problems emanate from a center. At its minimum, this suggestion means that educators will not make much headway into formidable challenges like sexism, class disparities, and cultural mismatch between students' families and schools, without simultaneously addressing racism. At its maximum, centering race is a bold announcement that these same dynamics will not abate *unless* racism is eradicated. This gives CRT a particularly strong explanatory position on education and its discontents, the daunting challenge of systemic reform, and a singular view on issues like the perennial achievement (read: racial) gap and stubborn attrition rates. It treats race as a defining principle rather than a variable within research for which scholars account (Omi & Winant, 1994). It lends CRT scientific credibility on questions of parsimony, origin, and causality. If it can argue convincingly for the first cause, even a meta-narrative of sorts, which explains why education assumes its current social shape and institutional form, CRT establishes itself as a scientific framework. Insofar as the claim to science is the guiding ethos of social science research, CRT becomes a competing paradigm vying for intellectual legitimacy.

Race—Assumed But Not Defined. Having established the centrality of race in CRT, it is then surprising that there is neither a concerted effort nor an agreement to define this driving concept. If race is indeed the privileged center, it is more often assumed than fully worked out. If this impression is correct, the lack of consensus about the meaning of race is not as worrisome as the lack of in-depth explanation concerning its usage. This is a problem not merely of definition but about setting conceptual parameters and analytical clarity. On the issue of consensus, it may be too much to expect CRT scholars to agree upon a given meaning of race. In this, CRT is like most other engagements, where a lack of agreement is often the norm. But it is not inconsequential.

For example, the absence of consensus around a definition of race may signal the lack of necessary cohesion around the main feature that defines the framework. Therefore, race becomes a proxy for social group, but there are other competing collectivities that organize people and schools, such as ethnicity or nationality. Without an agreement on the parameters of race, it is difficult to discern when CRT scholars are in fact discussing race, ethnicity, or nationality. Admittedly, there is no clean way to separate these concepts, as evidenced by Omi and Winant's (1994) claim that, at least within the sociological literature, ethnicity, class, and nation stand in for race. However, if race is not separated out as a distinct social phenomenon conceptually, if not also empirically, analysis cannot sustain its specific claims outside of folk theory or common sense. It cannot discriminate between culture, on one hand, and race, on the other. They slide into each other and elide a specifically racial analysis. They step on each other's toes and no one knows who is leading.

What Is a Racial Group? Critical Race Theory also enters the second difficulty of whom it includes when it stops short of defining race. For instance, there is a debate regarding whether Latinos and Asian Americans constitute actual racial groups. They may represent quasiraces or panethnicities (Espiritu, 1993). There are two reasons for this difficulty. First, because the White–Black binary is still the dominant framework for understanding race, non-White and non-Black groups exist in a vague and associative relationship to race. They are either White-like or Black-like, depending on the nature of the comparison. To Yancey (2003), the important distinction is not who is White, but who is not Black. When it concerns educational attainment, Latinos resemble more closely their Black counterparts, whereas Asian American trends fulfill White patterns. In assimilation studies, the test case for minority mobility is the extent to which its members achieve a modicum of Whiteness, whereas its opposite is termed downward assimilation (Portes & Rumbaut, 2001), which could be a euphemism for assimilating towards Blackness. Within skin-color studies, it bears out that lighter Asian Americans and Latinos fare better socially than their darker counterparts (Hunter, 2005; Rondilla & Spickard, 2007).

Regarding the second reason for the difficulty about what counts as a racial group, there are questions about whether Latino or Asian American experience is determined by race as defined by skin color, despite the fact that skin tone matters for those groups. That is, language and immigration status matter at least as much as skin color for non-Black minorities. By language, I mean a primary relation or proximity to English, standard or not. That is, Latinos and Asian Americans are socially defined by their relationship to a language outside of English, even if English is their main spoken language (see Bernal, 1998; Villenas, 2010). This assumed characteristic marks them as foreign or exotic (Park & Park, 2005; Wu, 2002), either of which becomes significant in their educational experience.

There are sound reasons for refusing the binary for its incompleteness and obvious limitations, and CRT in education should be lauded for broadening its analysis of race to include multiple forms of racialization. At the same time, the binary functions, indeed works, to explain certain racial phenomena, such as skin-color stratification among non-Black minority groups. This does not return the discussion to accept unproblematically the binary's implications. Its limitations have been well rehearsed, essentialism being only one of its bugbears (cf. Yancey, 2003). Rather it begs the question of what actually defines race as we know it—whether expanding its boundaries beyond the binary enriches or weakens CRT's analysis, and, as I take up later in Chapter 5, whether we should encourage the perpetuation of racial classifications, an interpellation reinforced when CRT includes more, rather than fewer, groups into its racial cosmology.

Because workers are directly involved in the material production of goods, Marxists make a distinction between historical classes and quasiclasses. The working class' experience with production generates knowledge about a historical vocation and human development that are revolutionary par excellence. This argument does not compare the amount and intensity of the worker's oppression with those of the middle class, or, better yet, people who are unemployed and cannot provide for even the basics. Within a strictly Marxist perspective, people without work may suffer a great deal but do not constitute a revolutionary group or experience. It is in this sense that Marxism, for better or worse, has defined the nature of classes and reduced them to two: workers and capitalists.

Establishing the Revolutionary Race

In a study of race, which groups count as races, as historical races, and as the revolutionary race, are unsettled questions. Often, the suggestion that there exists an ultimate victim group, such as Blacks, is enough to retreat from defining what constitutes, in roughly analogous terms with Marxism, the existence of historical races. This is not unreasonable because constructing the ultimate victim group tends to minimize the racial experiences of other oppressed races, whether they are quasi or not. Latino, Asian American, and Native American racial experiences quickly become judged on the basis of whether they approximate Black oppression. Often, the debate is framed as a contest over which group suffers most from racism. This tendency exists for a good reason. A group's claim for ultimate victim status represents an appeal to have its experience with racism treated with utmost seriousness and recognition. Treating it as less than this through parallelism or symmetry may minimize its severity, and a slippery slope is established. For a minority group whose plight has not been fully acknowledged and whose struggle is not yet resolved, the drive for recognition remains strong.

That said, it is enough to cause fundamental tensions among minority groups because the minimization cuts both ways, and the struggle for the center of the margins wages on. Critical Race Theory is right to resist this discourse, especially if there is a strong case for multiple processes of racialization, targeting each group differently. *But determining which group suffers most from racism is different from determining which dynamic represents the fundamental racial tension in history.* Therefore, reconciling this tension, like the one between owners and workers within Marxism, becomes an important discussion within race analysis. If this suggestion has merit, it is also consequential for a critical understanding of race and education.

The Question of Historical Races. Deciding which racial groups constitute the *historical races* is difficult but warranted. At the very least, it shifts the discourse away from establishing what Derrick Bell (1992) calls "faces at the bottom of the well," or a language of ultimate victim status, and toward a language of reconciling revolutionary racial contradictions. Marxists are very clear on the strategic point regarding the preference for the objective position of the working class, not its ultimate victimization. Within raciology, whether Black, Red, Brown, or Yellow represents the dialectical counterpart of White remains to be established. The easy answer is that the dominant frame suggests Black and White are the warring poles of a racial contradiction. For instance, the commonsense discourse of color pits Black as the absence of light, and White as its opposite. In school, children learn to use their crayons and pens with this understanding relatively unchallenged. Within this frame, no other two colors exist as antipodes. Yellow is not the counterpart of brown, red and orange are not at war, and blue and pink are gendered and only implicate race.

However, in other instances, ostensibly nonracial, opposing colors are not Black and White. In astrophysics, the phenomenon that American astronomer Edmund Hubble discovered, known as the Doppler effect, uses the language of red and blue shifts of light to explain how a source moving away from the Earth elongates its wavelength and appears as a red shift in the spectrum, whereas an object moving toward an observer displays a blue shift, or its wavelength becoming shorter. In color terms, red is the opposite of blue. An example closer to home is when children learn the color wheel and discover that yellow is opposite purple, and blue is opposite orange. If race is the discursive frame, it would sound bizarre to our racially trained ears to hear that Brown, Yellow, or Red is the opposite of White. It is more likely that Brown represents the amalgamation of all the racial colors rather than existing as the opposite of another color. These discourses do not override the Black–White binary, which is a naturalized racial understanding of color.

Some people trace the Black–White discourse to biblical passages where light is defined as good and darkness is evil. This is well rehearsed and its racial consequences are clear. Of course, we know that as a form of social organization, modern race does not date further back than roughly 500 years ago, with the arrival of the Age of Discovery, chattel slavery, and the biologization of difference. It is more likely that the biblical justification of race is just that: justification for our *current* racial order. It is the projection of a current state of affairs to a time when race did not apply or exist as a social relation. There were no Whites, Blacks, and other racial groups before the consolidation of Europe into the Occident and the simultaneous co-creation of the Orient, the Americas, and Africa. Jesus was not White, but saying that he is, has fundamental racial ramifications for salvation today. Whether Jesus was or was not White is not the point; that a society racializes him as White and behaves consistently with this belief system is more important.

Just as interesting is the forward projection of race to a naturalized perpetual status of foreverness. I will have more to say about this in Chapter 5, but for now, we receive the impression that race has always existed and will remain so in perpetuity. It is the racial equivalent of the Steady State Theory of the universe in cosmology. Everywhere you look, it seems like race is timeless.

Reflecting on Conceptual Parameters. Because CRT has avoided in-depth discussion of the constitution of historical races, it does not distinguish among different racial trajectories, which otherwise could be helpful. There are good reasons for this move because it behooves CRTheorists to avoid the oppression sweepstakes, which causes its own set of problems. But to reiterate, determining the status of historical races does not equate with a quantitative analysis of racial suffering, even if it qualitatively discriminates among different forms of it. Neither is this a position on which racial group subjectively best understands racism. If classical Marxism has anything to say to race analysis, it is that social analysis *begins* from the working class' objective position as a class-in-itself, not its cognitive development with respect to an accurate understanding of capitalism. That understanding, according to Lukács (1971), develops historically alongside the evolution of the mode of production and the particular needs of the working class (see also De Lissovoy, 2010).

Potentially a class-for-itself, the working class is the only class with universal, rather than self-, interests because it would rather generalize its project of negation against exploitation and realize human freedom. This progression is not inevitable because workers have to wade through the effects of reification, or the ideological process that distorts social creations into natural phenomena. If this theory marries with race analysis, then a revolutionary race is privileged not for its subjective apprehension of racism but for its objective position as a *race-in-itself* in relation to the master race (Leonardo, 2004c). It is not a matter of identity but of ideological development and maturity based on a fundamental social interaction. In other words, like the workers' exchange with material labor, the revolutionary race's interests guide the understanding of racial contestation and its negation. But also like the workers, this race's revolutionary potential is not guaranteed in advance as it must work through distortions and misrecognitions. Education, then, is precisely the process that transforms the race-in-itself into a *race-for-itself* when it realizes its historical function and universal interests.

There are several problems and caveats that must be headed off or entered into right away. First, the direction of CRT and race analysis is developing toward race coalitions, not a singular focus on one group's experience with racism. These developments are not incompatible with the discussion of a revolutionary race. The Bolshevik Revolution in Russia was a coalition among different classes but ultimately was guided by the workers' objective place in the relations of production. The urban industrial class joined with the rural peasant class as well as sectors of the middle and intellectual class, such as the movement's leaders, to topple the Czarist regime. Second, admittedly race relations do not proceed the same way as class relations. For example, there are multiple racializations within any regime of race. But here again, we note that there are multiple class experiences within any class regime, as previously suggested with the middle class. The question is precisely which class antagonism becomes the central and binding conflict that explains and implicates other levels of the class struggle. Likewise, race analysis in education would do well to pose a similar question.

Recent class analysis in education, particularly in public schools, suggests that the primary contact happens between working- and middle-to-upper-class children (Lareau, 2003). Middle-class *habitus* and culture represent the official capital that schools reinforce, which socially promotes children who enter school already embodying these codes. Working-class children are at a disadvantage, leaving them few options for success other than assimilating middle-class ways (Bernstein, 1977b), which becomes a form of cultural violence to their family and sense of self (Freire, 1970/1993). The problem with this analysis is that it obscures the fundamental and driving antagonism between the working and owning classes. Within the structures of capitalism, the middle class may represent difficulties for labor militancy because it has achieved a level of success within an otherwise exploitative system but, by and large, *it is not the problem.* Because public schools become a very specific node in social analysis, the larger problem becomes localized within a specific institution, and not in the manner that Althusser (1971) and Bowles and Gintis (1976) have suggested. Because capitalists and the superwealthy may send their children to private schools, they remain out of sight and out of mind within class studies of public schools. It becomes an analysis of convenience if the global picture of class relations does not make it into the frame (Cho, 2012). It becomes an intervention into the relations between the have-nots and have-some, while the have-everything fly above the fray.

Within CRT, focusing on a fundamental relation does not necessarily oversimplify the process and history of racial contestation. Many who are familiar with Marxism understand that the worker–capitalist model is very complex and much elegant theory production has been spun to explain this primary contradiction. In other words, there is plenty to explain in this binary. Likewise, the current argument does not vitiate against a nuanced understanding of race relations. In fact, a more convoluted race theory may explain less rather than more, and does not always represent an advance in social and educational thought. Rather than explain the inner workings of racism, less parsimonious theories leave one wondering what exactly is racial about the analysis. Nowhere is this becoming more evident than in some of the ways intersectional analysis has been appropriated in education to evade race analysis rather than add to it. At the 2011 British Educational Research Association Conference, the keynote session on intersectionality was very clear on this point. In their assessment, intersectional theory has been used in educational parlance to shift focus away from race, to discredit it with class or gender analysis rather than to bring race into sharper focus with a feminist or Marxist analysis.

In its original conception, intersectional analysis was a womanist, or feminist of color, intervention into White feminism for failing to integrate race into its analysis (P. H. Collins, 2000; Crenshaw, 1991; hooks, 1984; Mirza, 1997, 2009). It was not meant to dilute the effect of race but to enrich it by accounting for its gendered and classed modes of existence. It aimed for simplicity without being simple. In the same vein, Marxism inheres an intersectional argument without giving up its position on class analysis. CRT's revolutionary potential is found in its ability to reflect on its own conceptual parameters, such as determining the possibility and existence of historical races.

CRT's Relationship with Marxism and a Study of Capitalism

Critical Race Theory in law was originally a response to Marxist Legal Studies, on one side, and critiques of the Liberal tradition, on the other. Although it aligned itself politically with aspects of the former, CRT in law found that Marxism inadequately dealt with the racialization thesis of society, which cannot be explained simply by appealing to the machinations of a capitalist economy (Crenshaw et al., 1995). On the other hand, Liberalism falls prey to a nonracial idea of the social contract and sees itself as functioning outside of racial assumptions that affect both the construction and enforcement of the law (see Mills, 1997). Its most common iteration prides itself on the color-blindness of the U.S. Constitution (Gotanda, 1995). Both Marxist and Liberal discourses fail to capture the law of racialization and racialization of the law. When CRT makes it way to education, we notice a parallel history.

As explained in the first part of this chapter, Critical Pedagogy was sparked by Freire's 1970 publication of *Pedagogy of the Oppressed* and became a Marxist-inspired program in the educational literature (Gottesman, 2010; Leonardo, 2004b). Elaborated by Aronowitz and Giroux (1985) in *Education Under Siege*, Critical Pedagogy has since created an intellectual industry that favors a primary engagement with capitalism's influence over education. Even when Critical Pedagogy criticizes Marxist orthodoxy, it has the effect of centering Marxism as a main feature, with race as a matinée show. Like its predecessor in law, CRT in education shares a similar genealogy insofar as it points out the limitations of a singular focus on the economy as the privileged locus of critique. That said, CRT never went so far as to reject the implications of a class study of schooling. Instead, it assimilated some of the latter's concepts and concerns.

Unlike Marxism, or its educational cousin, Critical Pedagogy, which has had a tepid love affair with race analysis, CRT does not have an ambivalent relationship with class analysis, although it maintains a healthy suspicion about Marxism. Because it is a discourse led by scholars of color in education, who in general understand that racism is a function of economic strife, CRT has developed race and class insights alongside each other. At the very least, it gestures toward an elliptical argument with two centers. But in doing so, CRT ultimately superimposes a racial discourse over class issues. In effect, *class attains a color* within CRT discourse, but the basic discursive structure of CRT does not incorporate Marxism's problematic, such as a fundamental analysis of capital. Its argumentative structure is fundamentally unchanged by Marxism. Class is seen through racial eyes.

This section examines the manner in which CRT subsumes concerns with class within a fundamentally racial discourse and explanation. This is different from performing a race *and* class synthesis whose goal is to privilege neither framework and that instead offers an intersectional, integrated, *race-class* perspective. Coming from a slightly different direction, Brown and De Lissovoy's (2011) uptake of the Black radical tradition argues for the study of race within the larger development and foregrounding of capital, finding the "unity" of race and class relations therein. I will have more to say about the Marxist understanding of race in Chapter 2. My overall project has been to locate the unity between studies of capitalism, such as the division of labor, and themes of racialization, such as philosophies of personhood (for similar arguments, see also Preston, 2009; Stovall, 2006). My current argument regarding CRT's relationship with Marxism is twofold. First, how does CRT understand Marxist concepts, which shows up in the way it appropriates them? Second, how does CRT understand the role of capitalism, therefore both shedding light on its position regarding the class problem as well as framing the nature of race contestation by superimposing a racial understanding over class? It is no doubt attentive to class, but this is not the same as performing an immanent critique of capitalism.

The Concept of Cultural Capital. Nowhere is CRT's relationship with class analysis more clear than in its uptake of Bourdieu's (1977a) concept of cultural capital. It is one of the most frequently used and critiqued class-oriented concepts in the CRT literature on education. There are several species of the appropriation. First, in an endorsement of Bourdieu's concept, cultural capital is used to explain school biases against more or less essential(ist) cultures of color, their family value systems, and their priorities. Consistent with Bourdieu's ideas about class stratification but applied to race, CRT scholars indict the White standards of learning in schools, from the English forms that are recognized (Delpit, 1995), to the behaviors that are punished or rewarded (Ferguson, 2001), and the historical contributions that are valorized or omitted (Loewen, 1995). Through what Bourdieu and Passeron (1977/1990) call the cultural arbitrary, the dominant race's particularity is disguised as a universal. As a result, White racial worldviews are honored as objective standards for general student comportment and achievement. They remain unmarked, even unremarkable, that is, normalized.

It is easy to see the usefulness of Bourdieu's framework when the adoption of White standards by students of color confirms his sociological concept of symbolic violence (Bourdieu, 1977b), or how power is best hidden from view when it passes as objective or unnoticeable, scientific rather than ideological, and part of the order of things rather than having social origins. It may even become engrafted onto people's self-concepts, be sedimented at the level of their bodies and musculature, and affect their relations with others. Bourdieu refers to this agent–structure relation as one's *habitus*, which is at once a group sentiment, but apprehended as a person's subjective understanding of his or her objective chances for success within particular contests for resources. These struggles happen within the context of *fields*, or specific configurations of power and how they are regulated. At this level of understanding, CRT is harmonious with a Bourdieuan class analysis. However, when we keep in mind the idea that the descriptive function of theory may carry with it partial understandings of social phenomena, Bourdieu's framework begins to look suspect to CRT sensibilities.

Any critical theory, of race or otherwise, simultaneously consists of a descriptive and a normative component. To the best of their abilities, critical theorists render phenomena intelligible through the use of theories, usually based on empirical data and in recursive relationship with it (Anyon, 2009). In doing so, they build scientific explanations for how racial dynamics work. However, it is not as neat as that. As Said (1979) reminds us, no intellectual has ever successfully removed him- or herself from participation in social life and therefore exists within his or her interpretations and not outside of them. In this sense, theories, even critical ones, contain a normative dimension wherein intellectuals' own ideological preferences enter the conceptual framework. This does not preclude them from arriving at more or less objective descriptions of racial phenomena under study, but their positionality ensures us that something extra-scientific seeps into the process.

As I explained in the first part of this chapter, Eagleton (1996) points out that objectivity does not equate with neutrality. His example is Marx, who mapped the objective functionings of the capitalist economy, while maintaining a partisan hostility toward capitalism. The second did not prevent Marx from realizing the first. In our haste to reject the pretense of objectivity as the favored child of positivism, Harding (1991) finds that science is indeed objective, just not objective enough because it excludes from participation in it the mass of women, people from third-world countries, and other marginalized groups. Therefore, the goal is "strong objectivity," or the greater, democratic participation of hitherto excluded peoples.

For Althusser (1971), this intrusion is ideology itself, the opposite but complementary part of science. Ideology threatens science at every turn, as much as dark energy in the universe is the repelling force that may tear the galaxies apart from one another if it wins over the attractive force of gravity. So it goes with critical race thought. As intellectuals describe the motions of race, we render it controllable, intelligible, less mysterious. But we explain the social universe *as* racialized beings, and our explanations have racial consequences.

Application to Race. Bourdieuan theory's application to race is not without problems. To Yosso (2005, 2006), it is a lopsided attempt to speak to issues of racial domination. This is where the love affair with "cultural capital" turns south. Favoring the domination half of the story, Bourdieu fails to capture the agency side of resistance theories. Or worse, without reinventing his theory of cultural capital, race scholars recapitulate a deficit model of people of color. Conceived primarily through the master race's imaginary, people of color come out of the other end as derogated groups, whose culture lacks honor *in the eyes of Whites.* This could not be dismissed as simply untrue. However, by constructing cultures of color in this manner, a Bourdieuan-inspired theory cannot break out of the dominant frame that recalls Moynihan's (1965) criticisms of families of color (see also Glazer & Moynihan, 1970). Slightly different, Oscar Lewis's (1968) culture of poverty thesis gestures toward a structural explanation but one overshadowed and overwhelmed by the reception of its cultural argument.

Within this framework, people of color embody pathological cultural practices, lack moral principles, and do not persevere, again, according to the White imaginary. This belief in the fragility of people of color has long roots if we remember that Fanon (1952/1967) spent considerable text debunking the colonialist mentality that conceives of Africans as weak and prone to be dominated. But to people of color, being a minority is defined not by a fundamental lack but by the strength to withstand oppression, build beautiful cultures in the face of denigration, and even thrive when they were not expected to survive. If these criticisms are correct, Bourdieu's theory does not account for these resistant threads in minority lives and even aids in further marginalizing them when it reinforces the deficit discourse about them.

To some CRTheorists, if the situation were reversed, and Whites entered situations wherein their cultural codes were not dominant, the culture of people of color would be the guiding form of capital. For example, if White middle-class children entered the ghetto, they would find that their assumed norms did not guide interactions between people and they quickly would realize that they were out of place and even found to be lacking. Their daily culture would mismatch what was expected of them, much as the way children of color enter schools out of sync with the official milieu—what Lareau (2003) calls separation compared with the interconnectedness that middle-class people experience.

Whites in ghettos, barrios, and ethnic enclaves would discover themselves as Other, perhaps even feel the situation inhospitable. They would realize that *educación* is not mainly an academic exercise about abstract mastery of information but a way of relating to a community and maintaining communal ties (Valenzuela, 1999). Whites would discover that their English form would not be centered, but rather Black English vernaculars, Spanglish, and other hybrid forms of communication or code-switching foreign to many Whites (MacSwan, 2005). In short, White cultural capital would have little exchange value in these spheres of color, and Whites could not count on the usual privileges associated with their worldview and cultural practice. The cultural capital of color would be the privileged medium, and Whites would have to contend with it. Yosso (2005, 2006) extends the inversion of Bourdieu's framework even further to argue for the multiple forms of capital that people of color possess, such as aspirational, linguistic, navigational, social, familial, and resistant capital. Without going over each form of capital in this list, the upshot is that people of color have developed communal forms of cultural wealth in efforts to succeed in conditions that thwart their communities.

Taking her cue from Oliver and Shapiro's *Black Wealth, White Wealth* (1997), Yosso's (2005, 2006) innovation rests on the distinction between "capital" and "wealth." Whereas the former concept is limited to considering mainly income, salary, and wages, the latter is broader and includes accumulated resources over time. It is in this sense that Oliver and Shapiro's analysis of wealth disparities brings to sharper focus racial inequality amid arguments that Black income is catching up to White levels since the steady rise of the Black middle class in the 1970s. By including such indicators as home equity, stocks and savings, and levels of debt, Oliver and Shapiro convincingly paint a systematic portrait of Black disadvantage and overall White advantage. In general, White families bequeath wealth upon their children, whereas Black children inherit debt from their parents. This is ironic if taken in light of the wealth that enslaved African Americans created for the United States. It brings support for Ladson-Billings's (2007) shift of discourse from the deficit of African Americans to this nation's unpaid debt to them. The empirical data are convincing and the theoretical shift is elegant. Oliver and Shapiro are right to point out that the racial situation is *worse* if we shift the analysis from income to wealth.

But Yosso's appropriation of Oliver and Shapiro's framework travels in the other direction. With respect to communities of color, the shift from capital to wealth signals a *better* condition. This is made possible by a couple of working assumptions. The move from economic wealth to cultural wealth allows Yosso and others to affirm the redeeming aspects of wealth in order to argue from a position of strength rather than weakness. So the sting of capital à la Bourdieu is exchanged for Moll and Gonzalez's (2004) anthropological concept of "funds of knowledge," wherein marginalized communities bring with them a multitude of resources that schools ought to recognize and legitimize.

However, as Lubienski (2003) diagnosed, the conflation between Bourdieu's idea of cultural capital and Moll and Gonzalez's appeal for a funds-of-knowledge approach effectively "celebrates diversity and denies disparities." Although it would be too much to claim that CRT denies disparities when in fact it highlights them, the lesson here revolves around the hasty return to appreciating diversity as the antidote to disparity. This is a clear instance where the racial logic of CRT is grafted onto a class analysis. Bourdieu keeps his critical eye on the limiting situation of class inequality, *which he does not endorse.* In fact, as a critical sociologist, he considers private enterprise from the university to Univision, a sign of neoliberalism's hegemony, which intellectuals would do well to abate. He describes the inner workings of objective class structures as they work their way into the subjective and incomplete understandings of people. In his zeal to unveil this process, Bourdieu has been criticized for ignoring the role of agency in favor of an apparent cultural determinism. To these critics, Bourdieu and Passeron (1977/1990) provide a response in the Introduction to *Reproduction.* But my analysis is less concerned with Bourdieu's self-defense and more with CRT's relationship with class analysis, so I will put aside his quarrels with his detractors.

CRT and Class Analysis. In a class analysis, there is rarely an occasion where class diversity is celebrated. This is where both the endorsement and rejection of Bourdieu's thesis ironically share something in common. The appeal for different forms of cultural capital is a distinctly racial argument grounded on the appreciation of diversity. To scholars who appropriate Bourdieu, a framework for appreciating minority cultures becomes available.

To his detractors, Bourdieu does not go far enough and unwittingly contributes to the derogation of these same cultures. However, both sides of the argument converge on their use of capital. Critical race scholars fault Bourdieu for failing to appreciate minority cultural capital, which places his ideas alongside cultural poverty arguments from Oscar Lewis and others.

Within a Marxist understanding, crafting an argument to appreciate class diversity does not make sense because it would only perpetuate a society organized around class relations, this time with the added dimension of tolerating such differences instead of obliterating them en route to a classless society. There are nuances to this argument but this is a baseline understanding. Any effort to appreciate class differences as anything but violent is doomed to fail because it cannot structurally work. By definition, a class-based society is predicated on the exploitation of a class of workers by the owners. A diversity paradigm for class relations is incompatible with Marxism.

Furthermore, capital is a negatively relational concept. The bourgeoisie owns capital because it exploits the workers, extracts surplus value from them, and as a result maintains social advantage over them in all spheres of life, including education. This is Marxism's theory of power as possessed by some over many, much to the chagrin of Foucault and his proponents who argue that power is neither repressive nor something to be owned, let alone by one group. I will return to this concept of power in Chapter 4. For now, capital is a diabolical relation based on exploitation.

When CRT suggests that there are multiple forms of cultural capital, some dominant, some nondominant (Carter, 2003), it builds into the concept a certain amount of autonomy. It makes it possible to recruit cultural capital of color as a resource and effectively transforms the concept. In an institutional setting where people of color are experienced as a problem at best and demonized at worst, countering these tendencies with all the intellectual resources one can muster is a reasonable response. Robin Kelley's (1998) reaction is perhaps the most forceful example, critiquing a whole generation of social science research about Black communities that casts Black folks within a pathological and cultural light. This penchant, particularly within Sociology, was prominent for a few decades and popularized by scholars such as William Julius Wilson, whom Steinberg (1998) calls the academic reincarnation of Moynihan. The culture of poverty argument was reconsidered in a set of articles in a special issue of *The Annals of the American Academy of Political and Social Science* edited by Small, Harding, and Lamont (2010). It seems that the problem of culture just won't go away (for a thorough discussion of limitations in cultural and structural arguments, see Hughes & North, 2012).

These difficulties notwithstanding, it is worth insisting that a deployment of capital be informed by a project that demystifies power in all its forms. If CRT claims the concept of capital, then it becomes a form of power at the expense of somebody else. Otherwise, it simply goes by the name of "culture," or is amended as "cultural resources," "cultural repertoire," "cultural forms," or, in Moll's words, "funds of knowledge." Adding "capital" means something different–something that is hard to elude and even harder to elide–because of its Marxist pedigree in the realm of social theory from Bourdieu to Bowles and Gintis. Diversifying capital to represent racial difference uses only its conceptual shell and forsakes its explanatory kernel. In this, CRT is neither alone nor the first to discuss capital as a flattened or horizontal construct.

Decades ago, the sociologist James Coleman (1988) used a theory of social capital to describe its multiple forms (see also Coleman, 1966). In other words, the empowered group does not have a monopoly over capital, and it is more accurate to suggest that a society recognizes only its dominant form. The task is to create a situation where multiple networks are recognized as sources of economic exchange. This reiterates the fact that the concept of capital exists in different theoretical frameworks. But our interest here is firmly in the *critical* tradition, one that demystifies power relations, one of which is CRT. Given that, we are warranted to suggest that not all groups' culture converts into forms of capital because of existing asymmetrical arrangements of power. It would not be unreasonable to interpret this claim as overly deterministic. However, if all groups' cultures are capable of being converted to capital, then the concept withers away as an explanation of power differentials. It is difficult, on one side, to claim that White power derogates people of color, and then, on the other side, to reject a framework that attempts to describe this very process. It is hard to have it both ways.

When CRT speaks for the culture of the oppressed as dominant within its limited sphere of influence, such as ethnic enclaves, it lends autonomy to that culture within a larger field of cultural politics. One can appreciate that White subjects may feel out of place in spaces where they are not the dominant population or cultural viewpoint. But just as Memmi (1965) once wrote that the colonizer never feels not in charge in the colonies, Whites do not experience marginalization in non-White spaces. In the first, the colonizer is surrounded by the colonized, does not speak their language, and does not know his or her way around. He or she may even be lost and wander into a town, just as many Whites in the United States have been in similar situations. But just as the colonizer brings the signs of his or her power, Whites bring their privilege into the hearts and homes of minorities. *The colonizer knows it, and furthermore the colonized knows it.*

People of color are not in a dominant position by virtue of being the center of a localized situation because they are encapsulated by the larger influence of Whiteness. These fields of experience do not stand on their own, separated from the long arm of Whiteness, which represents their final limited situation. Whiteness may not be dominant in these spaces, but it is determining of them. Moreover, it is hard to imagine that segregated neighborhoods of color signify that people of color are in a normative position, when segregation is precisely the lynchpin of Whiteness that put them there in the first place. And as soon as they step out of these confines, the great wall of Whiteness awaits them. This is not an attempt to breathe more power into Whiteness than it already possesses in order to make it omnipotent. It is precisely a move to testify to its power, no more but no less.

In effect, CRT's uptake of class analysis grafts the logic of race onto economic issues. In doing this, *CRT gives class a color*, made evident by the fact that class hierarchy more accurately goes by the name of "classism," which is a class variant of racism. By achieving a color line, classism becomes the prejudicial framework for explaining the lowered life chances of working-class students, whose culture is at a disadvantage in schools. This is not untrue, but overlaying a race logic onto class issues does not fundamentally change the analysis to incorporate Marxism. In a sense, class becomes a synonym for race within the explanatory apparatus of CRT. Class is a tributary of race, from whose banks it flows. Race becomes the language, with class vocabulary superimposed on it. Within historical materialism, one finds a different focus, wherein class is explainable through its relationship with capital, which gives it life. Therefore, a thoroughgoing analysis of class relations necessitates critical knowledge of its structure, or capitalism. Understanding capitalism is obviously related to classism, but they are not the same.

A corollary of this investigation recognizes that the uptake of class is not always informed by a Marxist understanding. This is illustrated by both functionalist (Dreeben, 1968; Durkheim, 1933) and Weberian (R. Collins, 1979; Weber, 1978a, 1978b) frameworks on the economy and society, the first conceiving of the division of labor as a form of organic solidarity, and the second, redefining the economy as primarily a set of bureaucratic structures. In fact, it is very possible that Bourdieu's theory of cultural capital is informed by at least two intellectual trends: one Marxist, the other Weberian. As DiMaggio (1979) claims, Bourdieu's work is Marxist to the extent that it offers a theory of class warfare at the level of cultural production. The concept of "capital" is key in his understanding of power differences that are material and economic in nature. But just as profound, Bourdieu is Weberian when cultural capital is used to explain differences in status, prestige, and honor among the classes. Whereas Marxism is driven by a politics of redistribution, Weberian analysis is guided by a politics of recognition (see Fraser, 1997, for a dual theory of redistribution and recognition).

It appears that within the American appropriation of Bourdieu's work, the favored lineage is Weberian. This tendency is pronounced in the field of education for some good and obvious reasons. It allows educational scholars, particularly within CRT circles, to explicate the actual treatment of students of color, many of whom are working-class students: their derogation, dishonor, and cultural dispossession. This makes sense only if we consider schooling as autonomous from the productive system. But something about the power of analysis and the analysis of power is given up when the actual dynamics of class expropriation is translated into class privilege. Just as White supremacy is mystified through the detour of focusing on White privilege (Leonardo, 2004a), class exploitation cannot be explained through its effects.

The trappings and machinations of the capitalist system of production, which give rise to social relations in the school setting, become undertheorized in CRT, which is not the same as saying they are underappreciated. It means that CRT has yet to recruit fully the offerings of a Marxist analysis of schooling. This has definite historical and ideological precursors, not the least of which is what, in the first part of this chapter, I referred to as the suspicion that White Marxism demotes both race analysis and the lived experience with racism to secondary or epiphenomenal status. This being the case, Marxism still has much to offer CRT insofar as it can provide an endarkened historical materialism, a Black Marxism, or a racialized revolutionary class. This would make Marxism truly dialectical, for in the final analysis, a racist Marxism is not historical enough. Likewise, a CRT that sincerely incorporates Marxist analysis is that much closer to a complete understanding of racism.

CHAPTER 2

Marxism and Race
The Racialized Division of Labor

From the outset of this chapter, I want to make clear that a Marxist understanding of race is neither a call for an intersectional analysis of race within the matrix of race, class, and gender, nor a racialized position on class relations. Its primary focus is capitalism as an overarching social system that gives rise to secondary features, like race. Therefore, while it is affirming of race analysis at the level of politics, it does not promote it as the accurate way to understand the *real* relation, which is class. Marxism rejects race stratification, denounces racism, and abhors White supremacy. Its route to explaining these oppressive relations goes through the contradictions of capital and ravages of capitalism. In this sense, racism may be co-implicated with capitalism, but anti-racism and multiculturalism in no way fundamentally challenge capitalism's structures (see San Juan, 1994; Žižek, 1995). Anti-racism and multiculturalism may even strengthen capitalism as it finds ways to co-opt educational ventures and make them profitable. Certainly the market is able to produce paraphernalia and consumer goods to challenge racism, while promoting capitalist social relations and consumptive practices. Within a Marxist understanding, multiculturalism, one of the greatest upheavals in educational and curricular reform, comes under scrutiny as unable to challenge capitalism. Multiculturalism's militant form, or Critical Race Theory, does not dodge the bullet either. Because both discourses critically analyze racism but generally accept the presuppositions of race, they are suspect to Marxism.

FRAMEWORK OF MARXISM

The key to understanding the Marxist position on skin-color stratification is its view of the history of race creation. While historical materialism does not deny the near-complete racialization of Western societies, such as the United States, and just as it considers patriarchy an oppressive force with a long tradition, it frames these problems first as material relations, and second as functions of the ownership of the relations of production. That is, even if race is an idea, as a relationship of power it is secured through the material distribution of resources, which forms its basic architecture. Racial domination is not grasped or explained in terms of the circulation of symbols, such as skin-color status; valuation of cultural practices, such as proximity to civilized ways of life and educability; or belief systems about aesthetics, such as beauty. They would have been enough. These evaluations occur in the racist mindset and produce their own damage, particularly to people of color who are the targets of such processes, but racism is ultimately about control of the circulation of materials, such as access to jobs, housing, and income.

Without the material base, race's ideological relations lack force even if they have meaning. Without control of the material distribution among the races, White advantage becomes psychological but not social, symbolic but not solid. These consequences are the logical outcome or destiny of otherwise ideological or speculative comparisons between Whites and people of color. More fundamentally, their end point finds its resting place in the relations of production, now a global phenomenon, because it is here that race ultimately is made and White supremacy is secured.

The Conceptual Standing of Race

This being established, Marxism lays claims to race analysis as a species of class analysis. Racial events in history, such as slavery, colonialism, and immigration, become facets of the forward advancement of capital. To appropriate Marx's critique of Hegel, these events are racial only in their mystical shell, but economic in their kernel. For example, race was used as a "justification" for the colonization of lands peopled by non-Whites, enslavement of Africans for their labor, and promotion of immigration and diasporic movement to fulfill the bourgeoisie's endless search for cheaper labor and extraction of greater surplus value. Certainly these are racist structures and benefit the global White polity, but they primarily protect the interests of capitalists, some of whom may be people of color, who recruit the consent of the majority of Whites who live in poverty.

To affirm race as the source of the struggle is to see the process with one eye closed, not unlike Marx's critique of idealism as a *camera obscura*, or the ability to invert the real basis of history. It is a bit like being rear-ended by a car only to discover that an obstacle in the road 500 yards back is to blame for the pileup. One might sue the rear driver, and under current insurance laws in the United States the latter is likely at fault; but he did not cause the accident per se. Likewise, race struggle is the process wherein groups existentially jockey for power, but it is an effect of a more primary obstacle that explains it, which is class. Like the car accident, racial groups may determine fault in Whiteness, but they cannot resolve the larger contradiction of class. As a subset of the racial mindset, Whiteness is not responsible for capitalism or, more accurately, their conflation. That said, Whiteness cannot be reduced to a mere historical accident, but is part of the rationalization of a capitalist worldview as it matures—and as it matures, its own contradictions heighten. Race is one of those contradictions, and Marxism affirms it as a lived experience, whose resolution is found in promoting not greater race consciousness, but clearer class consciousness.

In education, a class analysis of race has some analytical legs. It is a well-acknowledged fact that class status is the strongest predictor of student achievement. About two thirds of schoolchildren reproduce their parents' class status (see Lareau, 2003). Lareau consistently argues that the ideology of race affects school outcomes but retains a role secondary to the processes of class, even in its cultural or less orthodox form as "cultural capital" (see also Lareau, 2000). Taking her cue from Bourdieu and Passeron's (1977/1990) general theory of cultural reproduction, or the way that the "cultural arbitrary" (p. 16) of institutions, such as schools, reinforces the dispositions and distinctions of middle-class ways of life, Lareau (2000, 2003) offers compelling findings of the primacy of class over race. She gestures to earlier research, such as the Coleman report (1966), which finds that no amount of school intervention can stem the tide of the awesome role of family class background and resources.

Bernstein's (1977a, 1977b) classic studies into class "codes" in England's schools describe the elaborated language practices of middle-class students when compared with working-class kids' restricted codes. Supported by Lareau's studies decades later, the insight is that Black students share more cultural similarities with White students of the same class than either group shares with members of its own race of a different class background. In public schools, middle-class students of any race have an advantage over their working-class counterparts. From culture to curriculum, the former experience an interconnectedness between home and school life, whereas the latter experience a separation between them.

It suffices to emphasize here that the race question has had a longstanding presence within Marxism. A bugbear on one hand and a necessity on the other, race has to be taken seriously, even if it is rejected ultimately, like the subplot of a movie without which the main story would not make sense. Failing to deal with race means that Marxism will not be able to reach the credits at the end of the movie.

Although Bowles and Gintis have been taken to task for their heavy-handed and Althusserian-inspired treatment of class reproduction, a process that is neither as seamless nor as inevitable as they portray it, their position on race's secondary status is generally accepted within Marxist analysis (Akom, 2008; Allen, 2002b). Bowles and Gintis (1976) clearly indicate that although race status affects students' experiences and place in the hierarchy of school rituals, it is secondary to the effects of class organization of schooling and its correspondence with the economic, not racial, system at large. As Bowles and Gintis (1976) observe, "Blacks certainly suffer from educational inequality, but the root of their exploitation lies outside of education, in a system of economic power and privilege in which racial distinctions play an important role" (p. 35). Their claim is unambiguous. "America" is a capitalist nation first, a racialized ideological system second.

The rebuttal to Bowles and Gintis from within Marxism comes from a Gramscian orientation (1971) to class hegemony, which emphasizes the relative autonomy of the cultural field and the permanence of political struggle between the historical bloc, no longer conceived as a ruling class but a conglomeration of interest groups, and the ascendancy of counterhegemonic movements, which include a race component (Apple, 2006; Buras, 2008; Giroux, 1999; McLaren et al., 2002). This development, stemming from the availability of Gramsci's collected writings while in prison, has much to recommend it. Staying with a focus on capitalist development, it is able to explain the multiple interests that (in)form a current hegemony.

Ahead of its time, Willis's (1977) study of the lads in England pays heed to race when he documents the White working-class students' ethnocentrism and racial animus toward their Pakistani and West Indian counterparts. The lads either summarily feminize them or treat them as a sexual threat; in comparison, the lads consider themselves deservingly and normatively masculine. This complication aside, Willis's analysis clearly is driven by a cultural Marxist framework that privileges class analysis, if not at the front end, most definitely in the final instance (cf. Althusser, 1971), or "how working-class kids get working-class jobs." Race identification is implicated but not co-central with class. Race produces contradictions for the lads, who cover over their class injury with their White and male privilege, but their praxis lies in recognizing their objective class interests and weeding out distortions, such as race or gender advantage, whether these are real or imagined. In other words, race serves class relations. The story's protagonists are identified by their true class interests and need to disidentify with their false race and gender interests.

Continuing along similar lines but within a U.S.-specific context, MacLeod's (1987) *Ain't No Makin' It* adds Giroux's theory of subjectivity and Bourdieu's concept of "cultural capital" (see Chapter 1). MacLeod argues that the Hallway Hangers (a parallel with Willis's lads) penetrate through the machinations and myths of meritocracy within an inherently unequal economic system. Like Willis's lads, the Hangers' destiny is bound up with increased class consciousness as race seems only to confuse them. By contrast, the Brothers, who comprise African Americans and recent Black immigrants, suffer from misrecognizing and believing in the same meritocratic system even though it produces little return for them. Not unlike Willis's lads, the Brothers emerge as naïve and lacking in any revolutionary potential. From this portrait, a classical Marxist uptake of race can be summarized as a class analysis of race relations, a materialist reckoning with an ideological concept, or the economization of a superstructural feature.

Race and Neo-Marxism

Neo-Marxism is an arm of historical materialism that is sensitive to the role of cultural struggle, which includes race. As a relatively recent intervention within Marxism, Neo-Marxists focus on the role of the superstructure, or the realm of culture, in the couplet of superstructure-base analysis. Neo-Marxism provides ideology and culture their own sense of autonomy as well as their ability to affect the economic base. As a result, the educational process is given its due weight in theoretical analysis (Apple, 2004). This is not an attempt to make real that which is ideological, or to melt into thin air that which is solid, but to launch a *proper relationship* between material and ideological processes. This transformation within Marxism owes some debt to Althusser's (1971) accommodation of questions surrounding culture, discourse, and subject formation. In a word, Althusser gave educators a language that delves into *ideology*, and not in the usual derisive way that classical Marxism framed the problem of ideational phenomena. I have written several interpretations of Althusser's work elsewhere (see Leonardo, 2005b), so I will appropriate only briefly his innovations regarding a way into race via Marxism.

Race as Ideology But Real. Simply rejecting race as an ideology, or a chimerical relation, does not advance an understanding of its effectivity. This is not the same as arguing that ideology is real, but that its modes of existence are real. Stuart Hall (1980) said as much when he suggested that race is a mode in which class is lived. This distinction is crucial if educators are to avoid reifying race, fundamentally an idea, into a natural social category. But the distinction also avoids dismissing race on the basis that the relation necessitates something inherently mental or psychical and therefore not directly observable, which is an unfortunate consequence of positivist social thought. So whereas for Althusser ideology retains its fundamentally unscientific status, it cannot be reduced as such if it has the ability to function socially.

As science's constitutive other, ideology exists in real forms even if it is not real in itself. It has a material and empirical life, as it were. This fact does not make it real but neither does it make race merely an illusion. For

example, although religion is based on the idea of a god who cannot be verified, religious institutions are themselves real and assume material shapes.
Thus, the idea of God produces material effects. Likewise, whereas race is an
idea and therefore relegated to the field of ideology, its institutions are real.
Recruiting Marxist science to understand these institutions is then appropriate, such as the study of schools, or what Althusser (1971) calls "ideological
state apparatuses," which are to be distinguished from the "repressive state
apparatuses" that function through coercion or violence, such as the police
or military. That is, although race is not a scientific concept in the strict sense,
educators may recruit science to understand it.

More to the point, neo-Marxism connects its understanding of race with
an appropriation of Gramsci's intervention. Specifically, Gramsci's (1971)
concept of hegemony, or the struggle over control of common sense, is generative in its ability to broaden economic struggle to the sphere of culture.
In the U.S. context, cultural struggle finds its expression in race. Shifting the
analysis from concentrating on the capitalist State (recall Bowles & Gintis,
1976) to a theory of civil society, Gramsci provides a complex picture of
both capitalist reproduction of the social relations of production and cultural
production as an autonomous activity with moments of good sense (recall
Willis, 1977).

Through Gramsci, educators gain a dialectical language of the compromise that is struck between the ruling bloc and the masses in the former's
attempt to secure consent from the latter. Gramsci's interest is informed by
his own particular context of Italy and Western Europe in general, where the
complicated earthworks of a developed civil society distinguish themselves
from the dominance of the State in places like Russia. In the latter, an all-
out war of maneuver characterizes the strategy against the State in order to
secure revolutionary change. In such nations, the State establishes its dominance and proceeds to reflect its will in civil institutions.

In modern societies, a more subtle war of position, no less significant, is
necessary in order to convince the masses through cultural communication.
In such nations, the State represents an outer ditch filled in by a complex
system of superstructural features. If we stop here, then this portrait is no
different from other Marxist writings on the ability of capitalism to satu-
rate the nonproductive sector, those spheres outside of work, such as leisure
life (Veblen, 1994), the culture industry (Adorno, 1991), commodity forms
(Lukács, 1971), and language practice (Volosinov, 2006). What distinguishes
Gramsci's opening is his focus on meaning, language, and common sense
as sites of negotiation over power, not just its expression. Raymond Williams (1977) joins him in affirming the truly creative aspects of culture, even
its revolutionary potential. In other words, Williams's more or less Gramscian orientation recasts culture as productive, a status previously reserved for

activities found within the means of production. Culture becomes, as it were, a form of labor. Not only does this allow educational scholarship to speak to the role of schools in political struggle, previously demoted to the realm of ideology in its pejorative sense. It also opens the door to analyses of race as part of the struggle over hegemony.

Kristen Buras's (2008) analysis in *Rightist Multiculturalism* represents such an attempt. Here she presents the struggle over the curriculum, reaching its heyday in the United States during the "cultural wars" of the 1990s, on the question of how multiculturalism has been incorporated into the language of the Right. Ostensibly recognizing the defeat of Eurocentrism and the purchase of diversity, at least in public language, the Right strikes a compromise. Without overplaying her hand on whether or not public schools are "doing multiculturalism the right way," Buras follows Apple's (2006) earlier argument of how conservatives have been able to appropriate popular trends and take advantage of social anxieties in order to argue for "education the Right way." Strategically inserting itself into the language of diversity, the Right presents its own (in)version of multiculturalism by arguing that White authors and the European canon represent part of the rich tapestry that is the United States.

As clever as it is seductive, the Right takes advantage of neoliberal restructuring of the capitalist economy and common sense by recruiting race logic into its national agenda. This reframing has economic dimensions that are, if not central, at least profound. The political economy of curriculum industries that serve large states, like California and Texas, is able to shift with the times and continue its dominance of intellectual production for public schools. The proceeds that come from this venture point to the argument that neoliberal restructuring is at once an economic project as well as a racial project. It benefits the economic elite and the master race. Of course, this perceives the struggle as half empty.

Looking at the same contest through the lens of hegemony necessitates an argument that is half full. The Right's compromise does represent not only its ability to secure political power but equally the portion of the struggle won and secured by the Left as represented by multiple political interests, some of which contain socialist elements and others, racial elements. Insofar as hegemony can be characterized as ongoing, it is a struggle over which kind of educational hegemony to support, and not counterhegemony as such. For there is no situation without a hegemony in place even if a social movement is positioned against a current one. In other words, while it is possible to be counterhegemonic, hegemony has no outside (see Laclau & Mouffe, 2001).

The transformation of capitalist common sense requires an understanding of extra-economic tendencies, such as race. Likewise, appreciating the full effect of racism brings into sharper focus extra-racial considerations, such as the economy. Last, these dynamics find their everyday expression through regimes of meaning that forge people's understanding through a naturalized set of assumptions. Their "nature" is questioned when, through ideological maturity, the subaltern work through the contradictions of practical consciousness as well as rescuing the germs of good sense contained therein.

Neo-Marxism's cultural explanation enables an analysis that emphasizes the partnership between economic development and racial contestation. It represents attempts to bridge the previously incommensurable perspectives of Marxist materialism and race stratification. This move is neither easy nor straightforward because it requires racializing Marxism and materializing race. It risks forsaking central aspects of both sides of the analysis, thereby weakening them. What it recommends, however, is a testimony to the co-implication of race and class systems, or their entanglement and mutual dependency. It is no wonder scholars find that wherever capitalism threatens democratic relations, it also comes with racialized justifications. For example, housing and school segregation in the United States is difficult to imagine without class and race analytics. Oakes's research on tracking practices, what Spring (1991) calls "sorting," is a concrete example of how working-class students, a disproportionate amount of whom are kids of color, are prepared by the public schools to take their place in the productive system as laborers in meaningless, repetitive jobs (see also Anyon, 1980; Willis, 1977).

Of course, it does not take Marxism to recognize that this disparity is happening, because it is somewhat overt. In some respects, class stratification within schools is not hidden at all, even though it contains a "hidden curriculum" that encourages certain ways of being and becoming. It is plain enough to see, and there is support for it on the following basis:

- It is not a closed system (Parsons, 1959), Oakes's (2005) depiction of tracking as a rigid system notwithstanding.
- The division of labor represents a form of organic solidarity (Durkheim, 1933).
- It is an unfortunate consequence of an unevenly developed social system, and tinkering with it through manipulation introduces even more violence to the system (Chubb & Moe, 1990).

Marxism is not just the apprehension that capitalism has something centrally to do with class stratification. It is equally about the way out of such a predicament, which is to say, the forging of a socialist consciousness. Not only does Marxism locate the problem in capitalism, but it also locates the solution in socialism. This point must be stressed for it represents not only the defining principle of Marxism but its position on praxis and where the analysis leads to certain actions. Attempts to wipe out racial inequality in schools will fail without a critical understanding of capital and a concerted effort to agitate against capitalism (McLaren, 1998).

Cultural Meaning of Race. In addition to the racialized division of labor, the cultural meaning of race circulates within a society's symbolic system. Reality takes a commodity form and necessitates an intimate appreciation for the transformation of everything social into objects for consumption (Lukács, 1971). This also presents the challenge of discerning the real from the real-like, or what Best (1995) calls the reality of commodification and the commodification of reality. At the very least, it is discomfiting to be uncertain of the boundary between reality and the real-like, and disarming to lack the analysis to discern the real from the reel. As the market logic rules every aspect of students' lives, from the thingification of their aspirations to the commodification of their desires, the consumption of race in the public sphere does not bring relief but intensifies minorities' experience with racism.

From college to knowledge, private enterprise threatens the entrance of students of color into the first and commodifies the appearance of the second (see L. T. Smith, 1999). With the fall in funding and withdrawal of state support for public education during economic downturns, such as the second U.S. depression during the late 2000s, students of color at urban schools, and the public universities into which they feed, become casualties of neoliberal policies that emphasize competition and individualism (Au, 2009; Lipman, 2004; Pedroni, 2007). Where they are able to compete, students of color face educational processes that transform their knowledge system into commodity forms for mass consumption, often distorting the worldview that grounds them. It would have been enough that these are examples of institutional racism, but they are symptoms of a capitalist drive to turn every social value into exchange value. Marxism acknowledges that people of color are casualties of an educational system that disrespects their personal development and group autonomy, but no amount of anti-racist schooling without a heavy dose of anti-capitalism will explain their predicament, let alone transcend it.

As the commodification of meaning and culture becomes the dominant way to understand race relations, success for people of color within a capitalist framework becomes an opiate. It mistakes the liberty to consume for freedom in general. Upward mobility for minorities within capitalism does not revolutionize race relations but co-opts them for profit, Black and White alike. From the 1990s on, the phenomenon of Black hip-hop moguls transferred control of Black music from White hands to Black hands. More than ever, Black control of music production in hip hop speaks to a progressive racial trend that breaks apart decades of White profiteering from Black artists since Elvis first wiggled his hips while appropriating Black music. All shook up, the current era showcases Black producers, like Dr. Dre, who lay claims to discovering White rap artists, like Eminem. It seems the proverbial table has been turned. From Jay-Z, P Diddy, Usher, Beyoncé, and J-Lo, the Black bourgeoisie of music control an unprecedented amount of the industry, which speaks to their artistic autonomy. There are two issues to speak of.

First, achievements of the superwealthy make the Black bourgeoisie partners in global exploitation through the material production that accompanies the industry. Not just a musical production, hip hop is a culture so all the associated paraphernalia and clothing pass through the hands of cheap labor, often attached to fingers of color. This does not minimize the amazing success that hip-hop artists and moguls have accomplished, which is a better storyline than the impoverished lives many of them once experienced, itself also a product of racist capitalism. It seems that capitalism was able to profit on both ends of the story. It also does not minimize the continuing racism that the superwealthy of color still experience inside and outside the entertainment industry. Recall that both Halle Berry and Denzel Washington won Oscars for best leading actress and actor, respectively, for roles that confirm stereotypical images of Blackness: the first a jezebel in "Monster's Ball," the second a corrupt thug cop in "Training Day." Recall also Oprah Winfrey's run-in with a worker in an expensive Rodeo Drive store in Los Angeles, where she was surveilled. These continuing assaults notwithstanding, minority success in a capitalist nation comes with class contradictions.

Second, the control of artistic production arguably is eclipsed by artistic consumption, which Blacks do not control. Because the United States boasts an overall 70% White population, any Black musical art form becomes "mainstream" when Whites consume it. This is the case for hip hop as it was for jazz decades earlier. Because consumption drives the profit motive in the entertainment business, Black self-representation in hip hop must go through the "tape" of Whiteness (see Du Bois, 1904/1989). This means that despite control over music production, mainstream Black artists' success is bound up with Whites' expectations of an acceptable Blackness. It is then no surprise that the narrowed choices for Black representation in musical lyrics, magazines, and other populist venues for *commercial hip hop* is tethered by White desires to either transform Blackness into palatable forms, such as Snoop Dogg's reality television show or Ice Cube's partnership with Martha Stewart, or criminalize it, as in the 1990s gangsta rap. The range in between, from the Black Eyed Peas to Nicki Minaj, becomes enjoyable spectacles that distract consumers from the workings of the political economy. Even when they produce socially conscious songs, such as TBEP's "Where Is the Love?" they pale in comparison and are dwarfed by the commercial success of clever songs about parties and material life.

At some point, Black hip-hop artists aiming for socially conscious music must choose between profit and popularity, or politics and obscurity.

It is difficult to succeed in both. This is not just a Black contradiction, but there are specific consequences for Black artists, whose mobility may be more concentrated in a couple of genres. Public Enemy is a favorite among activist-minded listeners, but their message may be too militant to have staying power. Tupac Shakur was an exception during the 1990s, succeeding in both revolutionary lyrics and locutionary rhymes, but it is difficult to guess how his career would have changed had he lived past 25 years old and outlived the genre of gangsta rap, as Snoop Dogg's transformation from realness to reality TV attests. Kanye West is a public intellectual of the 2000s, but his criticisms of former President George W. Bush's neglect of Blacks after Katrina in New Orleans are a blip on his road to stardom.

Despite the global popularity of hip hop, the growing control of a slice of the music industry by Black entrepreneurs, and the greater representation of minorities in sports and entertainment, racism is alive and well and not about to disappear anytime soon as long as capitalism has something to say about it. An even more grim pronouncement is that racism is permanent (Bell, 1992), especially in a world that conceives of no alternative to capitalist production and consumption. It is becoming increasingly difficult to discern whether Martin Luther King, Jr.'s, dream has turned into a commodified nightmare.

Limits of the Discourse of "Race"

The status of race is key in interpreting the form that capitalism takes in advanced societies, like the United States or United Kingdom. Because the threat of race reification is always real, it begs the question of how to tell or distinguish when this is not happening. It may even be possible that any talk of race is already a reification. Indeed, Marxism is not a "theory of everything" despite the fact that it has been able to explain many aspects of social life, including education (see Eagleton, 1996). It has, for example, very little to say about the mysteries of the Bermuda Triangle or why Pluto has been demoted to planetoid status. That established, Marxism has made a definite mark in entering the discourse of race.

One arm of Marxism insists that using the concept of "race" is dangerous since it invokes an ideological concept, which is not a social relation at all but a thoroughly ideological one and should be bracketed in quotation marks—what Warmington (2009) calls "scare quotes." Moreover, to the extent that it was once useful to describe early U.S. history as ensnared by the logic of race, it has since become obsolete to explain current U.S. society as such. Thus, eliminating "race" from educational discourse becomes the next logical step (Darder & Torres, 2004; Fields, 1990, 2003; Miles, 2000; San Juan, 2005; see also Cole & Maisuria, 2007; McLaren, 1997; Young, 2006; cf. Hirschman, 2004).

Expurgating race from critical theories in education (or at least bracketing it in quotation marks) is, at first glance, a strange proposition to the educational ear. Immediately, the question is leveled, "What about racism? Do Marxists believe that racism exists?" The suggestion to bracket "race" is argued by Robert Miles (2000), who does not reject the entire family of terms associated with "race," and considers racialization and racism as acceptable concepts. However, these terms do not point to race relations as such but rather to the class antagonisms found in capitalism, whose forms may take a different shape, such as "race," but whose ultimate function remains the same, which is the extraction of surplus value.

That racism is the mode in which capitalism is understood is not the same as apprehending the dynamic that explains it, which is class. Just as pre-Copernican scientists provided elegant theories and amazingly accurate predictions regarding the movement and location of planets and stars, their predictive value did not equate with explaining the fundamental laws responsible for planetary and stellar behavior. They could predict a spot in the sky where a planet was located but were unable to explain scientifically how it got there in the first place. In education, Marxists suggest something similar insofar as "race" represents the outward behavior of the internal, physical laws of class. Just as the moon shines but does not internally produce its own light, so is "race" illuminated by class, with "race" lacking its own source of heat.

Racism in education is outwardly a process that explains the stratification of racialized bodies. In other words, educators are accurate to register the phenomenon as a product of racial contestation because this is the appearance it takes. In the United States in particular, the history of "race" is undeniable. From colonization, to slavery, and then Jim Crow, Marxists do not deny that skin-color stratification and cultural imperialism took place and continue to shape social relations. Students in school learn these events overtly as products of White racism and a cruel past, which continue to affect the present. "Race" is an intricate relation and covers all facets of educational life, from curriculum (J. Banks, 1993), to student–teacher interactions (Oakes, 2005), to achievement rates (Darling-Hammond, 2010). In almost all worthwhile indices, Black and Latino students predictably lag behind their White and Asian counterparts. The challenge for educators and scholars is to explain the source of this inequality, which has equally to do with the solutions they pose in order to solve it.

Race—Not a Resource Owned. For the Marxist, the problem is that "race" is not precisely what is at stake here insofar as it is not a property over which social groups struggle. Unlike ownership of the means of production and how schools prepare students to take their place within it through the inculcation of skills and tastes (Bourdieu & Passeron, 1977/1990; Bowles & Gintis, 1976), "race" does not represent a form of ownership over a resource that prevents another group from sharing it. Whites do not own Whiteness any more than they own their skin color, which prevents people of color from owning the same. Unlike capital, which forms a negative relationship between workers and capitalists, to the Marxist, racial groups do not struggle over owning skin color. This may represent the battle, but it is not what the war is about. Whites do not hoard White skin like the capitalist accumulates wealth.

"Race" does not function like property other than in the symbolic sense. Whereas it may have functioned as a justificatory narrative for colonization and African enslavement, and became legally codified in the United States during the 18th century, "race" does not describe a relation whereby resources are owned by one group and not others. It is not literally something either group may possess; a trait inherent in them, such as culture; or something they "do" by virtue of belonging to a racial community. By contrast, as Marx insisted, labor—an activity that sets off humans from other animals—represents people's ability to produce history and confront its meaning.

As beings in labor, humans possess a level of consciousness that imbues their productions with significance beyond their utility and form. By externalizing their inner experience through labor, humans objectify themselves through the material world and realize their ties with history, others, and their own primordial make-up as laboring animals. Their genetic link is confirmed. Classroom teachers intuitively understand this process when they showcase students' work by pasting it on the walls, most evident during Open House. In this sense, education is a process of self-objectification. Although not hailed as a Marxist, John Dewey (1938) understood this organic and dialectical process as one of instrumentalism, or the pragmatic relationship between students and the environment, and the learning activities that form the arc between them.

On the other hand, "race" does not form a natural link with one's humanity and its general properties. Whereas a person is alienated when the otherwise free process of labor is turned into the drudgery of meaningless work (see Willis, 1977), wage labor, or, worse, unpaid slave labor, the same cannot be said when a person is prevented from having unadulterated access to a racialized identity. The first is an inalienable right of human striving, and the second is a product of a fabricated strife among human types. "Race" no more defines one's essence or humanity than do proper fitting clothes. Fields (2003) goes further to suggest that the creation of "race" identity was precisely the mechanism that made it possible to rationalize American slavery. Said another way, "race" was used to justify economic racism. It is then an added historical irony that centuries later, Americans hold on to the inadequate and antiquated discourse of "race" to describe the properties of certain groups, such as African Americans, or Blacks in general. Used against them, "race" is now something about them. Whereas the Big Bang of racialization began with the biologization of difference, Americans have since turned racial identity into a Steady State condition wherein racial identification all but assumes permanence. How is this possible?

Through the common sense of "race," racialization becomes the dominant framework through which social experience is rendered intelligible. Not much about American society makes sense without the filter of "race." From the economy to ecology, "race" becomes paradigmatic and represents the horizon of the nation's imagination. To use Gramsci's (1971) terminology loosely, "race" is hegemonic. Americans' daily interactions from the mundane to the newsworthy are interpreted through the framework of "race." In schools, Black children sit together in the cafeteria (Tatum, 1997); White youth prepare for racial domination; Asian Americans put their eggs in the educational basket because they lack access to other paths of opportunity (Sue & Okazaki, 1995); Spanish-speaking Latinos experience schooling as either incomprehensible through English-only instruction or irrelevant even when they share its language (Valdes, 2001). But there is a cost to this racial cosmology.

Racism as an Economic Phenomenon. Although certainly not a mere trick, racism is fundamentally an economic phenomenon. For one thing, racism is a material relation. Whereas racism commonly is experienced daily as a relation of attitudes, Bonilla-Silva (1997) argues for a more structural and materialist understanding of White supremacy. This means that ideational processes, such as racial beliefs, do not explain racial disparities. Beliefs are expressions of racism but not its cause. Rather, a preceding material relationship structured as institutional forms is responsible for the force behind racial ideas. This means that "race" is less in people's heads and more in their hands. It is defined not primarily with the circulation of ideas but with the distribution of goods.

To the extent that racial attitudes retain their force, they confirm a material inequality that is already in place. Without this material base, racist attitudes lack substance and power. Bigotry may hurt and is denounced by well-meaning educators, but attitudes without their material power do not produce limiting consequences for individuals, let alone groups of people. They are deplorable but not oppressive in the sense that Freire (1970/1993) talks about oppression as the unity between subjective or self-understanding and objective life chances.

Attitudes without material correlates remain at the ideational level. They do not explain why one form of racial attitude produces limited opportunities for its targets whereas another one does not. White attitudes toward people of color are consequential precisely because there is a material structure that supports them and that they instantiate. This explains why prejudice, while deplorable enough, does not always convert into racial power. When people of color express racial animus toward Whites, it does not graduate to institutional power even if it produces local consequences.

This difference is perhaps most clear in language use and the history of racial slurs. Whereas "nigger" comes with a long history of psychological terror *and* material consequences for Blacks in terms of how an idea is accompanied by material power, "honkey" and "cracker" remain terms of derision for Whites without the same force. Racial slurs for Whites lack any real sense of material history that limits individuals' life chances; they have little or no economic impact. No respected educator encourages them, but they also require a different analysis. Attitudes are a function of their material determinations.

An ideational definition of racism has a couple limitations, which a materialist framework goes a long way to ameliorate. First, wiping out racism in education would require attitudinal change as a primary component. Although this would likely take educators a great distance, it does not address the brutal deprivation of minority neighborhoods and the schools into which their children feed. Improved interpersonal relations between White teachers and students of color, without proper materials, such as up-to-date books, and an appropriate funding structure to support a challenging curriculum, result in an education that belies the name (see Dumas, 2009). Second, these material conditions prevent students from the self-objectification that forms part of the dialectic of knowledge (Apple, 1979/2000). Certainly, one could have an incomplete education even with access to appropriate materials if classroom relations were problematic or toxic. But without the prerequisite educational materials, students of color are unable to externalize their inner experience, short-circuiting the epistemological circle that is a hallmark of education. They do not partake in the historical experience of confronting their products, reflecting on them, and appreciating their genetic link with others through intellectual labor.

Having established that racism is a material relation, Marxists take the analysis a step further and argue that the base for this material relationship resides in the capitalist economy. Race is not just material in the general sense, but economic in the specific sense. The greater concentration of people of color within the lower ranks of the division of labor, the material deprivations of ghettoization and general housing segregation, and the preparation of students in an equally segregated schooling experience all point to the internal dynamics of capitalism. In all these instances, capitalists of all "races" benefit from racism, even if the White bourgeoisie benefits more than others. Racist behaviors and policies produce economic outcomes because racism strengthens and complements capitalism. Slavery is perhaps an obvious example, where its chattel form is an expression of capitalism's brutal face. The well-documented correlation between crime rates and race is also an urgent issue, but Marxism is able to explain crime as a product of both poverty and competition over labor (Robinson, 1993). These kinds of examples bring an added benefit to capitalists when citizens confuse secondary features with the primary issue. "Race" goes a long way to explain history, but the equal representation of people of color in all facets of social life, including the ownership of capital, provides only the illusion of democracy. For if this equality were to happen, it would only make people of color complicit with exploiting the working population, including minorities. The contradictions are apparent.

These instances bring up some of the inadequacy of organizing around "race" to address racism. Even less obvious and arguably progressive examples regarding "race," such as the election of Barack Obama to the U.S. presidency, are not so easy to celebrate when they do not challenge the juggernaut of capitalism. Education programs, like Race to the Top, follow in the footsteps of No Child Left Behind, heightening its neoliberal agenda. What NCLB left behind, Race to the Top was able to pick up. Ensconced in the language of choice and market metaphors, NCLB frames racial disparity as a product of people's inability to exercise the right to choose: their teachers, administrators, and curriculum. Falling short of these remedies, struggling schools, many of which are urban and dominated by working-class students of color, are natural extensions of the political economy of cities that have experienced decline and neglect for decades (Anyon, 1997, 2011). Their material condition is such that the discourse of the "right to choose" woefully fails to explain the political choices that are responsible for their lot. To recall Marx, these families make choices in conditions they had little hand in creating. Race to the Top's incentive structure uses competition to ameliorate this uneven development and does not touch the mechanism that makes it possible, which is capitalism.

The Realness of "Race"/The Reality of Class. In all, Marxism distinguishes between the realness of "race" and the reality of class. Whereas "race" is certainly a lived experience, not all lived experiences are based on real dynamics at their root. Religion may be the best example of a lived experience based on the impossible standard of verifying the existence of God. It makes real, by way of institutionalizing it, a relation grounded in an idea. This is the classical Marxist position on religion, which needs no rehearsal here. Like religion, "race" has built societies, such as the United States, on the idea that the master White "race" is superior to all other races, either biologically or culturally. These are justifications for the former's profiting from the latter's labor, extracting value from them while devaluing the people who perform it.

Racism would have been travesty enough, but capitalism provides the social conditions for the immiseration of people of color. No amount of honoring people of color under this system fundamentally changes their material condition without a simultaneous transformation of the relations of production whereby private ownership and avarice are replaced by public exchange.

Marxism in education recognizes the awesome influence of racialization. But from a scientific vantage point, if not also from a strategic position, it recommends economic analysis and organizing around labor struggles. Over and beyond "race's" suspect conceptual status, economics not only explains more accurately the real process of wealth accumulation and dispossession of people of color, but it captures quantitatively more people's objective interests that are not served by capitalism, obscured by racism, and confused by "race" analysis. Schooling has many purposes in this scenario, from personal and age-appropriate development to healthy dispositions toward learning, and at its best produces democratic social conditions free of coercion. But these goals cannot be realized under capitalism, which comes with its own educational agenda of producing workers and consumers before producing critical citizens. Organizing around "race" does not threaten capitalism as long as it projects the problem as one based on identity politics rather than group position in the economic system, which forms the primary social cleavage and whose resolution represents educators' historical vocation.

APPRAISAL OF MARXISM, RACE, AND EDUCATION

Very few discourses in education, which do not focus directly on race, have had as great an impact on race understanding as has Marxism. Because Marxism is explicitly positioned as a discourse against educational and social exploitation, it is ostensibly compatible with educators' concern over racism, itself an oppressive system. The clear overlap between the proclivity of White supremacy, on one hand, to hoard all things under the sun, and capitalism, on the other, to provide the desire and mechanism for accumulation of wealth, makes Marxism and race analysis at least accidental partners in tackling the 500-year-old problem of both capital and race power.

As pointed out earlier in this chapter, this overlap is better conceived by Marxism as the eclipse of class reality by race common sense. During solar eclipses, the life-giving light of the sun is covered by the moon, but the sun's dominant role in the solar system is never in question. The momentary throwing of the moon's shadow over the earth only reminds us that this is possible only because the moon is in fact "getting in the way." As the moon transitions past the path of the sun, the latter's full glory is revealed. Likewise, with race moving out of the path of class analysis, the true nature of social relations is at once unveiled. In Marxist science, class analysis outshines race analysis as the accurate apprehension of the laws of the social universe.

There is much in this move that demystifies the otherwise bizarre relation we know as race. Stratifying social groups according to their skin color makes no sense in either ethical or scientific terms. Race makes what is otherwise mundane, even incidental, of utmost importance. Therefore, organizing around skin color reifies the prior myth that people who are marked by an idealized skin color share primordial traits even if they now share political interests. Not much of this analysis may be disagreeable to race scholars, many of whom ultimately accept the emptiness of race despite the fact that political race continues to stratify U.S. society. But as educators peer into the logical structure of Marxism, various problems surface with respect to its uptake of race. While certainly not a deal breaker, these limitations are explained in the next section as:

- The general difficulty of determining the conceptual status of race within Marxism.
- The general inconsistency internal to Marxist philosophy regarding the status of race.

In other words, insofar as race is at best a secondary feature of social difference, Marxism is able to proceed in discrediting the rotten interpretation from the poisonous concept.

Race Interests and the Limits of Class Solidarity

As made obvious in the first part of this chapter, Marxism privileges class centrality conceptually and praxiologically. Class relations explain the current structure of modern capitalist states and the educational apparatus that reproduces them (Althusser, 1971; Bowles & Gintis, 1976). But Marxism also argues for class solidarity against this same system as a way to bankrupt it and drive its contradictions to a state of maturity whereby its center cannot hold. There are a couple reasons for this position, which are also informed by *realpolitik* and a concrete struggle for change.

First, class solidarity is assumed by way of the working class' objective position in the relations of production. Marxism crafts a theory of knowledge that is borne from the workers' interaction with selling their labor power. As a class-in-itself, the working class begins from a place of knowing based on its objective place in production. This knowledge does not automatically lead to the working class' scientific understanding of its own interest as a class-for-itself. This second state of knowing owes itself to increased maturity, politicization, and, in the end, education. Lenin once claimed that, based on

its objective location in society and the experience it produces, the bourgeoisie needs to be radicalized whereas the working class, based also on its
objective position, needs to be educated about its group interest, political
vocation, and historical mission (see Althusser, 1976). This suggests that the
political distance that capitalists would need to travel toward emancipation
is greater than that bridged by the workers. As a class-for-itself, the working
class reaches its potential as a revolutionary force.

A second reason for privileging the relations of production is that class
organization is a strategic point for political mobilization. In a nation like
the United States, where seven out of ten people classify as White, a race
struggle led by racial minorities runs into a quantitative quandary. Simply
put, people of color are outnumbered by Whites, even if a segment of the
latter is convinced of the merits of race equality. The problem is that more
Whites find purchase in the unearned advantages of being White. Of course,
people of color around the globe outnumber Whites, but an internationalist
race movement is not developing anytime soon.

By contrast, by its very nature, capitalism follows a pyramidal structure
whereby a small ruling class lords over a large portion of the population.
Even if the United States has outsourced much of its cheap labor to Asia
and Latin America, most Americans eke out a radically different existence
from the wealthy. Based on this real situation, class centrality has much to
recommend it, even for non-Marxists. Its logic casts a wider net and captures more citizens' daily existence. Because of capitalism's ability to co-opt
or commodify every nook and cranny of American life, it is not difficult to
convince people that class trumps race, especially in a context that is becoming increasingly color-blind. Class implicates a larger swathe of Americans
across race, and it can be said that poverty comes in only one color: gray.

These points to recommend Marxism notwithstanding, it appears that
race captures the imagination of Americans. For better or worse, race has
become the dominant language. From public figures to protection of private
property, Americans use racial common sense to interpret their daily lives.
Thus, from a purely strategic stance and based on recent history, race organizing appears to overtake class solidarity. Marxists are very clear about the
limitations of raciology, which is epiphenomenal, or remains at the surface,
at best and a form of false consciousness at worst.

However, if class hovers around our heads, it seems race is lodged in our
hearts. For example, understood to be a race-based mobilization, the Civil
Rights Movement and the legislation to which it gave birth are the most
sweeping examples of social change the country has ever experienced, perhaps second only to the end of slavery. To the extent that a class agenda was
present in the movement, it played second fiddle to race and failed to capture its imagination. Although class organizing makes sense quantitatively,

it misses the mark qualitatively. The strategic centrality of class gives way to the political weight of race. This does not mean that class relations are absent in race. Far from it, U.S. race relations are partners in crime with capitalism, and one cannot be understood without the other. The point is that Marxism has to be put on its racial feet in order to make sense of the particular context that is the United States.

As pointed out earlier in this chapter, the perennial problem of the "achievement gap" in schools is a euphemism for race-based disparities. The educational anxiety that disturbs many educators is driven by the White/Asian–Black/Latino divide. Simply put, even when research controls for class, the first group's rate of attainment outruns the second's. In short, there is a racial remainder that must be explained rather than explained away through class analysis. For Native Americans, this predicament has reached urgent status, where achievement is coupled with frightening rates of teenage suicide. For these students of color, schooling has become irrelevant, punishing, and even violent to their way of life. For these reasons, race relations are intimate with their individual lives, self-concept, and group experience.

Race as Ideology

Marxist-ideology critique suggests that race may be reduced to the status of an idea. Because it is something people are, rather than what they do, race identity does not fit very well within a Marxist understanding. By contrast, capitalists are defined not by their identity but by their place in relations of production. There is no physical basis for being a capitalist; capitalists are, outside of transposable markers, indiscernible from workers at the level of appearance; finally, capitalists' self-concept is borne from their social practice. A person is a capitalist by virtue of owning the means of production and entering into legally protected, yet unfair, relations with workers. Should a capitalist sever these ties, he or she no longer functions as a capitalist. The same body may well become a worker if the conditions were met.

Outside of ambiguities or exceptions to the rule, in race relations people are understood to belong to and are marked by race affiliations across gender, sexuality, and class. Even the phenomenon of Blacks "passing" as Whites confirms the fact that they have a "true" or private racial affiliation, which they hide, and a "false" public one. The concept of White "race traitors," or Whites who look but do not act White, which I take up in Chapter 3, is dogged by the idea that the race structure stubbornly interprets them as White despite their protestations and attempts to confuse it. Whereas Marxism recognizes a material world, race theory understands a corporeal one. Race-conscious people do not always support this facet of race, as Fanon (1952/1967) clearly demonstrates in *Black Skin, White Masks*, where he diagnoses Blacks' betrayal by the fact of their Blackness, their somatic marking from which there seems no escape. Only the evisceration of race relations would subvert it.

Rejecting the Social Contract. That race is an idea is rarely if ever debated, even by race scholars. It is well acknowledged that race was a European invention in order to justify both the ill treatment of subpersons of color and the elevation of European personhood. This moment usually came with the expropriation of racialized people's labor and natural resources. So far, this is compatible with Marxism. Yet there is disagreement in how causally to describe the actual social mechanism responsible for race as a social relation. Marxism recognizes the problem of racism, but considers it a symptom of capitalist relations, not race relations. This runs counter to much of critical race scholarship, which, while not rejecting out of hand the pivotal role of the capitalist division of labor in intensifying racism, does not find economic determinism convincing. This does not suggest that there is a shortage of card-carrying Marxists of color within and without education. However, as an explanatory framework, Marxism runs into limitations when it reduces race to an idea rather than a lived experience.

If relegated to the status of an ideology, racism does not warrant the seriousness that it registers in the lives of many people of color. It violates their common sense, and not in the way that Gramsci (1971) defined it. As a lived experience, displacing race with class invalidates

- The microaggressions (Kohli & Solórzano, 2012) and daily assaults (Ladson-Billings, 1998) that minority students and educators suffer.
- The lack of human recognition that makes it possible to treat them as disposable people (Bales, 1999).
- The structures that enable their marginalization in mundane affairs, such as affording them human decency (hooks, 1996), as well as large-scale disenfranchisement from governance, such as the right to vote and when they vote, the right to be counted.

In other words, the ideology of race defines the modern era, wherein the racial contract (Mills, 1997) becomes the actual reality masked by an idealized social contract. The social contract is a staple of Enlightenment philosophy, made popular by Locke and Kant, but which includes Marxism.

Marxism's reduction of race to chimerical status means that, as an ideology, race is neither part nor product of existing social relations. At best, it is derivative of them. Breaking with the Liberal tradition of social contract theory, Marxism argues that a materialist contract better explains and serves the plight of hitherto oppressed people. Because the idealistic social contract inherited from Locke focuses on inalienable private property rights, which then graduates to Kant's treatise on the inalienable respect for persons, Marxism strikes a blow to bourgeois theories of justice that protect propertied individuals. As a result, those segments of society that own only their labor are vulnerable to idealist social contracts that preserve property rights and therefore project an ideal, rather than real, sense of democracy.

However, to Charles Mills (1997), Lockean thought, Kantian ethical theory, and Marxism say nothing about *humans who are themselves properties of other humans.* If Marxism is an improvement over Liberalism through radical philosophy, it accomplishes this move through racial conservatism. This does not mean that Marx did not appreciate enslavement or the colonial form, but that he had incompletely grasped its racial content. As slaves, Africans in the New World fell outside of these theories in several problematic ways.

Within Liberalism, the assumption of property presumes the ascension of Whiteness as a form of property right, and Blackness as its chattel counterpart. The elevation of property rights penetrated social relations to the core, providing a paradigmatic understanding of race. As Cheryl Harris's (1995) key essay argues, Whiteness functions as a form analogous to property.

1. Whiteness becomes property through the objectification of African slaves, a process that set the precondition for "propertizing" human life (p. 279). Whiteness takes the form of ownership, the defining attribute of free individuals, which Africans did not have.
2. Through the reification and subsequent hegemony of White people, Whiteness is transformed into the common sense that becomes law. As a given right of the individual White person, Whiteness can be enjoyed, like any property, by exercising and taking advantage of privileges co-extensive with Whiteness.
3. Like a house, Whiteness can be demarcated and fenced off as a territory of White people that keeps Others out. Thus, calling a White person "Black" was enough reason, as late as 1957, to sue for character defamation; the same could not be said of a Black person being mistaken for "White." This was a certain violation of property rights much like breaking into someone's house.

In all, Whites became the subjects of property, with Others as its objects.

With respect to Kantian philosophy, Mills notes that a certain performative contradiction is at work. First, reason becomes the defining aspect of human life, which distinguishes the species from animals. However, rationality is afforded only to those who fall within the category of "the human." For example, the people of the African subcontinent did not merit the status of human, stuck as they were in a primitive, infant-like stage of development. In fact, Kant had damning statements for his perceptions of African backwardness. They may be people, but they are not human, and all the rights and privileges this title comes with are summarily abandoned.

Second, this premise implicates Kant's second and important principle: respect for persons. If Africans and indigenous people of the world fall into the category of "subpersons," then respect is not their birthright. Mills (1998) writes

> Naturalized *Herrenvolk* Kantianism has a population partitioned between White persons and nonWhite subpersons, with asymmetrical relations between them. Persons give each other respect but give disrespect to subpersons, who in turn, to show that they know their place in the scheme of things, are normatively required to show deference to persons. For nonWhite subpersons, disrespect is the norm, the "default mode" of this system. For Blacks in the West—*contra* official, ideal Kantianism—this *Herrenvolk* ethic means that moral standing and race, Whiteness/personhood/respect and Blackness/subpersonhood/disrespect, have been inextricably tied up together for hundreds of years. (p. 72; emphasis in original)

The concept of *Herrenvolk* ethics or democracy was coined by Pierre van den Berghe (1978) to describe a situation wherein a segment of the population experiences justice from which their counterpart is excluded. Or as Mills (1998) says regarding race, "Simply put: one set of rules for Whites, another for nonWhites. All persons are equal, but only White males are persons" (p. 70). The early and continuing treatment of people of color by Europeans and Whites worldwide provides ample evidence for the veracity of Mills's claim. From enslavement to genocide, miseducation to misrecognition, and disregard to disrespect, people of color are targets of Eurocentric philosophy enacted through centuries of European policy. As a form of *Herrenvolk* humanism, White democracy is a theory of justice for Whites.

Retaining Racial Overtones. Breaking with Liberalism, Marxism manages to retain its racial trappings. Although it recognizes racism as an outcome of economic strife, which is an improvement over idealist philosophy, it does not establish critical distance from Eurocentrism. If it is materialist, in the end it is not materialist enough to account for race. If it is anti-idealism, it does not appreciate the graduation of the race idea to a material fact. Mills (1998) is helpful once again and deserves to be quoted at length.

> Both mainstream/liberal and oppositional/Marxist political theory have been conceptually inadequate for the theorization of race and racism. For orthodox liberalism . . . the United States is basically an egalitarian liberal democracy

(though with a few admitted flaws), and racism is "prejudice" and is scheduled to disappear with enlightenment. For orthodox Marxism, the United States is basically a class society and race is unreal and ideal, attributable to the instrumentalist manipulations of the bourgeoisie to divide the innocent workers and is scheduled to disappear with class struggle. Thus in both cases, race is essentially external and ideational, a matter of attitudes and prejudicial misconceptions, having no essential link with the construction of the self, civic identity, significant sociopolitical actors, systemic structural privilege and subordination, racial economic exploitation, or state protection. In neither theory is there an adequate conceptual recognition of the significance of race as sociopolitical group identity. (p. 133)

Because Marxist philosophy comes with certain determinisms, teleologies, and priorities, it gives race analysis short shrift. This does not suggest that Marxism, or your garden variety Marxists for that matter, supports racism. It is not as simple as that. But its limited uptake of racial themes makes it an ambiguous ally in race struggle.

Not exactly known as hostile to Marxism, Churchill seems to concur with Mills. Assessing Marxism's ability to join forces with appeals to indigenous sovereignty, Churchill (1995) calls into question Marx's elevation of European development where

> it follows that all non-European cultures could be seen as objectively lagging behind Europe. . . . Marxism as a worldview is not only diametrically opposed to that held by indigenous people, it also quite literally precludes their right to a continued existence as functioning socio-cultural entities. (pp. 317–318)

To be clear, Marx affirmed the right of Ireland and other European nations to self-determination but "openly advocated the imposition of European colonialism upon the 'backward peoples' of Africa, Asia, and elsewhere" (Churchill, 1995, p. 32). As part of the forward and progressive movement of the historical materialist telos, these nations would be ushered into modernization by enlightened Europe's strident march toward the ultimate goal of communism.

To people of color or colonized groups, there is little, if any, justification for colonization. The forward drive to modernization is no consolation for the violence, community disruption, and cultural decay resulting from the colonial relationship. Centuries later and steeped in modernist outlooks even against their will, it is difficult to discern that colonized people are better off. It is even more difficult to argue that their second-class subperson status in the continuing "coloniality of power" (Quijano, 2000) of a global race system allows them to thrive within a modern system. In fact, one may argue that colonialism prevented them from becoming fully modern, marginalized as they are in its natural development. In general, Marx and Marxists also opposed colonialism so it would be problematic to lay this problem at their doorstep, Churchill's damning indictment notwithstanding. However, lacking an explanatory framework to lay bear colonialism's racial genesis makes Marxism at least an unwitting accomplice to the colonial project.

Ignoring the Personal. People of color will find Marxism's efficacy to explain their concrete existence—despite its claims to concrete analysis—uncompelling at best and disrespectful at worst. As long as it reduces race to an idea rather than a brutal fact, Marxism will be regretfully ahistorical in its uptake of history. Not unlike what radical feminists provide for gender relations, there is something "personal" about race, something intimate that touches the ontology of personhood. Within capitalism, the working class is denigrated and alienated, but they are assumed to be persons, even revolutionary persons, within Marxism. In contrast, Marxism has little to say about racialized peoples, who exist as ideas rather than concrete beings.

In schools, this intimacy is registered corporeally by students of color as the drive to *eraducate* them, or eradicate through education. As embodied instantiations of what Du Bois (1904/1989) once called a "problem," Black students are experienced as a burden on the educational system. As targets of what Fanon (1952/1967) calls negrophobogenesis, they suffer personal attacks to their dignity from anti-Black tendencies in the education apparatus. As pointed out earlier, they are overreferred to special education (Artiles, 2008); placed in remedial or vocational tracks at higher rates than Whites or lack access to high-status knowledge, such as advanced placement courses (Oakes, Joseph, & Muir, 2004); and disciplined disproportionately to their peers for similar infractions (Donnor & Brown, 2011).

To take another racial case, Latino children have long been *made to feel irrelevant* by virtue of their culture and ability to speak another language besides English. Trained for the bottom line of economic functioning as workers, Latino students register not only one of the most dismal attrition rates in the United States the longer they study in its public school system, but an alarming rate of disconnection from their parents, culture, and community (Bedolla & Rodriguez, 2011; Nieto, 2003; Portes & Rumbaut, 2001). They are not reproduced smoothly for the workforce, according to Bowles & Gintis's (1976) principle of correspondence, as Latino students exert their own will on the process through resistance or the like (Yosso, 2006). Certainly, Marxism goes a long way to explain their place in the division of labor, but the personal damage they incur as a result of racial stratification is not easily attributed to the economy's machinations.

Former White ethnics also lose ties with their primary culture and language, but Whiteness awaits them at the end of the day, where the process is not characterized so much as "White loss" as a trade-up. It is a bit like losing one's 1980s Toyota Corolla in order to gain a 2010 Mercedes Benz, which is hardly a loss. Assimilation for Latinos does not come with such consolation, and the sense of cultural loss weighs on them. Marxism's discursive structure does not capture the personal dynamics outlined above because they are racial in content even if they manifest themselves in economic form, such as the division of labor. That is, racism has economic consequences that are outcomes of racial processes, aided by capitalism but not determined by it.

False Class Consciousness and True Race Consciousness

Part of race's ideological status within Marxism comes with the logical conclusion that it represents a form of false consciousness. Although this rather classical Marxist concept has grown out of favor over the years, arguably replaced and softened by the concept of "misrecognition," the phenomenon of race thinking has not outrun its denigrated standing as ultimately ensnared in falsehood. As one of the world's leading Marxists, Terry Eagleton (1996) is right to point out that race domination is difficult to explain, since Whites and people of color are not exactly fighting over ownership of the means of coloration. Eagleton scratches his head as he explains the radical difference between the two processes. Whereas capitalists and workers are defined by the struggle over the means of production, which is clearly tangible, racial groups do not put on the gloves to struggle over owning skin tone since it is not what is precisely at stake.

Unlike the bourgeoisie, the White racial group does not own White skin and then prevent people of color from owning it. Whites do not exploit people of color by virtue of the material labor it takes to extract surplus value from skin tone. Race does not work this way. Therefore, defining the economic relation as epidermal (see Fanon, 1952/1967) is unsustainable. Something else is going on, mainly the accumulation of wealth, and race analysis ideologically gets in the way. Moreover, race divides the workers, creating what Bonacich (1972) calls a split labor, wherein traditional White labor does not see its destiny bound up with new or immigrant labor. Race fractures working-class solidarity, and its members are unable to realize their historical vocation as a class-for-itself. I will return to this point shortly.

Race as Ideological and Material. Insofar as race is a material relation, it is equally symbolic. Although the stakes are clearly material when wealth and labor relations determine the life quality and chances of people of color, the ideology of skin color serves as a proxy for arriving at these outcomes. In short, skin color is a literal, even biological, fact that race makes structurally meaningful. It becomes a metaphor in the most profound sense of that word as it begins to take on a meaning system that, completely arbitrary on one hand and yet predictable on the other, graduates to a brutal material fact. It is important to emphasize that race contains both ideological and material components. It is ideological in the Marxist sense that it introduces a fundamental distortion possible only through manipulation and the dissimulation of reality. How else do educators reasonably explain the perpetual derision of people and civilizations of color? Eurocentrism makes these seemingly ageless evaluations of non-European or non-White worlds appear neutral and nonjudgmental, even scientific. An ideological process divides the world in these pejoratively relational terms, with Europe and White as standards of humanity that appeal only to themselves for validity. This is an essence of the racial contract. Any attempt to question it through an alternative epistemology is evaluated by the stipulations and criteria of the existing racial understanding (Mills, 1997). Within the terms of the racial contract, these protestations appear like rantings of a madman. For they are unrecognizable and unassimilable within the contract's premises. Narratives counter to them are an illegible language to the contract. Race is thus ideological par excellence because it takes symbolization as fact, and representation as real. Arguing that race is only "real" forgets the amount of daily reification that is required in making it real, people of color included. However, to stop there leaves a Marxist analysis wanting.

To the extent that race is ideological, it graduates to a material relation. To maintain that it is only ideational, or a matter of attitudes and perceptions, violates the lived reality of many people of color. It would have been enough had the racism they face stayed at the level of ideas. In fact, this may be what Whites experience from people of color who harbor bigoted attitudes toward them. Because minorities cannot recruit structural power to buttress these otherwise harmful attitudes, they remain at the level of ideas. Bigotry of color lacks the appropriate force to limit White lives other than on a random or an individualized level, which hardly qualifies it as racial in the most useful understanding of that word.

For example, rarely does a White person even know what it means to be called a "honkey" or "cracker" outside of a negative gut feeling. These terms represent an attitude, even a hostile one, against Whiteness. In contrast, "nigger," "chink," "wetback," and other terms of derision for people of color are traceable to policies that regulate them as dangerous or unseemly, such as police profiling and real estate practices; dirty and foreign, such as immigration exclusion acts and language policies; and a threat to civilization, such as eradication through education. In other words, racism is about something more than the use of ideology; it is about the ability to make its meaning stick (J. Thompson, 1984). This "sticking" is the racial power to link the production of meaning to the means of production (Volosinov, 2006). This mode of analysis is already present within certain strains of Marxism that combine a race-conscious framework with critiques of the political economy, but the "unhappy marriage" continues.

The Attraction of Choosing Whiteness over Class. There is some truth in forwarding the thesis of false consciousness as a way to explain the distortions to working-class political development. Certainly, on the face of it White workers would do well to name the structure that injures them, which is capitalism. This seems at least part of Willis's (1977) analysis of the lads, whose objective condition is explained by the strictures of capitalism, with which they cope through a will to power via masculinity and ethnocentrism. But one senses that sexism and racism are complications that the lads need to overcome so that they can establish a clearer analysis of their real struggle, which is class. Although Willis avoids deploying the concept of false consciousness in favor of a more nuanced dance with Gramsci's (1971) concept of hegemony, he does not recognize race as an autonomous system in its own right. What results is an ethnocentric Marxism that couples Whiteness with class analysis.

McCarthy and Logue (2010) call attention to the fact that Willis's ultimate protagonists could not possibly have been the denigrated "Pakis" and West Indians in the ethnography. They more comfortably function as foils to the lads, the story's class heroes. For that matter, a certain First Worldism is in effect, which centers a U.K. metropolis like Birmingham, and not New Delhi or other postcolonial cities. In all, ahead of its time in the mid-1970s with what many scholars today might recognize as an "intersectional analysis" (see Crenshaw, 1991) of race, class, and gender, Willis's *Learning to Labor* is tethered by Mills's reminder of the limits of "White Marxism" (see also Allen, 2002a).

Answering the call to identify with the White race, workers endorse Rudyard Kipling's urging to take up the "White man's burden." When the prospect of complete class domination and the difficulties of unseating it undermine the White working class, they settle for the "wages of Whiteness" (Du Bois, 1935/1998; Roediger, 1991). Rather than topple the class structure, White American workers, for example, choose the coping strategy of race, specifically the flight to Whiteness. Race scholars may go a long way with the Marxist analysis that White workers are lulled, even coerced on some level, into accepting this compromise. Against their own class interests, White workers give up labor militancy in exchange for the triumphalist promise of prosperity under Whiteness.

Under this regime, White workers give up hopes of controlling the means of production in exchange for the means of honor. Denigrated as workers, they are elevated as White. Subordinated by capitalists, they are superordinate to people of color. Quite a trick, some may say. Perhaps. Called on to civilize darker peoples and places, it would have been enough to manipulate the workers into assuming their new roles under an equally brutal capitalism. But they willingly endorsed it, identifying with a characteristically White mission of *hidalguismo*, or son of God status (see Rimonte, 1997). If they were tricked, there was a treat at the end of it.

Roediger's (1991) history of the White working class is the poignant story of this compromise. Like Willis, Roediger avoids using the concept of false consciousness to explain workers' embrace of Whiteness, which is the favored Marxist narrative that is invoked. Roediger does not give us such an easy way out. Committed to, if not also preoccupied by, the root metaphor central to so much of Western philosophy, Marxist dogma traces the tributaries of race and ethnicity to the river of class (cf. Deleuze & Guattari, 1983). It is summed up best by Callinicos's (1976) distinction between Marxist determinism and the dominance of other social relations. Whereas the first characterizes class relations, the second is paired with race relations and others like it, such as gender. Race may be dominant in a social formation because it functions effectively and captures a people's imagination, but it is not determining in the final instance, something reserved for class (cf. Althusser, 1971). Or as San Juan (2005) explains, "Class as an antagonistic relation is, from a historical-materialist viewpoint, the only structural determinant of ideologies and practices sanctioning racial and gender oppression in capitalist society" (p. 335). Without rejecting causal explanations, Roediger argues that rather than prioritize class as the root of the problem, race signifies the low-hanging tree branches that people bump into, which break and scar their skin.

With respect to the invention of the White working class, we might say that *White workers exhibit false class consciousness but they share true race consciousness.* What do I mean by this? It does not benefit the White working class, as a primordial economic group, to displace an understanding of capitalism with the consolations of race. With all its baggage regarding scientific determinism and unadulterated access to truth, Marxism's branding of this detour in understanding as a form of false consciousness is not without merit. White workers' compromise with capitalism through the adoption of raciology does not deliver them from the exploitation they suffer. Despite the honor they accrue as White subjects within racialized capitalist relations, they still bear the markings of oppression as workers even if their Whiteness allows them some protection. They are not the "faces at the bottom of the well" to whom Bell (1992) refers, but neither are they free. Or as hooks (1984) argues, Whites are not oppressed or exploited by racism, but they suffer from and are limited by it. They are promised social divinity, but many live as paupers. It is this contradiction that prompts Roediger (1994) to ask whether it is worth it for White workers to be White anymore, suffering as they are from the ravages of capitalism and the unfulfilled hopes of Whiteness. Unfortunately, the answer seems to be a resounding "Yes!" (see also Allen, 2009). Whiteness seems more than enough consolation for the misery.

White workers within a U.S. context continue their loyalty to Whiteness because in some fundamental sense it is all they have. White workers cling on to proletarian Whiteness, Janus-faced as it is, for two reasons. First, the alternative is bleak as workers toil away at unrequited labor with only hopes of a projected revolution that may or may not occur within their lifetimes. Second, embracing Whiteness comes with material and immaterial interests. Nancy Fraser (1997) is helpful when she forms a "dual theory" to explain the recursive relationship between the politics of redistribution and recognition (see Dumas, 2009; North, 2006). They prefigure each other, such that the relations of distribution so central to socialist thought are complementary to relations of recognition.

Groups that suffer from a maldistribution of resources are targets of a symbolic relation that denigrates or derides them, which rebounds to the economic base to confirm the existing division of labor. With respect to race, this means that despised communities are also dispossessed races. They bear the markings of both material and immaterial oppression. To illustrate the point, in a memorable episode from the 1970s situation-comedy *The Jeffersons*, a White bigot who suffers a heart attack is saved by George Jefferson, a neighborhood Black businessman. When the White man awakens and his family members inform him that Jefferson resuscitated him back to life, the man looks over to Jefferson and whispers to his family that they should have let him die. In a more recent commentary, during his Washington, DC, concert the comedian Chris Rock challenges, "No White person in this audience would trade places with me. And I'm rich!" The upshot is that raciology is so deep in the ideological hearts of many Whites, including the working class and poor, that they would rather die as White than live as free people.

These two representations capture the sentiment of White racial entrenchment, even when Whites ostensibly would benefit from race consciousness. Of course, it is completely plausible that Whites behave in ways that forego short-term profit, such as those with the least medical protection refusing to support Obama's health care initiative or those who avoid sending their children to succeeding schools filled with students of color, in exchange for long-term racial domination. Recognizing the legitimacy or humanity of people of color, even if it alleviates Whites' immediate challenges, is tantamount to questioning the terms of the racial contract and its material and immaterial rewards. In the final instance, choosing social death in life has become the compromise for the White working class.

What's Race Got to Do with It?
The Reproduction of Racism Within Marxism

Raymond Williams (1977) is very helpful when he argues that a historical materialism without determinisms is hardly Marxist at all. But if it were to maintain its current forms of determinism, Marxism becomes a crippled intervention. In other words, determinism represents the blessing and bane of Marxist philosophy. It is what makes Marxism both compelling and fearful, not unlike Aristotle's (1970) theory of the tragic hero who inspires awe and pity at the same time. With respect to race, Marxist determinism is all but a deal breaker. Certainly, accounting for race in education without a powerful conceptual apparatus that indicts the political economy aids and abets capitalism, which is partners-in-crime with racism. It is a performative contradiction that fails even as it is annunciated. However, to condense race to class relations foregoes a racialization-specific thesis, which is not reducible to the inner workings of capitalism although its consequences may take on economic appearances. The economy (re)produces race as much as race articulates with the productive system. How this mutual entanglement happens has been the bugbear of a critical *raceclass* theory that is central to this book.

Whether Marxism and race theory are reconcilable without a good deal of conceptual violence remains to be seen. That said, I would like to avoid presuming their natural alliance as insurgent discourses in education. Instead, taking Marxism to task for its racialized moments represents the continuous search for a Black or endarkened Marxism, or Marxism of color. As I argued in Chapter 2, the same spirit of critique was laid at the doorsteps of CRT with respect to purging the bourgeois encroachment within critical race thought. The race question within Marxism has always been a source of theoretical tension. The pattern has been to account for "race" while purging race analysis in order to forge an authentic or "real" Marxism. However, I might suggest that a de facto racist Marxism is arguably not Marxist enough. If this sounds like a bold statement, then it takes seriously Marxist historicism's position on history as always specific rather than transcendental. Coloring in the lines of Marxist thought accounts for race history's impact on the economy.

As discussed in the first part of this chapter, one of the ways that Marxism deals with the race question is by using quotation marks around "race" to signify its immaterial status. Known to others as scare quotes (Warmington, 2009), quoting "race" is a Marxist semiotic device to discuss race while not legitimating its material standing. To the extent that it may be necessary to invoke the signifier, we immediately enter a strange dynamic where other social relations, such as gender or sexuality, are not bracketed with scare quotes. Even religion, Marxism's original poster child for all that is wrong with philosophical idealism, is presented naked without quotation marks. Why race? What axe is there to grind against race? It is possible that race, like religion before it, represents the new idealism. It certainly has captured the imagination of largely secular countries, like the United States. In schools across the nation, religion is under strict watch, but race walks the hallways almost unnoticed. Race is not the same as religion, but has achieved a status equal to religious common sense. With this in mind, it is consistent for Marxism to talk about "race" and refuse to legitimate race talk. This being the case, it is difficult to disentangle radical Marxism from race conservatism. At the very least, they share a certain color-blindness that makes race scholars suspicious of both their pedigrees. They converge on the point that portrays race-conscious scholars as essentially wrongheaded about the very thing that they are now beginning fully to apprehend.

Radical Questioning of "Race". There are several key works that showcase Marxism and allied discourses' tepidness toward race. Perhaps the first and best known is Oliver Cox's (1970) *Caste, Class, and Race*, which asserted a more or less biological definition of race as a collection of immutable physical characteristics. What distinguishes Cox's work from race-relations arguments is his incorporation of race within a properly Marxist framework, wherein race is introduced into society as a modern phenomenon in order to justify and facilitate the maltreatment of non-European workers in places like the Caribbean. This relationship would find its ultimate expression in U.S. slavery. In other words, race does not stand on its own analytical feet as an autonomous relation and becomes a species of class relations.

Robert Miles's (2000) interest in Cox is instructive in parsing out a couple of turning points in Cox's understanding of racialized class relations. First, Miles reminds us that proletarianization never realizes itself in master–slave relations, which are defined precisely as the absence of wage work. The slave does not sell his or her labor to the owner. This distinction was crucial for Roediger (1991), who argues that this is the lynchpin in creating the White working class, distinguished from Blacks as "free" laborers. Second, Miles's intervention is the radical questioning of the "race" concept, and Miles rejects Sivanandan's (1982) attempt to put race and class on the same level of conceptual legitimacy. To Miles, Stuart Hall (1980) and Paul Gilroy's (1993) early work put too much weight on the concept of "race" and went too far in arguing for its autonomy and effectivity. Here is Miles's position on "race":

This does not require denying that the idea of "race" is a constituent element of everyday common sense: the issue is whether or not such usage is transferred into the conceptual language that is used to comprehend and explain that common sense. I see no reason to do this. There are no "races" and therefore no "race relations". There is only a belief that there are such things, a belief which is used by some social groups to construct an Other (and therefore the Self) in thought as a prelude to exclusion and domination, and by other social groups to define Self (and so to construct an Other) as a means of resisting that exclusion. Hence, if it is used at all, the idea of "race" should be used only to refer descriptively to such uses of the idea of "race." (2000, p. 135)

Now, of course, since Gilroy wrote *The Black Atlantic* (1993), his own position has moved closer to Miles's (see Gilroy, 1998, 2000). Essentially a reification that turns a social invention into a social fact, race is as empty as the star-bellied sneetches' claim to superiority on the beaches by virtue of their markings.

Miles (2000) favors Guillaumin's (1995) pronouncement that "race" is ideological through and through, and "not a universal feature of social relations" (p. 137). Miles continues that, specific to place and time, "this process of signification was (and remains) an important ideological moment in a process of domination . . . [and] became understood as *natural*" (p. 137; emphasis in original). Miles takes to task both Marxist and non-Marxist scholarship for accepting the "reality" of races, indicated by their persistent use of the commonsense term "race." Reiterating the well-known Marxist trope that differentiates the real from the real-like, Miles declares, "The task is therefore not to create a Marxist theory of 'race' which is more valid than conservative or liberal theories, but to deconstruct 'race', and to detach it from the concept of racism" (p. 140). In all, "race" may be used on a descriptive level but remains outside of official analysis. It does not capture what is actually transpiring, or the division of labor, but hides behind naturalized assumptions of social groups based on something as arbitrary as skin color.

As I have described elsewhere (2009b), Miles's position is prototypical of Marxism's regard for race. Although Marxists of different dues-paying levels pay respect to race analysis, from dismissive to accommodating, one thing seems clear: Race is not real. Miles is particularly thoughtful and deliberate, but, as far as it concerns race scholars, he raises the stakes. A properly scientific (i.e., historical materialist) perspective should abandon race from analysis other than as a descriptor. There are no White or Black people, only those who think they are "White" or "Black." To his credit, he does not equate "White" history with "Black" history, the latter serving as a reactive force while the former is reactionary. That said, both are ideological constructs and the whole kit and caboodle of race-making crumbles at the conceptual level.

As we will see in Chapter 3, this position is also consistent with some strains in Whiteness Studies, some of them not necessarily Marxist-inspired.

Miles seems to have struck a chord with Marxist educators (see Cole & Maisuria, 2007; Darder & Torres, 2004; McLaren & Torres, 1999), who find purchase in the explanation that while racism surely exists, it is not a dynamic tension among racial groups and unresolvable through race struggle. Taken to its logical extent, explaining racism requires no analytical recourse to racial groups—since they do not exist—as primary actors or recipients of racial oppression. In nations like the United States and in state apparatuses like schools, it literally necessitates a shift in identifying self and Other. More important, it means that an overly punitive educational experience is not happening to students of color for racial reasons since they are "pigments" of the imagination (Rumbaut, 1996). Their White counterpart also vanishes. Because Miles cannot dig more deeply into the theoretical pocket than the otherwise helpful distinction between the real and the ideological, he is unable to explain actual racial contestation, how Whites from all economic classes materially benefit from believing in the idea of race, and how race explains a fundamental social cleavage.

Even class struggle, while not exactly isomorphic with race struggle, puts on a racial face. One might even go so far as to suggest that, particularly within a U.S. context, class becomes a variant of race in a society that Mills (1997) reminds us has forged no history of a transracial Marxist or feminist movement. With respect to class, Roediger (1991) acknowledges the ideological maturity of capitalism to create a flexible space wherein White workers find their dignity within the brutality of economic exploitation. But unlike Miles, Roediger does not consider this development as mere illusion. Since he is a labor historian, his ability to consider the economic as well as noneconomic material benefits to Whiteness provides a more expansive uptake of racial contestation that includes control of the productive, cultural, and symbolic system. This entanglement is key insofar as capitalism and Whiteness become the ideological moments of racial logic, where Whites hoard control of the means of production and the production of race.

Focus on Racism. Barbara Fields (1990, 2003) joins Miles in the attack on race thinking, adding more ire to the fire. She acknowledges a time when the concept of "race" may have been helpful in explaining actually existing relations. Regarding slavery, Fields joins Miles's analysis of what he considers is the declining significance of the race concept, particularly in sociology, whereas Fields hails from history. In its place, like Miles, Fields favors racism, which describes a process of class incorporation of racial group positioning. A bit less cautious than Miles, Fields (1990) makes the categorical mistake of defining any group animosity or social relation based on subordinacy or superiority as an example of racism. She cites the examples of the English/ Irish domination and the Russian nobility/serf relationship. However, race is precisely these relations assuming their modern racial form, where racial position is produced on the cotton fields through the performance of the slave's labor and master's entitlement. Although it would be dangerous to argue that racism under White supremacy is the worst form of social oppression, its global scope is unmatched (Mills, 1997).

Although anti-Irish sentiment and Russian experience with serfdom retain a family resemblance to enslavement and genocide, they are offspring from different parents. Nations like the United States became opportunity structures for hitherto denigrated White ethnics, like the Irish and later the Russians, as ethnic conflict between Whites gave way to racial solidarity. Fields acknowledges that this solidarity is not unconditional as "neither White skin nor English nationality protected servants from the grossest forms of brutality and exploitation. The *only* degradation they were spared was perpetual enslavement along with their issue in perpetuity, the fate that eventually befell the descendants of Africans" (p. 102; emphasis added). To drive home the point further, Fields continues with a longer list of atrocities toward "Whites" (1990, pp. 102–103), painting a universalized picture of slavery throughout history.

This signifies "only" the difference between being a person and being chattel or property. This "only" is the separation between the revolutionary subject of Marxism and being external to history proper even as one's lash marks record it. This "only" all but seals the fate of dozens of generations of one's descendants. Not many race scholars would minimize the enslavement of other peoples besides Africans, but only African enslavement affects current U.S. policies and development, such as inheritance laws and the failed attempts at reparations for descendants of African slaves. So parading the history of enslavement, even if that list included African leaders' complicity in selling other Africans, prevents a critical understanding of the specificities of modern slavery, as if it were like other slave practices of the past. Fields also is ostensibly unconvinced by fellow historians' accounts of the Irish as eventual White inductees (see Ignatiev, 1995), part of which meant a good dose of anti-Blackness (Roediger, 1991); the difference between White ethnic assimilation patterns and those for people of color (Omi & Winant, 1994); and segregation as a temporary holding pattern for Whites, like Jews, but permanent fixtures for Blacks (Massey & Denton, 1993).

Fields's understanding of segregation is perplexing. On one hand, she seems to grasp this process when she discusses Black incorporation, which transpires as much through commission as it does through omission. It seems all the more strange that Fields presents a contradictory commentary on what constitutes a racially divided society. This comes across in her rather flippant comment that Europeans would have accomplished segregation more ef-ficiently had they left Africans to their own devices in Africa. However, and despite White Americans' attempts to eject the Black body from U.S./Indian land (see Bell, 1992), this move would fail to create a *segregrated society* where Whites, from worker to owner, man to woman, would experience the honor of Whiteness and people of color its horror. Based on the lessons of Apart-heid, it seems plain enough to understand that in order to create a racialized society, a differentiated populace must exist, where a tiered somatic system is in effect. Otherwise, more homogeneous nations remain quasiracial or re-tain previous tensions that are based on ethnicity, which may or may not be articulated with race. Not aspiring to become a Critical Race Theorist, she states that rather than race explaining the law, "the law shows society in the act of inventing race" (Fields, 1990, p. 107). She rules out the possibility that the law not only produces and is produced by racial meanings (Lopez, 2006), but, because immigration and miscegenation laws regulate a citizenry's abil-ity to interact, physically creates what a nation's people look like.

To make clear her position on race analysis and therefore race as part of intellectual work, Fields offers her theory of ideology. It is not without some elegance. In what sounds like an homage to Althusser, Fields (1990) affirms that "ideologies are not delusions but real, as real as the social relations for which they stand. . . . They do their job" (p. 110). In other words, they sup-ply common sense, "a language of consciousness" (p. 110). So far, so good. Or as Fields (2003) writes elsewhere, "The more dutifully scholars acknowl-edge that the concept of race belongs in the same category as geocentrism or witchcraft, the more blithely they invoke it as though it were both a coherent category and a valid empirical datum," and in the end fall back on race as a "social construction."

To Fields, racism, unlike race, is not a hoax, which, paradoxically to some, does not mean that race is responsible for racism. Race has become something about the prey, or people of color, more specifically Blacks, rather than the racism of the predator. Yet, apparently this predator does not refer to Whites because that would be a logical conclusion that the "no races exist" analytic prevents. Like witches, Whites do not exist. In all, ideology is not tangible like a store-bought pair of Levi jeans.

Although Fields's theory of ideology extends beyond its classical defini-tion as simply distortion, she stops short of describing the connection be-tween ideology as an immaterial force, not unlike power for Foucault (1980), and ideology's material modes of existence. An alternative explanation to Fields's posits that although race, like religion, remains an idea-based rela-tion, it lives through material institutions. Like God's temples and churches, schools and governments speak to race's material form. They confirm the transformation of an idea to matter.

Critique of the "Critical" in CRT. In the field of education, a visible group of Marxist educators and education-sensitive scholars have taken up the challenges of Miles and Fields. Cole (2012), McLaren (1997), and Darder and Torres (2004) have all weighed in on the "race problem." Sometimes inspired to respond to race scholarship in general, sometimes to CRT more specifically, they question whether a "critical" race theory exists. Darder and Torres (2004) put it plainly when they titled a book chapter, "What's So Critical About Critical Race Theory?" in their book, *After Race*. From the Introduction onward, they carry out a race-as-ideology thesis that questions its utility. Promoting a study of racism without a parallel study of race, they dispel race scholars' anxieties about Marxist color-blindness: "To be clear, we are not arguing in the tradition of the color-blind conservatives . . . that the problem of racism has been ameliorated" (p. 2).

Their first target of critique is the Black–White binary. Here they offer anti-Semitism, which "disrupts the notion that racism occurs only within the context of Black–White relations" (p. 7). However, in this situation racism becomes a proxy for economic exploitation. It would be difficult to argue that race has anything at all to do with racism, which is precisely their point. So the attempt to expand the Black–White race binary, which belongs in the family of race analysis, becomes an awkward dance without reference to race groups, instead favoring explanations centering on racism. Broadening definitions and victims of racism is not new, but the question remains whether any expression of group hatred falls under the category of racism and not xenophobia, nationalism, or ethnocentrism, despite the fact that racism may recruit each of them to do its work (see Balibar & Wallerstein, 1991). In the U.S. context, there is a lot of appeal to Darder and Torres's intervention and certainly a case to be made for a multiple racialization thesis beyond the Black–White binary while recognizing its continuing and structuring presence. But their plea for a theory of racism that extends beyond the "necessary reference to skin color" (p. 111) begs the question of whether or not they are referring to racism and not cultural imperialism and the like. Generalizing racism as any form of group hatred (i.e., race as a *class* of people, and not in the economic sense of class) is ironically ahistorical for a perspective that focuses so much on history, such as Marxism.

Rather than going with Bonilla-Silva's (2003) notion of "racism without racists" to describe the prevalence of color-blindness, Darder and Torres instead find purchase in Balibar's "racism without race" (in Balibar & Wallerstein, 1991) in hopes of provoking the end of race discourse and prioritizing class struggle. Their assertion that scholars are more interested in race than racism does not seem to hold up in light of the voluminous writings on the 500-year-old problem of racism. To my occasional chagrin, race theory in education may need revitalizing, CRT's popularity notwithstanding. I fear that

Ladson-Billings's (2004a) warning about CRT's steep learning curve may not have been heeded. These criticisms aside, the charge that race is undertheorized is also without much substance since within the Marxist purview, race is nothing but a theory anyway. Marxists more precisely prefer a historical materialist theory of race, so a race-relations theory of race likely will never get out from under the badge of being undertheorized.

It is true that, as Darder and Torres assert, race analysis is guilty of essentialisms, full of unnecessary excess, and replete with dichotomies, but these same critiques have been laid at the feet of Marxism. That Marxism somehow has answered them satisfactorily is only true to gold-card Marxists. That "class is implicated in all social arrangements of oppression, including racism" (Darder & Torres, 2004, p. 109) easily can be said of race, which permeates all modes of production, particularly in a multiracial context, from capitalist America, to socialist Canada, to communist Cuba. And that race struggle is bankrupt seems an excessive point since the major social upheavals, such as the Civil Rights Movement, and school reform, such as the 1954 *Brown* decision, that the United States has experienced in the past several decades have revolved around race. In all, the Marxist compromise to legitimate racism while bracketing "race" at best is not without difficulties or at worst reproduces racism at the level of theory. This is unfortunate if Marxism otherwise could help explain the experiences of students of color. As it stands, there is no marriage, which precludes divorce.

CHAPTER 3

Whiteness Studies and Educational Supremacy

The Unbearable Whiteness of Schooling

In the spring of 2011, I took part in a plenary at the Center for New Racial Studies Conference at UCLA, which was organized by leaders in the field of race studies. As a new initiative, the UC-wide Center for New Racial Studies is an ambitious undertaking that brings together race scholars from the University of California system and those who have affiliations with it. After 2 days of energizing and exciting conversations about the current state of race relations and the changing face of new racism with the scholars who make it their preoccupation to understand these matters, I walked away with a rejuvenated sense of the importance of our intellectual strivings.

The morning after the conference ended, the experience of my ride in the airport shuttle provided a timely juxtaposition with the conference. The van driver was an older White gentleman, who was a friendly character, even chatty, and he asked me about my visit. I remarked that I had attended the New Racial Studies Conference at UCLA, to which he responded with what might have been a predictable "huh?" So I explained that I was an academic who studies race, to which he replied that, of course, there is really no such thing. Such a comment had an immediately deflating effect on me, having just come from the conference, which ensured me that race is indeed real.

His remark struck me as both brazen and cavalier, but sincere and heartfelt at the same time. I decided that it would be more interesting to engage, rather than interrogate, him. He continued to explain how as an Italian American, he had lived in Los Angeles for a long time, specifically in Long Beach, which went through a racial transformation when more Blacks moved into the area. Since I am an Angelino who lived and worked in Long Beach between 1999 and 2007, we shared a geographical frame of reference. The driver was in his 60s so I asked why he was still working, driving a shuttle and not retired. He explained that he has multiple grandchildren and his wife has not worked because they preferred that she stay home with their own children. He needed to work to support the family. He looked older than his years, his skin weathered and his wrinkles deeply set in. Yet his demeanor was generally cheerful, even a sparkle in his eyes. He struck me as a worker and answers to that interpellation.

When the driver stopped to pick up new passengers, we discovered the man and woman were visitors from Argentina, so the driver proceeded to talk to them in Spanish. He explained that having worked with Mexicans throughout much of his adult life, he had learned how to speak Spanish functionally and fluently, considering it an important skill he now values. He informed the other passengers that I was a professor, to which they responded in English with some interest and mentioned that they are students in one of the main universities in their country. The conversation flowed and shifted from one topic to another as we travelled south across a surprisingly uncrowded 405 Freeway that Saturday morning. When we arrived at the airport, the driver helped me with my bags, and I gave him a tip as he bid me a nice farewell.

The interaction was innocent enough but pregnant with meaning. There are many things to say about this event, but in line with the purpose of this chapter, I merely signal the apparent "normalcy" in his throw-away statement that race does not exist, a hallmark of the White racial mindset that typifies our color-blind era. In addition, there was not an ostensible intent to offend me or my sensibilities; for him, it was just a way of relating. Finally, his deployment of Spanish to relate to the two other passengers came with ease and trespassing confidence but without the benefit of self-reflection that they actually might speak English fluently—which they did. One is tempted to call it mock Spanish in Jane Hill's (2008) sense of Whites' experimentation with "foreign" languages in public spaces.

FRAMEWORK OF CRITICAL WHITENESS STUDIES

Since the late 1980s, education has witnessed the creation of a new subfield of study called "Whiteness Studies." Beginning with the arrival of Peggy McIntosh's (1992) essay on White privilege, David Roediger's (1991) documentation of the history of the White working class in the United States, and Ruth Frankenberg's (1993) interviews showcasing White women's vacillation between evading and recognizing race, a veritable explosion of writings centering Whiteness has given educators a new arsenal for analyzing schooling. Overall, the innovation of Whiteness Studies has helped educators focus on the contours of racial privilege, or the other side of the race question that has long been neglected. Rather than the usual, "What does it mean to be a person of color?" it asks, "What does it mean to be White in U.S. society?"

Traditionally, race analysis focused on the experiences and developments of communities of color, their struggles with racism, and their hopes of one day ending it.

In *The Souls of Black Folk*, Du Bois (1904/1989) posed the question to African Americans: "How does it feel to be a problem?" Partly ironic in the sense that African Americans were on the receiving end of racism, the question was nonetheless profound in extrapolating what life is like when you are *perceived* to be a problem within the audacious assumptions of American democracy. The turn to Whiteness, which is now in full swing only 2 decades after the initial works, perhaps asks Whites the same question without the implicit irony: "How does it feel to be *the* problem?" This time, and coming mainly from White scholars writing about Whiteness, the tone is more literal, even accusatory.

The Turn to Whiteness

How do we scaffold educators to adopt the study of Whiteness in a critical way? There are some immediate challenges to implementing a "pedagogy of Whiteness." Immersed in multiculturalism, many schools have taken minority studies seriously. We can hardly find a school that does not, in some form or another, take up the cultures and histories of people of color, from additive approaches that incorporate a teaspoon of ethnic studies and stir the pot, to more transformative approaches that revamp the curriculum and entire school culture (J. Banks, 2005). In a word, multiculturalism has become hegemonic; it is the common sense. That suggests not that educators are somehow "doing it right," but that most educational initiatives now have to contend with diversity, even if superficially. These victories notwithstanding, it is problematic to focus solely on the margins, which negates a critical look at the center and reinforces the invisibility of Whiteness, including Whites' racial investments and general process of racialization in schools. Once again, they escape critical scrutiny, historical accountability, and moral culpability.

Familiar and Then Made Strange. What does it mean to be critical of Whiteness? In schools, first this means that educators would encourage locating Whiteness. Passing as unremarkable and even unmarked—from which books count as "the canon," to whose perspectives are legitimated and whose voice is relegated to "special interests," to the hidden racial referents of policies like NCLB, to the implicit norms of "safety" (whose safety?) in public dialogue about race—the ideology of Whiteness becomes familiar and then made strange. Familiarizing students and educators with the codes of Whiteness allows them to understand the taken-for-granted, or Whiteness passing as simply good values or a universal human nature, when in fact it is particular and partial. It is partial in two senses of the word: part of the whole and a form of investment.

Once Whiteness is made familiar, then it must be made strange. No longer able to disguise itself as normative, Whiteness becomes peculiar once it is located. However, unlike ideologies of color, which are not simply false but whose history has produced rich legacies of resistance to educational inequality, Whiteness has had a bad track record. As Roediger (1994) says, it is a bad idea. It has no cultural content other than the enforcement of racial hierarchies. Students learn that the strange machinations of Whiteness include the law. For example, in 1923 the Supreme Court rejected Takao Ozawa's plea for citizenship on the basis that he might have claims to be White through culture (defined as "American"), but in no way was he Caucasian based on scientific evidence of the time that traced Whiteness to the Caucasus Mountains (see Lopez, 2006). A mere 3 months later, the same Justice wrote the decision against Bhagat Thind, whose citizenship, based on Caucasian status because of his origins in the Caucasus region of Indo-Asia, was revoked. We should note that Thind's reasoning is compatible with Blumenbach's (2000) "scientific" typology of the races. This time, the court ruled that Thind might be Caucasian, but common sense said he was not White. Where the court ruled on the side of science in the first and thwarted Ozawa, it ruled on the side of common sense in the second and frustrated Thind. Strange indeed. The upshot is that "White" is whatever Whites and Whiteness say it is. Whiteness has no essence, and its shape shifts according to the whims of Whiteness as long as its overall interests remain intact.

Limitations and Innovations of Whiteness Studies. Whiteness Studies is interesting equally for its limitations as for the dynamics it is able to illuminate. As a generative race framework, its scholarship is appreciated as much for its fallibility as for its fierceness. To be accurate, scholars of color have been doing this work at least since Du Bois's writings at the turn of the 20th century. It seems that Whites have not been taking heed of this scholarship, and it took White scholars and public figures to repeat or appropriate the message of intellectuals of color in order for Whites in general to assimilate the insights. This is not surprising. Whites are more accommodating when they hear the same message from a White messenger, which preserves White comfort zones and inevitably feelings of safety. How this intraracial interaction translates into transformed White action toward or regard for people of color is less clear. As Andersen (2003) notes, "There is an assumption here that if White people would only become conscious of their Whiteness, more just behavior would follow" (p. 25). Thus, just as there is some need for all-White race encounters that deal with White privilege but that inevitably become insular and narcissistic, Whiteness Studies by Whites for other Whites runs into similar problems.

For Whiteness Studies, the most obvious of these hurdles is of existential proportions. How does a privileged group work through the reasons to dissolve its own advantages? What could possibly motivate Whites to undo their domination after they have enjoyed it for so long? How could Whites be trusted to lead a movement against their own interests, indeed against themselves? People of color have every reason to doubt that such an event would take place since few, if any, examples of social change in world, let alone U.S., history provide evidence of a group in power that willingly gives up that power without an overwhelming demand. The ironies are clear, which leads insurgents like Derrick Bell (1992) to launch his "permanence of racism" thesis. He bases this pronouncement on the observation that throughout history, Whites have found purchase in racial change when it was convenient for White interest to do so. As a result, Blacks and other people of color have been third parties to change, often fortuitous and unintended recipients of reforms, such as the end of slavery and, later, school desegregation (Bell, 2005c). Bell argues that a certain "interest convergence" is at work, which allows Whites to consider legal and political changes only when White interest is preserved and Black progress does not threaten it. I set these caveats aside until the second part of this chapter. Here I want to consider the innovations discovered by Whiteness Studies as a tributary of race theory.

A singular focus on Whiteness in the academic literature is relatively new. It is not the case that scholars and intellectuals only recently discovered Whiteness. From Du Bois (1940/1984), we are treated to stories of how he navigated the White world, its mysteries, and its cruelties. And who could forget his haunting descriptions of Whiteness in *The Souls of Black Folk*, through which Black self-representation filters the distortions, measured as they are through the "tape of another world"? From James Baldwin (1991), we learn of White society's contempt for Black people even as Baldwin shares his struggles regarding his own Black community. On the other side, the literature is replete with White accomplishments, from the discovery of science to the recovery of civilization. This latter phenomenon received sharp criticisms, giving birth to multiculturalism and allied movements.

However, if the claim signals the invention of an academic topic, a field of study, or knowledge industry, Whiteness Studies is only a little over 2 decades old. It is driven by the commitment that *racism is ultimately a White problem.* Therefore, short of this guiding principle, educational solutions that claim to "fix" students of color and their families can go only so far because Whites and Whiteness are what need changing. In its infancy, Whiteness Studies gropes its way forward, trying to find its voice and place in race scholarship. But like childhood, it is also brash, captured best in David Roediger's

(1994) charge that "Whiteness is *nothing but* false and oppressive" (p. 13; emphasis in original). In short, Roediger argues that the ideology of Whiteness, which is not to be conflated or confused with White people, should be abandoned or, better yet, abolished. That said, the abolition of Whiteness comes with the concomitant result of expurgating the concept of White people.

White Reconstruction or Abolition. In education, the uptake of Whiteness immediately responds to Roediger's challenge with the strategy of White reconstruction, the favored child of Whiteness Studies. Although abolitionism and reconstructionism arguably share a family resemblance traceable to the discourses about U.S. slavery, they differ radically in their conceptualization of both Whiteness and its future (see Chubbuck, 2004). After the early years of Sleeter's (1993, 1995) investigation into how White teachers make sense of race, almost without exception educational scholars have favored the strategy of rearticulating Whiteness, which attempts to purge its oppressive dimensions while affirming its progressive moments (G. Howard, 1999, 2000; McIntyre, 1997, 2000). Ironically, against the neo-abolition of Whiteness, reconstructionism proffers White apostasies that educators might find conveniently in the actions of original White abolitionists, like William Lloyd Garrison and John Brown. Arguing for a nonessentialist understanding of Whiteness, Giroux (1997a, 1997b) launched what has since become the dominant frame for a theory of Whiteness in education that excavates what it means for Whites to be something other than racist.

What Preston (2009) calls the move from "troubling Whiteness" to "treason to Whiteness" has not taken hold of the discipline after the discourse wars over Whiteness during the mid- to late 1990s. Twine and Gallagher (2008) speak of a "third wave Whiteness" that avoids the pitfalls of an essentialized Whiteness. The first wave, starting with Du Bois, was sparked by the uptake of Whiteness by people of color; the second wave, mostly by White scholars on White privilege and the history of Whiteness. Between abolition and reconstruction of Whiteness, it seems we have a winner. What it has won is the subject of the second part of this chapter. For now, we consider the archaeology of Whiteness Studies.

White reconstruction is made possible by two scholarly trends in education. On one side, the strategy is flanked by a programmatically reconstructionist collection by the contributors to and editors of *White Reign* (Kincheloe, Steinberg, Rodriguez, & Chennault, 1998), and on the other, the industry promulgated by McIntosh's writings on White privilege from 10 years earlier (e.g., see Rodriguez & Villaverde, 2000; Rothenberg, 2002). McLaren's (1995, 1997, 1998) writing from this period inches up to abolitionism with a language of "unthinking" or "dismantling" Whiteness, which arguably leaves behind pieces of Whiteness rather than completely expurgating it. However, it seems clear that a reconstructionist logic is in place when McLaren (1998) pronounces, "Here I adopt American studies scholar Ruth Frankenberg's (1993) injunction that cultural practices considered to be White need to be seen as contingent, historically produced, and transformable. White culture is not monolithic, and its borders must be understood as malleable and porous" (p. 65; see also McLaren & Torres, 1999). After much consideration, McLaren's intellectual feet land firmly on White reconstruction.

Against abolitionism, the language of reconstruction breaks up Whiteness (into pieces, rather than abolishing it) and exposes it as many things all at once. This ethos is confirmed by Ellsworth's (1997) elegant poetics when she claims that Whiteness is "always more than one thing, and never the same thing twice" (p. 266). It is fluid, multiple, and constantly changing. To Kincheloe and Steinberg (1998), "A key goal of a critical pedagogy of Whiteness emerges: the necessity of creating a positive, proud, attractive, antiracist White identity that is empowered to travel in and out of various racial/ethnic circles with confidence and empathy" (p. 12). Ian Haney Lopez (2006) agrees that Whiteness may be many things at once but concludes that these traits do not vitiate against the judgment that, in the end, Whiteness is nothing but false and oppressive. In fact, to Lopez, the call for a positive Whiteness betrays an ironic understanding of the history and general portrayal of Whiteness as already *nothing but* good. Arguing for a proud Whiteness conjures images of "White pride," whose history with White supremacy is intimate and familiar. The clarion call for an attractive Whiteness forgets that the racialization of aesthetics already rewards Whiteness with a virtual monopoly over beauty. Finally, for centuries Whiteness has felt empowered and confident to travel in and out of spaces of color in the formal sense of colonization and the informal sense of cultural appropriation.

Gary Howard's (1999) journey into Whiteness perhaps represents the archetypal story of what this sojourn might look like in theory and practice. In *We Can't Teach What We Don't Know,* Howard chronicles his stages of development from the desert of Whiteness, or more or less racist history, to the tropics and warm climes of anti-racism. However, although Howard promotes the otherwise appealing border traveler (cf. Giroux, 1992), he is clear that it does not include, for Whites, a journey beyond Whiteness. Howard (1999) writes, "Those who claim to have discovered such a pathway *out* of Whiteness merely demonstrate their limited awareness of the depth and complexity of our journey" (p. 115; emphasis in original). He bases this reasoning on a seductive analogy that "telling White people not to identify with Whiteness is tantamount to telling Black people not to identify with Blackness" (p. 112). Ingram (2005) questions the symmetry in arguments that put Blackness side by side with Whiteness, as if they serve similar historical purposes. This is a basic distinction between abolitionists and reconstructionists of Whiteness, wherein the first imagine an end to Whiteness, and the second end in Whiteness, albeit a transformed one (Leonardo, 2002). But as I address in the second part of this chapter, the question remains whether or not Whiteness is transformable.

All in all, the discourse of dismantling Whiteness conjures up a machine whose parts and accessories remain after a kitchen appliance has been taken apart. Even the manual for piecing it back together is preserved, albeit useless for remaking an apparatus that bears little resemblance to its predecessor. This is a different situation from razing the machine to the ground altogether, a discourse that is more consistent with abolition. What is left after the abolition of Whiteness are its ashes. There is no phoenix here, but instead a funeral. Just as Lenin (1963) once asked the famous question, "What is to be done?" I invoke the same spirit in the current discussion. What is to be done with Whiteness?

From Center to Margin: Issues with Recentering Whiteness

The turn to Whiteness disrupts the focus on minorities, indeed recenters Whites once again. Certainly educators might do well to suspect that Whiteness is up to its old tricks again. In fact, Whiteness Studies arrives on the scene precisely at the moment when minorities have gained a legitimate foothold in curricular, instructional, and cultural reform of education. These days there are workshops on raising race consciousness for Whites, educational videos showcasing the White mindset, and conferences on White privilege. In short, Whiteness Studies has become an industry. That said, if Whiteness Studies centers Whiteness, it places it in an atypical, even uncomfortable position. It puts Whiteness on trial without indicting White people as individual embodiments of an ideology called Whiteness. When Roediger (1994) wrote that Whiteness is *nothing but* false and oppressive, he was careful to distinguish between Whiteness and Whites. A focus on Whiteness surely centers Whites in an analysis of racism, but this is not the same as saying that Whites themselves are only false and oppressive. There have been examples of Whites who fought and continue to fight on the side of justice, the abolitionist John Brown being an obvious instance, but as an ideology Whiteness has no redeeming characteristics because it has functioned primarily to stratify society. This is what led Roediger to suggest that it is nothing but false.

The center–margin discourse is a staple of scholarly work on race. This geometric or spatial metaphor, which sometimes goes by the label of center–periphery, explains a centripetal force that gathers what or who matters in the center while spinning the extraneous material out to the margins (see Mills, 1997). For example, bell hooks's (1984) text *Feminist Theory: From Margin to Center* argues that it is necessary to bring the experiences and analytics of women of color to the center of feminist scholarship. In education, Maisha Winn (2010) examines the school-to-prison pipeline discourses and moves incarcerated youths' voices from margin to center. Dolores Delgado Bernal (1998) and Sofia Villenas (2010) apply the metaphor when they argue that education should take more seriously the immigrant lives of Chicanas, who face not only racism with respect to skin color but also linguicism and a problematic relationship with immigration policies. In general, the turn to post-studies, such as postcolonialism, interrogates the assumption of centeredness, from which an origin emanates and which defines its relationship with the margins through a discourse of derision and derogation. Scholars of color have waged this battle, which is as material as it is discursive.

It is discursive or representational when the metaphor positions subjects of color as dependent on and inferior to Whites. In fact, the cover of Morley and Chen's (1996) edited book, *Stuart Hall*, depicts one of the founders of Cultural Studies posing as a docent in a museum, behind whom is a picture frame hanging on a wall. The frame is ornate in gold with no picture in the middle, suggesting the richness of the margins and simultaneous emptiness of the center. Against the history of empire that characterizes the West as the educator of all the rest, representing the margins as teeming with rich traditions and robust with civilization shifts the focus away from the Occident and toward its complementary Other. The cover of *Stuart Hall* strikes back against empire with a representation that resists centering the margins in order to replace an original center and instead re-evaluates the entire relation of center–margin as a whole. It does not replace the center with the margins but appreciates the insights brought about by the concrete conditions of living in the margins. This representation against the grain does not wish to recuperate the center's logic and reproduce its predictable failings and tragedies, that is, turning the sword toward the master (Freire, 1970/1993; Lorde, 1984).

Without romanticizing life at the margins, which is marked by both dispossession and dishonor, this cultural politics testifies to the possibilities that such a life brings as well the knowledge produced by having to survive its daily assaults. Living in the margins is *productive*, which is not the same as saying it is *positive*. Very few social groups elected to be in the margins; it is more likely that they were put there. Nevertheless, life in the margins produces knowledge that neither the marginalized races nor the master race could have predicted or over which the master race could exercise complete control. Life in the margins points out the limitations of both the center and margins. It is a predicament neither to be grieved over nor celebrated.

It is completely possible, even reasonable, to suggest that with respect to public race discourse, people of color have always occupied the center and not the margins at all. Most educators imagine a face of color when issues of race are invoked: race = people of color. "Diversity," or the accepted equivalent of race, becomes a code word for people of color at the same time as it assumes that "White" is just another racial difference. This is made possible by a color-blind understanding that performs a sleight-of-hand with respect to racial disparities in structural life chances. Although White may be a site of difference, it is not a racial difference like all others.

In other instances, "urban" is the preferred term to replace "diversity" (Noguera, 1996). In fact, teachers are wont, sometimes even proud, to announce that they teach urban or diverse students when in fact, once pushed to be more specific, they refine their statement with the admission that they teach mainly students of color. Often, they mean one or two racial groups of students, such as Black and Latino. This hardly qualifies as diverse. The upshot is that *people of color are already at the center of the racial imaginary, whereas Whites are arguably at the margins.* The opposite case, when a teacher instructs mainly White students, does not count as diverse, urban, or racial. It goes unmarked as such. The discursive move that locates Whiteness at the center of race analysis comes with the purpose of being critical of it, not recentering it in the usual manner.

The center–margin pairing is material when the spatial configuration of the relationship ghettoizes or segregates bodies of color from White spaces within neighborhoods, academies, and nationhoods. Gulson's (2011) multicity, multinational analysis of the relationship between race and cities reminds us of how the configuration of space creates race, as in the ghetto (Massey & Denton, 1993; see also Lipman, 2004), which then gives birth to ghetto schools (Anyon, 1997). Similarly, the space of race dialogue is itself constitutive of race, which is forged in the context of the classroom and gives race its intelligibility, shape, and form.

The well-grooved and global discourse of central and peripheral nations has found its way into education through Lave and Wenger's (1991) sociocultural argument on the nature of "legitimate peripheral participation." In this sense, the "post" in post-studies (e.g., postmodernism, poststructuralism, postcolonialism) signifies a fascination not only with temporality (see Jameson, 1993) but with spatiality as well. For the *post* signifies not only an "after," which suggests periodization, but potentially a place, as in an outpost or a colonial post. Whiteness Studies brings the White racial post into the center of analysis in order to locate it, demystify it, and, if possible, discontinue its hold on education.

It is in this sense that analysis of Whiteness within Whiteness Studies takes the risk of recentering Whiteness in order to marginalize its power and unveil its mysteries. By this, what I mean is a certain accounting for White privilege, normativity, and general invisibility. For example, in curriculum, Whiteness is a dominant framework for the valuation of knowledge that is

most worthwhile, history that counts because it confirms the reality of Whiteness and the Whiteness of reality (Loewen, 1995), and in general a perspective that reinforces a portrait of *Herrenvolk* progress, or White advancement at
the expense of people of color (Mills, 1997). At its best, *Herrenvolk* democracy
produces what Derrick Bell (1995) calls "interest convergence," whereby
Black advancement is predicated on maintaining the priority of White interests. Revoking these entitlements is the general goal of Whiteness Studies.

Membership Has Its Privileges:
White Advantage and Other Entitlements

The beginning of official Whiteness Studies was guided by a rather simple question: "What is life like for White people?" Peggy McIntosh (1992) is
most closely associated with starting the shift, but many others have joined
to unveil what daily White privilege looks like in informal, taken-for-granted
ways (Bush, 2005; Rains, 1997; Wise, 2007), as well as its formal, institutionalized manifestations (Gillborn, 2005, 2006a; Gillborn et al., 2012; Preston,
2010). Its first expression is the luxury to claim oblivion to these entitlements.
As McIntosh's list of over 40 taken-for-granted aspects of Whiteness compel-
lingly portrays, Whites live in a world structured after their own image. This
means that Whites rarely have to ask, "What does it mean to be White?" The
answer is plain enough. Whites may have struggles and challenges in life,
but race is not one of them. Certainly, Whites are a complex set of identities
and histories, some of which are the targets of social denigration, such as
White women, LGBTQ Whites, and Whites with disabilities. Jackson Katz's
(2010) analysis of presidential masculinity delves into the way that Whiteness
recruits the work of manhood as a constitutive moment of becoming White,
which requires an understanding that distinguishes it from feminized forms
of Whiteness (see also Dyer, 1997; Katz, 2006). It goes without saying that
social and educational structures do not punish Whites for their Whiteness
but reward them for it, even if it comes at the cost of obfuscating the actual
injuries they legitimately suffer as Whites with other social identities (Bell,
2005d; see also Allen, 2009). This point is worth elaborating.

Now that intersectional analysis has reached popularity since Kimberlé
Crenshaw (1991) first argued for a decentering of social identities and arrived at a more complex picture of their mutual reinforcement, to some the
study of Whiteness becomes unnecessarily myopic and essentialist. Whether
Crenshaw was arguing for de-emphasizing White privilege is debatable. In
fact, it is possible that in conversation with White feminism and Marxism,
Crenshaw (1991), P. H. Collins (2000), hooks (1984), and a host of feminists
of color coming from multiple disciplines wanted to create a more thorough
analysis of White privilege rather than prohibit focusing on it. P. H. Collins's

(2000) phrase, "matrix of domination," in *Black Feminist Thought*, gestures toward a more expansive theory of White domination, which incorporates the history of Black women's labor experiences within White households as "outsiders within," their informal place in knowledge production in daily life, and the reconstruction of academic knowledge within disciplines, like sociology. Not to be outdone, hooks's (1984) contribution takes White feminists to task for their a priori assumption of solidarity among women without taking into account White women's sordid history with Black women, as well as the latter's intimate relationship with Black men. In all, intersectional thinking brings White privilege into sharper focus by coloring in the lines that are left dotted by either White feminism or color-blind Marxism. It does not prevent a critical uptake of Whiteness but enables and advances it.

To speak of White domination as a power package includes an appreciation of patriarchy and capitalism as constitutive moments in the creation of Whiteness. David Roediger (1991) is clear about this interaction when he chronicles the history of the White working class as a response to both capitalism and racialization. A laboring body on one hand and a carrier of racial honor on the other, White workers accrue what Du Bois (1935/1998) earlier called the "public and psychological wages of Whiteness." Not only did the White elite convince them to adopt their Whiteness, but White workers gladly endorsed it as a way to differentiate themselves from unpaid, slave labor. In this sense, social structures not only intersect but interact to produce multiple contradictions that make up Whiteness. An *interactional theory of Whiteness* then focuses on White privilege, which does not end the analysis but arguably begins it.

Peggy McIntosh's (1992) celebrated essay is a good place to start. Arguing that the male privilege against which women swim represents an analogical relationship with the phenomenon of White privilege, McIntosh is credited by Rothenberg (2002) as having inaugurated the break. Formerly, race scholarship focused almost exclusively on the experiences of people of color with racism. When White privilege is invoked, it is described in relation to its effects on minorities. With the turn to Whiteness, the history and upkeep of a privileged identity become central to educators' understanding of the daily and institutional maintenance of race. White privilege is not defined only as an advantage based on perceptions, although that would have been enough. It is not the case that educators merely perceive White children with bias but that these subjective preferences translate into structures that benefit Whites. From mundane practices, such as daily classroom management, to formal structures, such as school finance and curriculum forging, White children are presumed to be more deserving than Black and Latino children. Much of this unfairness goes undetected and proceeds as part of normalcy and racial common sense. That said, White privilege has not gone completely unnoticed, particularly in the past 20 years of educational research under the aegis of Whiteness Studies.

One of the improvements introduced by this new field of study has to do with the reframing of Whiteness as an ideology rather than simply an identity. Roediger is helpful here. Insofar as the ideology of Whiteness gave birth to the identity of Whites, it is difficult to appreciate the pervasiveness of Whiteness if educators reduce it to the concept of identity. Rather, the turn to ideology in studies of Whiteness allows Roediger to argue for the dissolution of the entire conceptual apparatus that makes it possible to utter and perform the identity of Whiteness (see also Ignatiev, 1995; Lopez, 2006). However, unlike the pejorative status of ideology within the Marxist framework, discussed in Chapter 2, White abolition gives ideology its full measure of power while acknowledging the emptiness of Whiteness.

The Problem of the Center and the Center of the Problem: The Limits of White Supremacy in Schools and Society

In terms specific to the subject matter of this book, racial oppression more accurately is called the problem of White supremacy. Here, White supremacy is understood less as the image of extreme and hateful Whites, such as the Klan or neo-Nazis, which are specific historical forms of it, and more as a general political system that serves White interests (Bonilla-Silva, 2001, 2003; Gillborn, 2006b; hooks, 1996; Mills, 1997, 2003b). White supremacy is an entire political system, not unlike the political economy or a liberal society. It is not simply an explanation for the reprehensible actions of a White group or an individual. Delgado (2011) notes:

> Critical historians have shown how seemingly neutral laws (like the GI Bill) and practices (like school choice) have enabled Whites to secure wealth, jobs, and influence at the expense of non-Whites, and to hang on to them. They have shown how White supremacy is more than the occasional practice of favoring one's kind, but an interconnected system of rules, customs, and privileges (such as union membership) that consistently enable the majority group to remain ahead. (p. 9)

Rather than define racism as individual entitlements, using Lukács's (1971) concept of "totality" *sans* its Marxist problematic, a Hegelian race analysis of the whole suggests that isolating parts of the racial system may appear rational to its observers, but accounting for the totality of race relations exposes its fundamental and ultimately indefensible contradictions. To Whites, the racial system makes sense, with merit deservedly coming to those who work hard. As CRT figurehead in the United Kingdom, Gillborn (2011) describes,

White supremacy no longer looks special to Whites, especially when we re-member that they have lived through it all their lives. It becomes the norm.

The turn to White supremacy in education is in fact a return to a pre-vious language that was assumed to have faded with a cruel past. It was abandoned because of the assumption that U.S. society had moved past its "old fashioned, unapologetic [racism]" (Delgado, 2011, p. 8; see also Vaught, 2011). This word choice does not come from a place of White-hating, but precisely from trying to explain its opposite, what Fanon (1952/1967), for example, earlier called negrophobogenesis. In fact, in a world saturated with loving images of Whiteness, people of color find it hard to hate Whites and Whiteness, and much easier to adore it or, worse, turn the necrophiliac gaze on themselves through self-hatred. The turn to *White educational supremacy* is a politico-intellectual choice to establish clarity about a situation that is increas-ingly difficult to detect in the color-blind era. It recognizes the fact that race privilege has changed forms over the centuries, but as Charles Mills (1997) tells us, the terms of the racial contract may be amended without changing the fundamental relationship between the mythic superiority of Whites and equally false inferiority of people of color, which, to the CRTheorist, is still in effect. Favoring the explanatory framework of racial supremacy neither exaggerates nor understates this racial predicament but names it in the most realistic way possible that accounts for current racial arrangements, such as the ghettoization, patterned disregard, and systematic (not to be confused with conspiratorial) neglect of students of color. Just as the image of White supremacy is not fixed in the image of a hooded White person, the image of a CRTheorist who invokes White supremacy also cannot be reduced to the rantings of a lunatic Leftist.

From curriculum to comportment, schools require that students adopt an obsessive-compulsive White mindset, even in its instrumentalist forms (see Fordham, 1988; Fordham & Ogbu, 1986). Even when students of color do not wholeheartedly adopt White normativity, they assimilate it in order to succeed in schools. This process does not happen seamlessly, without disrup-tion, and it does not suggest that students who identify with their own group orientation do not draw strength from it, which then propels them to achieve. It acknowledges what Du Bois (1904/1989) once called the "tape" that is used to measure the worth of Blacks in schools and society. The imposition leads to the formation of double consciousness, whereby Blacks develop twoness as a result of self-valuation as well as having to navigate a White value system in order to survive, let alone thrive.

In schools, this measuring tape overwhelms students of color as it ulti-mately compels, even coerces, them to adopt or adapt to its codes. The im-age of coercion used here is less the strong-arm tactics that Whiteness may utilize in times of civil unrest, as has been the case on many occasions from the Civil War to the Civil Rights Movement, and more Durkheim's (1956) sense of social coercion that compels people to participate in a social milieu. It is a process admittedly more sinister in Whiteness Studies than when perceived through Durkheim's functionalism. In effect, successful students of color live in two worlds: inside their own community and the White standard imposed from outside. They may resist Whiteness at every turn, but do not emerge from many years of formal schooling unscathed or unchanged. As Fanon (1952/1967) might suggest, their destiny is to be White (see also Kirkland, 2010). Students of color have to become "White" on some level, at least culturally, in order to achieve—otherwise they confirm White fears about their uneducability. This is not a hopeless situation as many students of color lead successful lives as a result of having to master Whiteness, even surpassing Whites, as in the case of Asian American students (Lee, 2005; Sue & Okazaki, 1995). If they resist, they may be marginalized or stigmatized, which are not preferable options outside of the romantic and essentialist notion that dropouts, burnouts, and the down-and-outs represent unqualified radical identities and perspectives on schooling (see Willis, 1977).

Of course, Du Bois's point is precisely that this burden is at the same time the gift of double sight, a racial epistemic privilege of sorts. It provides Blacks an intimate perspective on freedom precisely because it has been taken from them. Tempting as it is to consider the possibility that anti-racist Whites, even the abolitionist strain, experience double consciousness, it would be a misappropriation of Du Bois's insight. Whites may experience the gift but never live with the burden of their Whiteness, other than the "White man's burden" that Rudyard Kipling encouraged Whites to take up, which is another matter altogether. In fact, many Whites are happy temporarily to put or paint on Blackness as long as they retain property rights to their Whiteness in the end, or when the police come, as Spike Lee so aptly put it. To the extent that they appropriate non-White understandings, Whites have the option of "leaving" if the going gets rough (DiAngelo, 2006, 2012). Nor do Whites live with the burden of Blackness weighing down on them and frustrating their self-actualization. Whites do not navigate a compulsory Blackness that imposes itself on them as a coercive force. White double consciousness is a myth, seen from a Du Boisian framework. *There is no such thing.* Whites may live *with* Blackness, even be fundamentally influenced *by* it, but they do not live *under* it, which is the critical distinction in the concept of double consciousness. Or as Fanon (1952/1967) puts it, as far as Whites are concerned, there is no ontological resistance attached to the Black body. Whites do not live with a veil other than the proverbial protective White sheet that produces forms of color-blindness and an opaque grasp of the racial formation. They have a fragmented, rather than double, consciousness.

One reaches a reasonable conclusion that Whiteness Studies is a discourse of Whites talking to other Whites, those with relatively higher levels of race consciousness convincing others with race amnesia how race really matters in their lives. It becomes a White Whiteness Studies. What does a Black Whiteness Studies or Whiteness Studies of color look like? Watching idly as Whites take one another to task, usually where liberal Whites disarm their conservative or color-blind brethren, people of color marvel at the spectacle from the sidelines. It is a bit like watching two Whites call each other "racist," one accused for wanting to return to the "good ol' days," the other as lowering standards by placating a complaining group, or what former President George W. Bush once called the "soft bigotry of lower expectations," which became the backbone logic of No Child Left Behind. Bizarre indeed. Whereas racism is ultimately a White problem, this does not suggest that it is a problem for Whites. Whites may have many social problems, but race is not one of them. Rather, people of color bear the injury so that insofar as their voice is muted within a critical analysis of Whiteness, Whiteness Studies replicates the very problem it seeks to solve.

To be fair, scholars of color in education do not rush to be included in Whiteness Studies. Instead, it is more respectable to join the ranks of Critical Race Theory or multiculturalism. Be that as it may, much is at stake for them in the uptake of Whiteness, and their future is bound up with its destiny, for Whiteness represents their ultimate limit situation with respect to race relations. One might go so far as to argue that people of color, instead of Whites, are precisely the ones who should lead the charge for the abolition of Whiteness. In fact, this has not happened, and I will diagnose the problem in the next part of this chapter.

APPRAISAL OF WHITENESS STUDIES, RACE, AND EDUCATION

There are several challenges to pose and resolve in a critical study of Whiteness, some obvious and well-documented anxieties, like the dangers of re-centering Whiteness indicated earlier in this chapter, while others are less apparent and evidence of an immanent problem within the framework itself. The language of Whiteness Studies is implicated in the very dynamic on which it sheds light. Because language practice, whether written or spoken, is located within the racial history that interpellates it, Whiteness Studies becomes a symptom of its own racial predicament. This characterization does not paint the discourse into a corner but acknowledges that scholars of Whiteness Studies do not just use language to describe their conditions, but they go *through* a language that is populated with history and power relations. They describe Whiteness from within, rather than from outside, its structures. Because "race has no outside," even critical race thought will not succeed in resolving its contradictions. At times, it may even reiterate those contradictions whereby Whiteness becomes the limiting condition of Whiteness Studies.

The popularity and leadership of White scholars within Whiteness Studies, which is a growing industry, are not lost on scholars of color. The fear is that race scholarship will become another White-dominated field of knowledge. A chorus of "They've done it to us again!" from people of color may be a reasonable response. Of course, the caveat is that much of Whiteness Studies calls for an end to racism so that Whites are not the only ones to benefit but people of color benefit equally. That said, like capitalism, racism has a recuperative logic whereby even threats against it are incorporated into its logic. In this case, as long as general White preferences and priorities are maintained, Whiteness can withstand internal cleavages and discord among Whites, just as it has survived through hundreds of years of ethnic strife among them. A few thousand White abolitionists seem to pale in historical comparison. Inevitably, a brutal self-reflection becomes necessary for Whites if Whiteness Studies is expected to avoid reproducing racial privilege at the level of intellectual production, despite the best intentions.

Finally, what does any of this have to do with people of color? The dissolution of Whiteness intimately implicates the lives of people of color and the choices they make, yet one receives the near-universal impression that the dissolution of White privilege, or the more radical abolition of Whiteness itself, is up to Whites. It is captured best by Linda Alcoff's (1998) central question, "What should White people do?" (see also A. Thompson, 2003). Relinquishing racial change to Whites displaces racial minorities and reduces them, once again, to the status of bystanders.

Discovering the Continent of Whiteness: Whiteness Studies as the Age of Discovery at the Level of Race Theory

For people of color, race and Whiteness have always mattered. From colonization to canonization, Whiteness appropriates land and knowledge, an unwelcome gesture almost always inappropriate to sensibilities of color. So when Whiteness Studies arrives on the intellectual scene, scholars of color raise an eyebrow, much as they did when Pat Boone and Elvis "discovered" Black music. The explorers were on the move again. It is now a well-known criticism that when Europeans claim to have discovered North America, it was peopled by a thriving civilization in its own right. Therefore, Eurocentrism betrays its narcissism by claiming to know a land better than its own inhabitants. If, after this trenchant critique, the narrative is altered to suggest that North America and other lands like it were discovered by Europeans *for* Europeans, then indigenous people apparently can rest assured that they are not being cast aside. Yet an epistemic move replaces a militaristic one, which controls how a people and land will be precisely known, made known to others, and become targets of power equally damaging (see Grande, 2004; L. T. Smith, 1999). Often, this knowledge is intended for Europeans, not people of color who are its targets.

In the tradition of Edward Said's (1979) path-breaking work in *Orientalism*, Linda Tuhiwai Smith (1999) lays the groundwork for global indigenous education through her documentation of the continuing colonization and colonial education of Maori people in New Zealand. Although one certainly may read postcolonialism as the temporal end of a certain form of colonialism, such as administrative colonialism, it does not signal the end of colonialism as a relationship. The spatial reconfiguration of colonialism may lead to the wrong conclusion that colonialism has ended, only to hear Sykes' sardonic response, "What? Postcolonialism? Have they left?" (cited in Smith, 1999, p. 24). There is rather compelling evidence that in fact this has not occurred. And, even when the colonizers have left formally, their institutions and colonialism's legacy have remained (Smith, 1999).

Scholars of color have been doing race work for quite some time now, although admittedly more concerned with colorness than with Whiteness. So there is something quite new and refreshing about Whiteness Studies as a bona fide intervention. But by and large, critical scholars of color in education, aligned more with CRT, have stayed clear of critical studies of Whiteness. Why is this the case? Some of this development is unfortunate because, if my earlier assertions are reasonable, neglecting Whiteness forgoes a deeper engagement with the primary investment in raciology. In Whiteness Studies, a sense of topical takeover reminds people of color of Whites' ability to appropriate and take credit for practices around which minorities have built traditions. White discovery of race critique recalls previous transgressions that made it possible for Whites to claim lands that were not their own. In intellectual terms, the continent of critical race scholarship on Whiteness had existed, and it took Whites' traveling to its shores to make it known. This does not mean that Whiteness Studies in education is mainstream in any sense or that its proponents receive adulation for being "race traitors" (Ignatiev & Garvey, 1996b). Far from it. From McIntosh to McLaren, White scholars on Whiteness receive plenty of derision from Whites and people of color alike. It also does not suggest that something new has not been forged out of the old. Whiteness Studies is innovative, particularly as it concerns White participation in anti-racism. These facts notwithstanding, it is a racial practice that carries contradictions, one of which is the danger of White appropriation.

Part of the language of discovery is, of course, discovering one's Whiteness. With the advent of Whiteness Studies, more Whites are now discovering their Whiteness and outing themselves as such. Many works that hail from Whiteness Studies begin with narratives of confession about one's Whiteness. Having found an intellectual space in which to discuss their Whiteness, Whites experience an almost cathartic event in disclosing their Whiteness for the purpose of illuminating the utter oblivion that many Whites share about their privilege. But written over and again, it has the unfortunate effect of violating the sensibilities of people of color by intensifying the well-known history of White privilege through the act of repetition. Whites' sheer amount of repetition regarding their overprivilege produces a violence that reminds people of color about their lack of advantage. As a result, the act of reading or hearing repetitively about White privilege becomes assaulting for people of color. It is they who live the effects of White privilege that Whites are only beginning to discover. The repetition serves to reinforce those privileges when it stays at the level of confessionals. People of color are well aware of the racial privilege they lack; White privilege is rarely, if ever, a mystery to them (Essed & Trienekens, 2007). Thus, White discovery of racial advantage is new mainly *to* Whites.

In her early work, Ruth Frankenberg (1993) was one of the first scholars to unveil these dynamics in her book, *White Women, Race Matters*. Frankenberg documents the way White women vacillate between color-evasive and race-cognizant discourses on race. In essence, she discovers in empirical fashion their penchant for building a race architecture that protects them on one hand and a counter-discourse that penetrates the inner workings of racism on the other. She avoids painting Whites into a corner by depicting them as racial subjects in the making and thereby provides hope that they may emerge from race evasion and into the space of race cognizance. But, as is typical in the genre, Frankenberg succeeds in framing White normativity as taken for granted. Of course, from the perspective of Whites, this is entirely believable. But as Ahmed (2004) notes, this is possible only through Whites' reification of their opaqueness, their pale/ontology (Leonardo, 2009a). Similar to Ellison's (1952/1995) thesis about Black invisibility in the White world, Whiteness Studies launches a parallel insight about White invisibility. In other words, both Blacks and Whites are invisible to Whites. Racial groups vanish right before our eyes, which is convenient and typical of color-blindness in its most literal sense. This time, the insight is forged without the irony that color-blindness is a misnomer since color-blind pretenders selectively see race to maintain a certain equilibrium.

In 2001, Frankenberg announces, "The more one scrutinizes it . . . the more the notion of Whiteness as an unmarked norm is revealed to be a mirage" (p. 73) (cited by Hartmann, Gerteis, & Croll, 2009). The move from

discovering the continent of White invisibility in the 1990s to its denuncia-
tion less than 10 years later speaks to the ability of Whiteness as an ideology to seep even into anti-racist discourse. Having pronounced knowledge
of what people of color knew all along, Frankenberg establishes a second
discovery by denouncing her first finding, thereby staking a claim to two
insights that cancel each other: the fact and myth of White invisibility. She
discovers twice what people of color knew all along. Meanwhile, minority
knowledge about White privilege is unaccounted for. Five hundred years
ago, Whites "discovered" a land already populated by people of color; this
time, with the credibility and Leftist credentials of Whiteness Studies, Whites
explore a discourse already populated with the ideas of people of color. This
encapsulates the tragedy in the methodology of Whiteness Studies. Because
it caters to the White racial mindset, it discovers what people of color already
know to be true. Thus, racial knowledge moves at the snail's pace of the
White imaginary.

The discovery discourse entails stories about travel. From forays into
race theory to deeper journeys into the heart of lightness, or what Lugones
(2007) calls the light side of the colonial/modern gender system, Whiteness
Studies describes White educators' willingness to leave their comfort zones.
There is much to recommend in this move. Whiteness Studies encourages
Whites to go into exile, if only to experience the disjuncture of having to
leave familiar surroundings. For too long, Whites have lived with the luxury of either avoiding racial others through segregation or displacing them
through colonization. On the other hand, historically speaking many White
ethnics immigrated to the United States and other nations, arguably forming
the basis for Whites' understanding of exile. However, history also informs
us that Whites have transformed other peoples' homes into their own either
through force or appropriation. Exile requires something else, which is the
feeling of unrootedness, of homelessness, rather than putting down roots in
someone else's land. It is the feeling of restlessness (Freire, 1970/1993; Said,
2000), even rootlessness, and not resting on other peoples' soil without their
invitation (see Espiritu, 2003; also cited in Coloma, 2006).

Being (White) and Nothingness:
Compulsory Whiteness and the Challenge of Abolition

Just as feminists have argued that schools promote compulsory heterosexuality (Rich, 1993), we might perform a parallel argument that they also
reinforce a compulsory Whiteness. That is, because Whites enjoy a monopoly over many social processes from the means of production to the production of meaning, it is difficult for people of color to imagine or accept a race
movement led by Whites or their racial imagination. In the first instance, a

race movement dependent on White uptake of race struggle is marred by the challenges of White racial consciousness. This does not suggest that, as individuals, Whites cannot experience transformation in the way they apprehend race. It speaks to the overwhelming disincentive for them to make this leap. Cognitively, they are habituated to think of racism as a problem of attitude or perspective. Indeed, Peggy McIntosh's intervention is already too transgressive for most Whites, even though it may not go far enough for others, particularly people of color who favor the White supremacy over White privilege framework. That anti-racism is beyond good White intentions (Bush, 2005) escapes the sensibilities of many Whites. For these and other reasons, the idea that critical change in race relations requires White readership, let alone leadership, becomes a difficult premise for people of color to accept. For many of them, the movement is doomed before it begins. It is a non-starter. For why would a privileged group willingly relinquish its advantage, especially when its majority believes the privilege was earned meritoriously? Very few, if any, examples of historical upheavals bear the imprint of such altruism.

More to the point, Whites enjoy their social honor, especially poignant for Whites who carry a legitimate injury, such as working-class Whites or White women. For them, Whiteness is all they might have. Abandoning it would put them at risk with little protection against either sexism or capitalist exploitation. Whiteness adds a modicum of privilege that allows them to cope with their suffering. Without overstating the case that working-class Whites and White women control the administration of race relations, they are invested in their own share of White spoils. *They may not call the shots, but they frequently pull the trigger.* In the army of Whiteness, different Whites play specific roles in guarding the fortress. It depends on its foot soldiers as well as officers; rarely do they defect to the other side because they pay a high price for being "race traitors," not the least of which is giving up the honor of being White. Convincing them to put aside their proverbial guns is likely to meet with their resistance.

As difficult as this sounds, racial transformation does not need the agreement of most or every White citizen. The abolitionist's goal is to convince enough Whites to find purchase in abolitionism so that a vocal group may act so flagrantly against the political structure and social expectations of racialization that it would create a culture of treason against Whiteness (Ignatiev, 1997; see also Ignatiev & Garvey, 1996a). This counters the popular refrain and criticism that abolitionism ultimately will fail to convince all Whites to abolish their Whiteness. The simple answer is that abolitionism does not require all Whites to commit race treason. Mass White enrollment in the abolitionist cause is not a prerequisite, and it betrays a certain shallow understanding of history to critique it for failing to come through with card-carrying abolitionists en masse. That said, if at least for strategic reasons, a certain threshold criterion is missing from abolitionism. The complex answer requires multiple levels of analysis. If it is indeed unnecessary for the entirety of White educators to buy into abolitionism as their cause célèbre, what is, at least theoretically speaking, the tipping point? 10,000? 100,000? Do we need a Million White Man March to wave the flag of abolition?

After Whiteness, What? What Whites will become after the abolition of Whiteness is a central anxiety in both progressive Whites and people of color. If not White, then what? Admittedly, this question is more of a preoccupation within the White reconstructionist literature than within abolitionism. Reconstructionists, like Kincheloe and Steinberg (1998), pose the pragmatic concern that abolishing Whiteness leaves nothing for Whites to cling onto in their need for identity, even if the ends are justified. Indeed, abolitionists have been silent on this issue and will likely fail to resonate with Whites and will attract suspicion among people of color. The first will insist on filling the void left after the dissolution of Whiteness, while the second will raise the issue that the absence of Whiteness is tantamount to color-blindness. White nonraciality recalls Whites' consistent attempts to disappear into personhood and individualism, which people of color are justified in questioning. Moreover, the pretense of nonraciality becomes a form of White privilege at the level of theory. After all, people of color do not have the luxury of entertaining an identity untethered to race (Wright, 2003). They are betrayed by their own body, as Fanon (1952/1967) so aptly put it: "I am overdetermined from without. I am the slave not of the 'idea' that others have of me but of my own appearance" (p. 116). This move is not contrary to race relations but becomes its lynchpin.

In addition, precisely at the moment that Whiteness Studies succeeds in "locating" Whiteness, abolitionist scholars announce the disappearance of Whites as a conceptual category. It is reminiscent of postmodernism's arrival, pronouncement of the death of the subject, and the problem of meta-narratives, such as justice, precisely at the moment when racial minorities, women, and other marginalized groups were developing cohesion (Hartsock, 1987). Although scholars of color, from James Baldwin to Larry Bobo, would likely not find much to disagree with in the idea that race is a social construction, they might find it difficult to accept the strategy that "White people do not exist" is a prelude to radical change since it smacks of commonsense race conservatism, or at least makes it difficult to tell the difference.

On the other hand, abolitionists, some of whom may be influenced by situationist or anarchist philosophy, may be suggesting a strategy that highlights a certain irony in the uptake of Whiteness. If all it proferred were a racial disappearance on the part of Whites, this would be easy to refute and reject. This is already Whiteness' modus operandi, its claim to be every-where and nowhere at the same time: everywhere because it is the standard, nowhere because it efficiently hides its normative status. It is possible that abolitionists recognize that the abolition of Whiteness requires the double move of remembering *and* forgetting one's Whiteness. First, remembering one's Whiteness serves to mark and locate White privilege and dominance. Much of the "White privilege" literature, from McIntosh (1992) to McIntyre (1997), succeeds in highlighting this fact and ways to counteract it. Videos, from "Blue Eyes, Brown Eyes" to "Color of Fear," treat educators to stories of White oblivion, of Whites' failure to remember their Whiteness until forced to confront it. These lessons' powerful effects on Whites notwithstanding, they ultimately encourage White subjects to remain White, albeit a trans-formed notion of it. To the abolitionist, other than a wish fulfillment, White without dominance is not sustainable. Abolishing the latter eviscerates the former. That said, Whiteness Studies in education proceeds *as if* it is possible to recreate Whiteness, which represents its regulative ideal.

In an attempt to generate a developmental system that parallels the stages of Black identity, Janet Helms's (1991) innovative answer to Wil-liam Cross's (1978) "nigrescence" model comes in the form of the "White identity development" model. Here, Helms creates a stage schema wherein Whites, like Blacks, progress from more or less provincial and self-centered attitudes about race to more authentic, autonomous self-understandings. Al-though Helms, like Cross before her, builds in the dimension of nonlinearity through the stages, wherein Whites do not simply travel from point A to B of Whiteness and may revert to previous stages, the model's telos is for a transformed Whiteness. The model ends with a White subject who accepts his or her racial difference as part of a constellation of differences rather than assuming a superior place among them. It would be hard to argue against its strategy to provide options for Whites to become something other than participants of racial supremacy.

However, it is clear that at the end of the day, the conceptual category of Whiteness is preserved. That is where the model stops, or stops short as it were: a compulsory Whiteness. What is this Whiteness *sans* racial domina-tion? In the history of race, what are Whites without their presumed superi-ority? Without this self-appointed sense of *hidalguismo* (Rimonte, 1997), the very center of Whiteness collapses, becomes emptied of its historical content. In fact, one might argue that they are White no longer, and Helms's model reaches its conclusion as prescribed by the logic and limits of White recon-struction. It does not take into consideration that Whiteness at the crossroads of racial equality signals its own demise or, to borrow from Marx, creates the conditions for its own grave diggers, wherein its last stage of development is not autonomy but the final throes of a historically disappearing concept.

Remembering and Forgetting Whiteness. It is nothing short of an irony that much fear and anxiety surround the disappearance of Whiteness, particularly for Whites. The literature is compelling with respect to Whites' color-blind tendencies, their penchant for perceiving themselves as nonracial subjects. Finding after finding, we receive a portrait of White preference for personhood over racial affiliation. They are portrayed as "ignorant" of the racial formation and of their own racialization as Whites. If this consistent finding has veracity, then it would seem paradoxical for Whites to balk at the abolition of something about which they seem to care very little. To many Whites, being White seems to matter as much (or as little) as choosing paper over plastic bags at the grocery store. But the suggestion of abolishing Whiteness receives an uncharacteristic response from Whites, one filled with possessive investment in Whiteness (Lipsitz, 1998), like an irrational anger at the thought of banishing from the family an uncle one was not aware of. Given this resistance, it is very possible that Whites intimately know their Whiteness, even its dividends, and abolishing Whiteness threatens their livelihood and entitlements. It may be the case that publicly recognizing this privilege makes them realize that *people of color know it as well.* This comes with some horror, like learning someone presumed to be invisible has been watching all along (hooks, 1997).

If this is accurate, then Whites do not need to be reminded of their Whiteness, a default strategy so many anti-racist educators are quick to adopt and central to so much of Whiteness Studies in education. If Whites know their Whiteness, then reminding them of this fact seems redundant and may reify through repetition the same privileges. At the very least, Whiteness Studies proceeds from the White imaginary and its apparitions rather than the endarkened epistemology of people of color (Wright, 2003), wherein Whites' deduced conclusions about their supremacy were the premise of people of color from the start. This does not suggest that Whites necessarily *understand* the historical causes of their Whiteness and the general process of racial accumulation. For, as Mills (1997) informs us, Whites suffer from an inverted epistemology of the world, not unlike the *camera obscura* that Marx and Engels (1970) reserved for capitalists and idealist philosophers. It argues that although encouraging Whites to remember their Whiteness is helpful, it is not an end in itself. It must be complemented by a simultaneous appeal to forgetting their Whiteness. This takes us toward a *schizo-subject of Whiteness.*

James Baldwin (1985) once wrote that as long as Whites think they are White, there is no hope for them (cited in Roediger, 1994; see also Aanerud, 1999). Although thinking is different from remembering one's Whiteness, because the latter is arguably more active and assumes a lesson ultimately was learned, Baldwin's observation points us to the importance of encouraging Whites to forget their Whiteness. Because of their uncommonsense appeal to check their Whiteness at the proverbial door, abolitionists cut against the anti-racist grain. They insist that Whites already know they are White and enjoy the privileges. In fact, racial supremacy was inaugurated when Europeans began to think they were White. Today, as long as Whites think or remember their Whiteness, there is too much temptation—and with it, a structure that recognizes the rightness of Whiteness—for Whites to assume their place as the center of anti-racism, even within a critical uptake of Whiteness. So inasmuch as Whiteness Studies insists that Whites remember their "peculiar" place in race relations, White abolitionists ask them to forget they are White, to the extent that this is possible. While sounding problematically cozy with color-blindness, this second apostasy serves as a reminder that signifying one's Whiteness is part of the problem. It is a circle of loyalty that Ignatiev (1997) argues must be broken through a praxis of anti-Whiteness, even anti-White. Of course, he is not invoking a White identity but more profoundly an ideology of Whiteness that must be challenged.

This double move or helix of remembering-and-forgetting is not unlike the strategy of people of color and other historically marginalized groups. With respect to historic events like the Jewish Holocaust or African enslavement, it is a well-known fact that remembering one's victimization is part of building group memory. In both cases, the Holocaust and enslavement remind Jews and Blacks of what may happen again despite claimed protections against their recurrence. They cannot leave it up to others' promises that a similar atrocity will not occur. Even if laws exist to prohibit such atrocities, in the case of slavery *it was the law of the land!* In other words, laws are only as protectionary as the society that produces them. In the United States, people of color both depend on the law to protect them as well as fear that the law will not protect them from prosecution, let alone persecution.

Critical Race Theorists, like Derrick Bell (1992), Ian Haney Lopez (2006), Angela Harris (2008), and Cheryl Harris (1995), have produced trenchant critiques of the law and its racial intentions and outcomes despite pretenses of color-blindness. In fact, color-blind legal discourse further exacerbates and hides Whites' racist motivations. During Passover and Black History Month in U.S. schools, remembering becomes the operative pedagogy, and studies of Whiteness would do well to follow suit. Of course, relegating Black history to the shortest and coldest month of the school year serves to ghettoize Black life, to the chagrin of the creator of Black History Month, Carter Woodson (2000). But this fact speaks more to Whites' power to resist integrating Black existence into the formal curriculum (see also Apple, 2012). In other words, the issue is not whether or not schools should remember Blacks during February; this is not the problem. Rather, the target of criticism is whether or not a more or less White-centric curriculum can accommodate its constitutive other throughout the entire year. The fact that there is no "White month" is

not the same as forgetting Whiteness but points to its perpetual and normative status in historical memory. It hardly requires remembering.

However, because reminders of victimization sometimes produce victi-
mology, there is also the simultaneous effort to forget one's otherness when
people of color are concerned. Claude Steele (2004) and his collaborators
(e.g., Aronson, 2004) have all but verified the existence of what they call
"stereotype threat," wherein the mere priming that one's racial (or gender)
identity is relevant to educational events, such as test taking, lowers the performance of Black students, particularly in domain-identified areas where
they either excel or care deeply about their performance. These are not purely psychological phenomena but social cues about intelligence that victimize
people. They are located not in the test takers' heads per se but in their social
environment. Although Steele's point is not about Blacks' internalization of
inferiority (see Gates & Steele, 2009), it speaks to the difficulty of remembering one's identity in a context where it is derided.

In order to combat this daily assault and concentrate on succeeding in
school and other evaluative situations, students of color may desire to forget
their racial identity in order to forge a state of racelessness (Fordham, 1988).
Although Fordham and Ogbu's (1986) evidence suggests that Black students'
attempt at racelessness is ultimately a form of "acting White" (therefore not
raceless at all), it represents their schizo-subjectivity wherein they must remember their Blackness and its social disadvantage while forgetting it in order to avoid stereotype threat. They are reminded of the external standards
of Whiteness against which they are measured as well as affirm their nonra-
cialized yet elusive humanity in order to forget their victimization.

Likewise, White abolitionists require a schizo-orientation to their Whiteness. This is not a double consciousness of sorts in Du Bois's sense, but a
sensation of restlessness, of falling into Whiteness to understand it but falling
out with Whiteness to break away from it. Simply becoming aware of one's
Whiteness, even critically at that, answers only half of Baldwin's injunction
because as long as Whites think they are White, they cannot trust their own
ability to divest hegemonic Whiteness of its power to define them. People of
color will not be so quick to embrace this new Whiteness either.

In his scathing but incisive criticism of White anti-racists, Ewuare Osayande (2010) questions the recuperative logic of Whiteness to regain what it
loses through radical critiques of Whiteness by rewarding individual Whites
who dare speak publicly against Whiteness. At the center of Osayande's criticism is the White anti-racist Tim Wise, whose book *White Like Me* (2007) is
popular in courses on race or Whiteness. Many people of color consider
Wise an ally. Of secondary consequence to Osayande are people of color
who exalt Wise as the "great White hope" against racism. It is tempting to
read Osayande, himself a public *but* Black anti-racist intellectual, as having a

specific axe to grind against the charismatic Wise, whose public talk sched-
ule is booked for a couple years to come, whereas Osayande struggles for
air time. In addition, insofar as Wise helps build an anti-racist culture, he is
not the only one who benefits but arguably people of color benefit as well.
These caveats aside, Osayande brings insight to the phenomenon of White
anti-racism and refuses to localize the problem in a personality figure, such
as Wise. His point is farther reaching than that.

Osayande's main bone of contention is with the industry that produces
White anti-racists, which includes Whiteness Studies, a political economy that
rewards Whites for a message that people of color know firsthand through
experience. In fact, Wise often expresses his gratitude for the sages of color
who have come before him, invoking the images of Du Bois and Baldwin,
retelling the lessons they have taught him.

At issue here is Whites' ability to appropriate knowledge of color *for other
Whites' consumption.* They remind other Whites of their Whiteness and White
privilege; they also remind people of color of their denigration. This same
message is not received well coming from a speaker of color, whose analysis
is suspected as self-interested and self-serving, whereas Whites' indictments
are self-effacing and self-sacrificing. That is, if Osayande is correct, to the extent that White anti-racists are popular among White audiences, they eclipse
the ability of anti-racists of color to reach White educators, who would have
to confront the living image of a person whom they are, at the very least
indirectly, accountable for having created.

To be fair, insurgent Whites, like Tim Wise, are not universally beloved
by Whites, and probably even less so by Blacks, and they are accused of being either race traitors or outlaws, wannabees or race tourists. Moreover, too
Black for Whites and too White for Blacks (Lipsitz, personal communication,
2011), White anti-racists experience exile from both sides of the racial aisle.

These existential crises and political negotiations aside, the White anti-
racist industry comes with problems. It reifies Whiteness, which is the risk it
takes when it testifies to its power and social reality. Forgetting Whiteness is
arguably the complementary half of remembering it. If Whiteness is to disappear as a relic of history, it requires that Whites commit the unreasonable act
of retreating from their Whiteness. Whether Whiteness Studies in education
encourages this move remains to be seen.

What Should People of Color Do?
Minorities as Co-Participants in the Abolition of Whiteness

The apparent audience of the majority of Whiteness Studies is Whites, in
particular those with liberal racial sensibilities. This preference is politically
and educationally consequential. From educators, to students, to scholars,

Whiteness Studies peers into the lives of racial privilege and determines ways to disinvest in it (see Giroux, 1997b; Kincheloe, Steinberg, Rodriguez, & Chennault, 1998; Richardson & Villenas, 2000). In short, what acts and decisions must Whites commit in order to transform Whiteness? As suggested, one of the answers to this question includes the abolition of Whiteness (Ignatiev, 1997; Ignatiev & Garvey, 1996a; Roediger, 1994). To the extent that this is the preferred *goal*, what is the preferred *strategy,* and who is its *revolutionary subject*? If the abolition of Whiteness is a provocative question *for* Whites, what is it that people of color should do? This is rarely, if ever, asked in Whiteness Studies. If abolishing Whiteness includes, along with structural changes, an educational component that eviscerates a social identity and ideology, this process is not completely up to Whites, individually or at the group level. In fact, we might go so far as to say that it is dangerous to suggest this as the preferred strategy.

Whites Abandoning Whiteness. Within abolition and following the discussion above, the preferred strategy is to compel Whites to abandon their Whiteness. After getting over the initial shock that this means something beyond the pretenses of color-blindness, this process includes flagrantly breaking the codes and expectations of White solidarity. It means disidentifying with Whiteness and its communities through race treason, or defecting. The immediate problem is that defecting suggests joining another group, in this case another racial community. Although it is hard for most people to imagine what this action looks like in practice, it is even more difficult to imagine which group abolitionists would join. They will be exiled by other Whites, and because they are still scripted as and "look but not act" White, they will likely be unacceptable to people of color. White race traitors have not stopped being White because the racialized social system still (mis)recognizes them as such. It is more likely that anti-White abolitionists will spawn their own group, replacing the comforts of the White home on which they previously counted. They will experience the social stigma as traitors to the White nation. This is difficult but imaginable. So far, so good.

The strategy's essence is a politics of disruption so flagrant that this will make it nearly impossible to discern White abolitionists, at the level of behavior, from many people of color, thereby making it at least inconvenient to enforce Whiteness in the usual way. Discombobulating Whiteness includes thwarting the police, who are inclined to enact less harsh tactics toward Whites; calling into question racial favors from everyday interactions, like car salespeople who charge less to White buyers; and the subtle yet felt dynamic of presumed agreement, such as participating in racial jokes about people of color. We should note that White abolitionists, like Ignatiev, overplay their hand when they equate Whites *acting* flagrantly with *being* Black. In fact, for White abolitionists, acting against Whiteness is a means of inviting its ire, whereas people of color are its victims merely by being minorities. In other words, Black men do not invite the police to pull them over; racial profiling occurs absent suspicious behavior by people of color. They are suspect by virtue of their identity. Therefore, it is a sign of race privilege to invite the attention of authorities, who otherwise would look the other way. Nevertheless, the abolitionists' point is well taken insofar as they aim to disrupt racial expectations and establish an "outsider" White status within Whiteness. They will become a version of Patricia Hill Collins's (2000) "outsider within," or, more accurately, White race traitors as the "insider without." In acts that amount to a form of racial sedition, these betrayals to Whiteness send tremors into the architecture of Whiteness, one feature of which is the predictable acquiescence of most Whites. In all imaginable instances, the response they encourage is consistent: look but do not act White. Abolitionists will resign from Whiteness instead of being resigned to it.

There is much about White abolitionism that is sound. Its radical questioning of racial expectations suggests that the knee-jerk reaction that Whites simply will stop calling themselves "White" depends on a simplification of the actual philosophy. It is not a politics of renaming as much as it is an undoing of an ideology through the performativity of opting out, not unlike the original slave abolitionists. However, in their unrelenting focus, they project an image of a hermetic movement that occurs among Whites, even if it is a minority within the majority. Missing is an argument that not only includes participation by people of color, but begs the question of how they are affected by a nearly all-White strategy. This is not surprising if we keep in mind that Whiteness Studies, abolition in particular, is largely a White scholarly intervention. Arguably staying with what they know best, Whiteness Studies educators speak to their own racial formation as Whites. But this is incomplete at best and reinforces the invisibility of people of color at worst. I would like to end this chapter by discussing these provocations with respect to racial minorities and what their participation would look like in the abolition of Whiteness, which then implicates identities and ideologies of color in the process. In other words, the transformation of Whiteness necessitates the transformation of "color" and race relations in general.

Partners in Unthinking Whiteness. If White abolition's suggestion is for Whites to undo their Whiteness (after all, what are Whites but people who think they are "White," according to James Baldwin?), this implies that people of color also would need to stop thinking of Whites as "White." What would this mean, and how is it different from color-blindness? The problem with the abolitionists' formulation is that Whites are not the only ones who think they are White; people of color also think that Whites are White. White abolitionists not only break rank with Whites who assume they are White, but also must challenge people of color who insist on constructing White people in everyday life. This strategy is tricky because it will be received unfavorably by people of color who will suspect that Whiteness is up to its old tactics again. As a result, White abolitionists have to establish trust with minorities if they are to become mutual partners in the abolition of Whiteness. These difficulties notwithstanding, what is the minority's task? To the extent that the abolition of Whiteness is the goal, then people of color must partake in the strategy. They also consider what it means to stop thinking of Whites as White.

People of color recreate Whiteness daily. As part of identity development, Whiteness is the constitutive outside to an identity of color. The livelihood of people of color is framed by the limit situation of Whiteness. On this, scholars from Du Bois on have been clear. This means that disidentifying with Whiteness is not a task left up to Whites alone. People of color who assume that the body to which they speak is White also benefit from critically reflecting over the naturalized and naturalizing tendencies of racialization. In short, Whiteness will not disappear if people of color insist on its facticity and foreverness. This comes with certain presumptions that White bodies will behave as White people, which is a reasonable and learned expectation. But if anything is clear about the role of people of color in history, it has been marked with sacrifice. In this sense, the abolition of Whiteness requires another sacrifice from them.

Suspending naturalized expectations of Whiteness means that Whites receive the trust they have not sufficiently earned but is necessary if the larger goal is the abolition of Whiteness. This requires the recognition from Whites that a gift, in Bataille's (1985) sense, has been rendered. A gift is less a present and more a challenge. In order to reciprocate, Whites would have to return the gift with a more extravagant one, in this case, by living up to the expectation that they will not reinforce their Whiteness. In return, people of color will issue the further challenge of increasing their trust in Whites, and the stakes continue. This "economic" exchange is terminated by the abolition of Whiteness, the ultimate gift.

Minorities Abandoning the Ideology of Whiteness. Because Whiteness is an ideology and not simply the property of White bodies, it lives through the choices and performances of people of color. Being a person of color is shot through with the ideology of Whiteness, which makes its abolition a personal undertaking. Previously, White scholars compelled to abolish Whiteness left this task up to the whims of Whiteness. But because Whiteness threatens minority self-perception through stereotype threat, internalized racism, or colonized mentality, abolishing Whiteness means purging the Whiteness within people of color. Not only must Whites stop thinking they are White, but people of color must resist allowing Whiteness to enter their being. If this is true, then abolishing Whiteness is not about the historical task of Whites, but a shared one with people of color. If it is difficult for Whites to shed their Whiteness, it is not a forgone conclusion that people of color so easily abandon an ideology they have learned to negotiate for so long, something Fanon (1952/1967) once said is the destiny of every Black person. Nothing short of abandoning one's tormentor cleanses Black development into a new form of humanism.

Whiteness has created its other in people of color. As much as the latter are inclined to reject the former, the two identities interpenetrate each other. In Whiteness' projection, this other is a problem that needs to be contained. In the minds of people of color, this Whiteness is a terrorizing force (see hooks, 1992, 1997; McLaren, 1995). Contrary to the impression that people of color engender animosity toward Whites through their racial indignation, minorities have been subject to an education that valorizes Whiteness. The logical outcome of this process is the default adoration of everything White, which takes significant effort to avoid on the part of people of color. In fact, from science to literature, beauty to art, Whiteness becomes the standard. The abolition of Whiteness requires that people of color de-internalize this tape that measures their worth. It requires abolishing the Whiteness in them.

This point differs from Michael Eric Dyson's (1998) assertion that promoting the abolition of Whiteness denies the certain amount of Blackness that went into making Whiteness. That is, because they interpenetrate each other, Blackness is intrinsic to Whiteness. Therefore, abolishing Whiteness is in part calling for the abolition of Blackness. Some part of Blackness may be lost. To Dyson, Whiteness is an institution, ideology, and identity. While these distinctions make sense existentially, since it is difficult to separate ideology from identity, the conceptualization of Whiteness fails to differentiate it from the category of "White." Whereas "White" is an identity, Whiteness represents an ideology. Other than those who pass as White, people of color do not occupy the first, although they may embody the second. When educators define Whiteness away from the specificities of White bodies, they attest to the ideological autonomy it needs in order to do its work.

To the extent that Whiteness includes Blackness, it is the distorted or appropriated form of it. This is the image that people of color receive of themselves from Whiteness. From the lazy native to the violent urban youth, the otherness mirrored by Whiteness to people of color is not uplifting. In fact, one would conclude that it is an image of otherness for Whites' consumption. Equally a distortion, the Whiteness that people of color often mirror for Whites is an embellished one, this time a flattering image. People of color would need to exorcise both reflections as they participate in the abolition of

Whiteness. This leads us into the final point regarding the entry of people of color into abolition.

Ending Racial Otherness. The abolition of Whiteness implicates identities of color. Dismantling White identity simultaneously calls into question non-White identities. Because they are dialectical unities, White and identities of color were once co-created and now exist alongside each other as complements. The abolition of Whiteness implicates this complementarity, White and minority as woven into each other. This does not suggest that they are symmetrical (Ingram, 2005), since they exist within an asymmetrical relation of power. Otherness is not just the mirror of Whiteness because they serve different historical functions. Whereas David Roediger (1994) tells us that Whiteness has been nothing but false and oppressive, Laurie Garrett-Cobbina (personal communication, 2011) reminds us that *Blackness has been nothing but falsified and oppressed.* This establishes a differential orientation toward racial domination, where Whiteness encourages the obfuscation of racial accumulation, and otherness does not. This does not mean that people of color have a crystal-clear understanding of racism at all times; in fact, they may be as confused as many Whites. Nevertheless, it is not in the interest of people of color to support racism, despite the temporary and personal dividends that result from being in bed with White supremacy.

All this being said, the abolition of Whiteness implies the eventual disappearance of the category of racial otherness. As a relation, they are burst asunder because their mutual interdependency is compromised, particularly for Whiteness, which is parasitic on otherness. But this implosion does not leave otherness intact and in fact ushers in a new era of post-raciality, and not in the sense of a current condition that conservative scholars and pundits portray as a *fait accompli,* but as an aspiration for a world after race stratification. I will have more to say about this in Chapter 5, but here I want to signal the preparation for people of color that comes with participating in White abolition.

People of color who accept the abolition of Whiteness would contemplate the end of racial otherness and its centrality for their identity and history. If White abolition succeeds, there will be no need for the racial category of people of color other than the transitional period of change that generalizes their understanding for the whole of humanity, not unlike the "dictatorship of the proletariat" within Marxist doctrine following the abolition of capital. People will be neither White nor of color, but free.

CHAPTER 4

Cultural Studies, Race Representation, and Education

From the Means of Production to the Production of Meanness

In this chapter, I describe and appraise the framework of Cultural Studies in order to introduce the offerings of a more or less recent discourse on race. I will not spend much time on the history of Cultural Studies as an amalgamation of schools of thought, which I have written about elsewhere (Leonardo, 2010). My specific interest here is how scholars might deploy a Cultural Studies understanding of race in education. En route, I focus on several, but not all, key concepts, such as representation, discourse, and subjectivity. A privileged medium for understanding these processes is language, where meaning is both expressed and constituted. Said another way, from its spoken to unspoken varieties, language becomes a cultural apparatus for constituting and understanding the known world. It may not be made of matter, but language clearly matters and produces material consequences (Volosinov, 2006; Vygotsky, 1978). It is both cause and effect of educational action when educators are informed by language practices, and language becomes an outcome of these cultural activities. In education, language is both an incredible human capacity that distinguishes us from the nonlinguistic slug and also one that humans use to wound one another.

FRAMEWORK OF CULTURAL STUDIES

The cultural politics of race relations signifies the totalizing effect of racism. It recognizes the ubiquity of Whiteness *from the means of production to the production of meanness.* That is, controlling the division of labor on one hand and monopolizing the apparatuses of representation on the other, Whiteness exercises free reign over power relations in its multiple forms. Not only does White capitalism benefit from the exploitation of non-White labor, but a politics of recognition under the sway of Whiteness also produces racism as a form of meanness (see Bell, 2005b). The terrain is decidedly complex when people of color fight the two-headed monster of labor relations and cultural representations. As if it were not enough to experience discrimination on the job or second-generation segregation at school, people of color return to their homes to watch disparaging images of themselves stare back at them on the television and other social media outlets.

With respect to race, Derrida (1985) suggests that racism exists because language provides its intelligibility. Without language, racism would likely not exist, or at least racism requires language to do its work. In privileging language, a Cultural Studies approach to race broadens its appeal from the study of languages, such as English, Spanish, or bilingualism, to the general linguistic environment of education. It is related to language socialization (Solis, Kattan, & Baquedano-López, 2009), but has a specific conjunctural history that recalls Stuart Hall's (1997) work on the politics of representation, Foucault's (1982) ideas on subject making and forging of subjectivity, and Giroux's (1995a) contention that the circulation of discourses defines how social life will be made intelligible.

With respect to race, we enter the educative functions of representation and what students, particularly of color, learn about the inner workings of race, their place within its circuits of meaning, and how power is deployed through the image to accomplish certain ends. Of course, by image we mean not only pictures or icons but also the ability of language to frame the content of race as part of social imagination. It is perhaps more accurate to privilege meaning over language, but this would be a false or convenient separation between the two.

The Educational Politics of Race and Representation

In *Representation*, Hall (1997) argues that representations are not ephemeral things but rather a process whereby the social world itself is constituted through a chain of meanings. More accurately, cultural meaning is established through difference whereby terms, in this case racial identities, are defined through their relational properties with one another, such that Whiteness, for example, is not autonomous of Blackness but is complementary to it. One does not exist without the other. Representations are not incidental to reality or imperfect renditions of it. They constitute that reality as they offer racial subjects a way into it. Hall (1997) explains:

> Cultural meanings are not only "in the head." They organize social practices, influence our conduct and consequently have real, practical effects. . . . It is

what distinguishes the "human" element in social life from what is simply bio-logically driven. Its study underlines the crucial role of the *symbolic* domain at the very heart of social life. (p. 3; emphasis in original)

Representations are part of the reality they apprehend, like the spoon's particles become part of the contents in the bowl with which they mix. They are durable because they accomplish political tasks and may have staying power. Once institutionalized, the effects of representation have a way of perpetuating themselves, creating even more intricate webs of images. They have material consequences, especially representations that tap into a society's collective racial unconscious. We only have to recall former President George H. Bush's use of Willie Horton's picture and accompanying crime narrative to open the racial archive and mobilize the nation's racist construction of violent Black males. This does not suggest that social life is synonymous with language, but a Cultural Studies perspective apprehends how it works like language. As a system of oppositional differences and circuit of meanings tied to changing terms, race maintains a linguistic structure that is crucial in order to understand its functions.

Race as a Field of Representation. Establishing some distance from a purely structural analysis of language, Hall reminds us of important and recent studies of discourse as a way to assess the effects and consequences of language: that is, its politics. In this sense, race is understood as a field of representation where power is defined as the ability to control its intelligibility. Not unlike a regime of meaning (Foucault, 1980), race comes with material consequences because our social understanding of somatic, or bodily, relations becomes the fulcrum for policies that directly affect students' life chances, such as the link among racialized perceptions of intelligence, standardized tests, and tracking practices. However, while possessing a materiality, race resists being reduced to a simple material fact when its effectivity happens precisely on an ideational level (Lopez, 2006). As an ideological construct, race is susceptible to political practices that attest to its shifting status based on configurations of power.

Ian Haney Lopez (2006) uncovers this ideological process when he analyzes prerequisite legal cases involving race. As cited in Chapter 3, they vacillate between justifying rulings based on "scientific" understandings of race (denying Takao Ozawa's bid for U.S. citizenship) or based on race common sense (revoking Bhagat Thind's citizenship). These cases hinge not only on interpretations regarding whom to exclude from citizenship but precisely on whom to include: in short, free White persons.

Representations are flimsy because they always require upkeep, updating, and upping the ante. While not easy to destroy, representations are contested even after they have been established. While they aspire to the status of incontrovertible truth, more often images manipulate our ability to reason, going around, rather than through, it. Representations whose motives and intentions are either too nefarious or difficult to accept depend on a good dose of affective work in order to tap into emotions, which are not free floating but part of the "structure of feeling" (Williams, 1977). Hence, as explained in the Introduction, a hermeneutics of suspicion (Ricoeur, 1986) is sometimes necessary in order to peel back what is hidden through the representation. This does not mean that the truth is behind the image, separate from it, but that it takes place through the image, is bound up with it.

One reasonably might ask whether or not people actually believe images to be representations of the real world. The simple answer is that race representations are not direct correspondences with reality and more accurately refract it for the purposes of certain interests. Because racialized societies, like the United States, are stratified along what Du Bois famously called "the problem of the color line," these interests are not usually made transparent. But the difficult answer is that there may not be a once-and-for-all reality to capture absent some detour through a symbolic system already one step removed from it. As such, children in schools learn that they construct the racial world the moment they partake in representing it. As educators kick and scream against the power of images to affect children, we discover that the story and old saying, "Sticks and stones may break my bones, but names will never hurt me," is just plain wrong. To underestimate the power of representations, some quite harmful, is not to be a serious educator. For every educational interaction takes on some form of representation: from history, to literature, to art.

Myth of Science and Math as Culture Free. Even the subject areas educators presume are immune from representation do not escape. Science and math often are touted as beyond symbolization, as culture-free representations of otherwise natural phenomena, other than in their use of equations. However, in order to communicate otherwise cultureless meanings, scientists recruit language to explain physical or biological laws. In summoning the work of language, scientists enter the domain of representation where words contain sign value, rather than the use and exchange value central to Marxism (see Baudrillard, 1981). In Emily Martin's (1992) classic study of biology textbooks, she finds that conception or birth is described through the use of metaphors, usually consisting of military and war imagery. The woman's womb and egg have been described as passive receptacles waiting for the deluge of sperm depicted as active soldiers deliberately seeking their target. In "reality," these sperm flail about, the majority of them dying before reaching their destination. Martin's points are instructive on a couple of educational fronts. First, she elevates the role of language in arguing for a theory of metaphor within scientific discourse. By doing so, she extends Kuhn's (1970) work on paradigms as subject to the standards of normal science and implicates science in the practice of cultural politics.

Second, Martin makes the link among language practice, school scientific texts, and larger gender relations that construct women as passive and men as active. Because she does so, the real lesson in her analysis is that apprehending science through language is not an innocent process of plainly representing reality as it exists. Rather, because the scientific enterprise is literally made up of human ecologies, science becomes a human cultural activity. This does not diminish scientific discoveries and explanations, or open the door to a cultural theory of gravity, but acknowledges that teaching science is sometimes most effective when culture is recruited to give it form. More important, it provides students the opportunity to decode cultural assumptions reproduced as objective scientific facts, such as gender roles. Last, the analogical basis of science does not doom it to relativity but arguably creates what Harding (1991) calls "strong objectivity," that is, a more inclusive truth, a democratic and participatory science.

With respect to race, racial representation enters many subject areas regarding the assumed cognitive capacities of students. Here are just a couple. In science and math, Asian Americans have become the poster children for ideal students. In fact, the racialization of math may be the only racial stereotype educators are aware of that is connected to a subject area (Nasir & Shah, 2011; Shah, 2013). Even if these stereotypes have some factual basis in Asian students being overrepresented in these subject areas in high school and later as majors in college, they do not occur absent a sociocultural system that enables and regulates them.

Victims of linguistic discrimination, Asian students receive the message that they may fare better in subjects that are not as intensive in training with respect to English-speaking or, worse, writing ability. Sue and Okazaki's (1995) theory of "relative functionalism" may go a long way to explain these students' plight as they make cultural choices based on their sociopolitical predicament. That is, they are reproduced à la Bowles and Gintis's (1976) correspondence theory, this time with a bit of racial twist to the story, but they do so as participants who interpret their social surroundings, albeit incompletely (cf. Willis, 1977). In other words, Asian students in the United States make choices in a social condition not completely of their own making. But they make choices nonetheless. Their dominant representation as math whiz kids does little to alleviate their outside status as perpetual foreigners in an English-only climate (Macedo, 2000a). It may confirm it. They are model minorities as long as they remain subalterns who do not speak (Spivak, 1988).

By contrast, Black students struggle with math and receive the opposite message. They are thwarted from building a math-specific identity because, at least in part, they are surrounded by representations that do not encourage their math competencies. This does not mean that Black students do not face real challenges in school, and specifically in math. However, as explained in Chapter 3, it provides evidence for Steele's (2004) work on stereotype threat, wherein the link between a student's cognitive evaluation and the recognition that he or she represents a racial group is enough to cause a drop in performance, especially in math.

Representations of Race as Relational. Representations work through suggestion and sometimes complicity. Images are not coercive representations of racial existence and require some amount of persuasion in order to work. In this sense, they retain an educative function because something is taught and something is learned. This does not prevent protest against them, which may produce counter-representations as a result. But even here, it may be too much to claim that counter-images are more accurate portrayals of race reality "out there." As representations, counter examples do the work of convincing their audience that another interpretation exists, even if it is not the final stop for meaning. To assert these contra-significations as truth, simply speaking, falls into the gap that dominant meaning systems have dug for themselves as the arbiters of reality. For as much as each representation sheds light on social issues, it is guilty of covering others. Insofar as it clarifies race, it manages to obscure it or other social relations. This is not an unhappy or hopeless state because it opens up the field of possibilities and emphasizes the task of historical change, which is never closed off.

In schools, this means that interconnection is more the norm than the exception. Representing race is always a relational enterprise inasmuch as it works through the politics of difference. Children learn that Europeans are the symbol of civilization, but they also learn that darker places on the globe are stuck in their own backwater. In fact, race is relational par excellence; it works only through the intimacy of difference. Representations of White and Black depend on each other, whereas being ethnic Laosian does not depend on the history of Luxembourgians. For nearly every representation of Whiteness, there is an existing, although admittedly absent and disparaged, representation of Blackness.

This seems to be Toni Morrison's (1993) point in *Playing in the Dark*, where she analyzes the deconstructive presence of Blackness within the official American literary tradition. And who can forget her almost casual but powerful question, paraphrased here, "How do you know a literary character is Black? Because the book tells you so." Her point questions the normativity of Whiteness in literary representations, its taken-for-granted status as an unmarked subject that needs no name. By contrast, Black characters are made visible, are named as such, and are specific rather than universal humans. As subordinate to Whites, they have less to lose but that much less to achieve (see Dyer, 1997). In race relations, representations of Whiteness are parasitic on Blackness, and a Cultural Studies framework is arguably the best way to teach young people to appreciate their power.

Making Racial Subjects

Schools are places where language happens. Children enter them daily and interact in language forms, from informal chat among peers to formal instruction in the classroom. In the United States, it does not take long for them to discover that this language is also racial, and they notice that race calls them each day. They answer. Schools are also places where race is made and recreated. This process happens in subtle ways as students and educators interact with the world more or less as unquestioned racial beings. Especially for the master race, it goes without saying that its members are White. Labeling Whiteness (McLaren et al., 2001) is a jarring experience because it locates the pervasive, stops the One in constant motion. Therefore, a racialized social system assumes the existence of racial subjects.

Race and School Structure. As U.S. schools currently exist, they are difficult to understand without the structuring effect of race. I appropriate "structuring" here in Giddens's (1986) sense to emphasize the process whereby the race structure creates race subjects who are limited by it and who in turn recreate it. In other words, racism and race relations function because they shore up racialized identities that do not precede them but are constitutive of them. This observation suggests that there is no race structure in the abstract outside of the creation of racial subjects and their performances. It affirms Judith Butler's (2004) basic insights with respect to gender, a system that does not exist a priori "out there" independent of the subjects who constitute it through performativity and by doing so give life to gender relations.

Similarly, Deborah Youdell (2010) claims that race injury is a matter of repetition, of general social subjects transforming into specific racial subjects through repeated interpellations. Race becomes a social phenomenon at the point when it becomes the prism through which subjects in public institutions, like schools, see themselves. Race and student subjectivity are not genetically linked in an originary way, which attests to the power of race to define how students and educators interact in an everyday way despite its bogus status. Whereas many people would admit, if push came to shove, that evaluation of social worth on the basis of skin-color affiliation is bizarre, educational practice continues to function as if it were legitimate.

In order for race relations to become a formidable force in education, teachers must fashion students' subjectivity in racial terms. This means that race is as impressive as it is because we have the compulsion to think through it despite the pretenses of color-blindness, which, as Gotanda (1995) rightly claims, must recognize race in order then to ignore it. For race to capture its subjects, it must traverse school life relatively unnoticed. This does not equate with race being completely undetected. Scholars have documented students' and teachers' recognition of race (A. Lewis, 2003; Pollock, 2004), using it for evaluative ends (Oakes, 2005). It means that in order for educators to recognize race, they must enter its meaning system and adopt race identity as something central to the way they see or understand themselves. It also means that race becomes axiomatic to the way that schools function and process not just information but also people.

Race subjectivity is a key element in the politics of race representation, which is part of how race groups are rendered intelligible. This is not a deterministic process that seals how groups necessarily understand themselves. When Black and Latino students observe their image thrown back to them as either criminals or school dropouts, it is not enough to reproduce these outcomes. Over the years, they have built counter-discourses to combat the barrage of pathological representations that affect their self-concept, not to mention self-esteem (see Yosso, 2006). But when these representations become the dominant and consistent public association for students of color, they begin to "believe" the representations. These beliefs are not fueled completely by representation absent structures that support them. For example, Black students' subjective understanding of their objective chances for school success arguably forms the arc of their habitus (Bourdieu & Passeron, 1977/1990), which confirms and in turn is confirmed by social practices that fulfill it. One is tempted to blame them for their perceived lack of resilience, evidenced by their lower achievement rates, but they are not the only ones who recognize these subject positions.

Whites also are invested in the perceived lower cognitive capacities of many students of color. White sense of intellectual superiority completes the circle that allows cognitive relations based on race to continue. This is Lopez's (2006) point when he stresses the relational dimensions of subjective or self-understanding: "Because identities are relational, inferiority is a predicative for superiority, and vice versa. This implies that there can be no positive White identity without commensurately negative minority identities" (p. 22).

If the suggestion is for Blacks and Latinos to rise above public representations of their lowered intellectual capacities, then it is equally true that Whites would need to fall below their overvalued intelligence. As explained in Chapter 2, Mills (1997) notes this epistemological racism dating back at least to the Enlightenment, wherein Europeans launched a *Herrenvolk* episteme between a backward Africa and Americas, and a transcendent knowing Occident. Of course, this negative relationship is most clear if educators recall decades of eugenics and scientific racism. Admittedly, this is evidence of a cruel past that now is easily dismissed by even a casual observer.

It seems that Whites' investment in their intellectual superiority continues to be a formidable force today, if only in a kinder, gentler form. The subjects of knowledge, Whites are beings-of-knowing. When students survey U.S. history and development, they receive the overwhelming impression that advances in knowledge came as a result of White innovations. From inventions to conventions, Whites have created a world of technology and mores unrivaled by any other civilization.

By contrast, as beings-to-be-known, people of color are objects of the knowledge industry called schooling. They are either victims of its imposition or targets of its improvement such that school reform's success is dependent on the alleviation of their plight. In the Native American case, boarding schools are evidence of the attempt to replace indigenous knowledge systems with Eurocentrism. In more recent years, NCLB could be dubbed No "Colored" Left Behind as the Black figure arguably became the litmus test for the initiative's ability to decrease the achievement gap. It also could be renamed No Chicano Left Behind, as it flails about in its attempt to address the undereducation of English language learners.

As a power/knowledge relation (Foucault, 1980), race power is the master race's ability to control how subordinated races become known, objects of knowledge, or subjects of race as a regulating discourse. Not only does it distinguish the knower from the non-knower, but it constitutes how they should be framed or made known. As a discourse, race positions people within circuits of meaning, usually through the privileged medium of language. As subjects who are inserted into statements, racialized people are not just socially constructed. This would have been enough, and most educators appreciate the constructed nature of race relations. That race is socially constructed does not equate with it being less real, than, say, the political economy. As long as race functions as what Paul Warmington (2009) calls a "mediating" tool, race serves certain social and political ends. He writes, "Race is understood as real not because it is an essential category but a historically specific means of effecting certain forms of social organization, of mediating human relations" (p. 289).

Because educators' comprehension of social relations informs how they organize educational interactions, in effect they racialize the classroom. They rely on their knowledge base, which is a combination of personal experiences, racial positioning, and understanding (or lack thereof) of the structural nature of race. In this way, humans become subjects of race, which is one of the prerequisites to race's mode of efficacy. Its mythical status notwithstanding—in the sense that it was an invention based on false prem-ises about human worth—race graduates to a representational scheme that affects all facets of schooling, from curricular decisions (J. Banks, 1993), to teacher–student interactions (Milner, 2010), to school disciplinary patterns (Ferguson, 2001; Parker & Stovall, 2005). These processes are made possible by raciology, or the elevation of race discourse to the status of "reality."

Reach of Curriculum. One mechanism for making racial subjects in schools is through the curriculum. Selecting knowledge of most worth on one hand (Kliebard, 1995) and legitimating particular sets of values on the other (Beyer & Apple, 1988; Giroux, 1995b), curriculum creation is one of the central functions of education (Apple, 2012). From the humanism of William Torrey Harris to the romanticism of G. Stanley Hall, knowledge selection is the process of representing the fundaments of human civilization. From Bobbit's focus on efficiency to Counts's emphasis on the social order, forging the curriculum is important for deciding the "what" of schooling, but equally significant for determining the "what for." In other words, struggles over the curriculum represent debates about not only what students will read, write, and believe about history (Loewen, 1995), but also the particular kind of life to which they are introduced (Giroux, 1988). Curriculum introduces them to a life that accepts their knowledge at face value, but the curriculum also can encourage them to interrogate knowledge's taken-for-granted status. In this manner, curriculum is not only a way to forge knowledge but a facet of life itself, not unlike Dewey's (1938) claim that education is not a dress rehearsal for life but is a form of living. By saying this, Dewey affirms the life-giving or life-taking properties of schooling. So it goes with curriculum, which makes the educational subject we know as the child.

With respect to race, the curriculum's ability to structure knowledge is constitutive of how racial subjects come to know themselves, are perceived by others, and are inserted into the educational project. Because knowledge is imbued with actors, some of whom are constructed as agents while others are not, the racialization of the curriculum and the hidden curriculum of race become powerful forces in the educational endeavor. For instance, Brown and Brown (2010) unravel the representation of Blackness in history and social studies textbooks to discover that, more often than not, racist violence against Blacks is attributed to the volitions of maladjusted Whites. Forsaking a more structural explanation of violence accomplishes several tasks.

Textbook representations construct the racialized social system as more or less acceptable and make aberrant the violent moments and people in his-tory as they "distort, minimize, or oversimplify the story" (Brown & Brown, 2010, p. 36). For example, regarding enslavement, they write that "textbook narratives do not position slavery as a fully institutionalized system that afforded a foundation of economic stability and wealth [for Whites] that can be traced to contemporary institutions and families, but rather as the actions of a few 'bad' (or less 'bad') men" (p. 46). In this way, violent Whites are depicted as autonomous agents, free from social forces.

Combining the frameworks of cultural memory and Critical Race Theory, Brown and Brown suggest that an "inclusive and racially balanced" (p. 38) yet flawed representation of history becomes a proxy for racial progress rather than reflecting it. In their study of 19 textbooks, from 5th, 8th, and 11th grades, the authors also find that Black resistance was reduced to deliberate or "violent insurrections" (p. 51), rather than including everyday forms of disengagement, such as work stoppage or feigning sickness or insanity to escape work. In this way, Blacks are portrayed as making history without necessarily participating in everyday, mundane forms of it, that is, concrete history.

One might object that these events happened long ago and therefore representations of them do not affect current affairs. Insofar as these violent acts are stored and remembered in problematic representations, they make up the very stuff of people's understanding with respect to racial inequality. To the extent that they create the limited script for students' comprehension of the nature of the "race problem," students are robbed of more sophisticated analyses of racism.

Historical representations are not fleeting moments that children and young adults freely take up. They enter the representations' structure and learn their place within its horizons. These signifying practices have the ability to symbolize what is meaningful about race, especially for events in history in which students did not participate and are, in practical terms, at the mercy of their representations (see Swartz, 1992).

Racetalk and Race Discourse

An important node in educators' understanding of race is language. Saying that race and language are inextricably tied underscores the fact that language, as mental thought and social practice, is constitutive of what we believe about race, racial groups, and what is meaningful about them. That Americans constantly talk about race is indisputable. Especially in a mediatized and modern society, like the United States, race fills up every information venue, from newspaper stories about crime and famous spectacles, to television sitcom shows about family life in ghettos and suburbs, to social networking gadgets. In education, race discourse is as common as the day is long. From official processes, like student placement in schools (Welner, 2006) and federal reform initiatives, to informal settings, like Open House and pep rallies (Pollock, 2004), race is an American preoccupation turned into an obsession. In U.S. education, its most common iteration goes by the topic of the "achievement gap," which is a more acceptable way of signaling that a racial disparity exists in schools across the nation. It represents one of the fundamental anxieties in education today.

Pervasiveness of Racetalk in Education. What we avoid disclosing about race says as much about it as what we choose to say about it. This confirms Pollock's (2004) discovery that the racialization process can happen through both "racetalk" as well as "colormute" discourse. By this, she means that race is constituted as much through overt race naming in schools as by silence about it. In the first, racetalk names racial dynamics, such as attempts to explain the high attrition rates of African Americans and Latinos. In the second, race-evasion testifies to a fundamental discomfort Americans, particularly Whites, feel about labeling an event or interaction as racial out of fear that the invention we call race will graduate to reality (see Frankenberg, 1993). Although a critical perspective on race would frown on the latter, the former is not without its problems, a point to which I will later return in Chapter 5. Both moments contribute to the racialization process because the first, including its progressive version, constructs race through ready-made assumptions about the naturalness of race, whereas the second, with pretenses of color-blindness, avoids explicit racial referents and codes them in apparently nonracial language. In all, racetalk and race silence contribute to the architecture of race.

When educators and students participate in racetalk, their annunciation of race themes confirms race's existence without at the same time verifying its realness. This distinction is important because a perspective, such as Marxist orthodoxy, that brands race as chimerical runs into the formidable force of race as a lived experience. An ideology as such, race lives through language as a material practice. This does not conflate language with matter, but argues that where race language is articulated with institutional arrangements and power relations, it comes with material consequences.

Through language, race becomes intelligible as a social relation. Not only do we speak of race, but race also speaks to us. Education would be unintelligible without race because so much of what transpires in schools owes itself to race relations, which does not suggest that it is the only game in town. From the history of U.S. nation creation (Loewen, 1995; Zinn, 2005) to assertions that we now live in a hip-hop nation (Chang, 2005; P. H. Collins, 2004; Dimitriadis, 2012; M. L. Hill, 2009; Rose, 1994, 2008) and beyond (Alim, Ibrahim, & Pennycook, 2009), children's school life is surrounded by race language. From the moment they step foot in homeroom and recite the pledge of allegiance, to the moment they leave campus and converse with friends on the way to their segregated neighborhoods, race is there, at least implicitly, if not overtly.

White Racial Framing. As conceived here, race discourse is a group's ability to direct or influence the public's understanding of racial meaning. It includes terms, statements, and frames of understanding that regulate racial subjects' uptake of race, which then becomes part of the functioning of the racialized social system (see Bonilla-Silva, 2003; Feagin, 2009; Foucault, 1972). Discourse includes chatter but also implicates the ordering of matter. Taken seriously, language as racial practice affirms the powerful role of ideology, and not simply in its pejorative sense.

Language ideologies of race constitute somatic politics at the level of the word. Teachers and students understand this process intuitively, as most educators have strict rules, if not zero tolerance, for racial epithets or animus. A critical study of race discourse takes this sensibility one step further by revealing the entire domain of language itself as racial, extending well beyond the accepted norm that racism is always overt. Absent direct references to race, racism can thrive through value-rich statements about racial groups apparently targeted at individual members.

In fact, we might argue that the hostile environment most children of color experience is precisely one where race referents are muted or coded because they are ambiguous situations. Ripe for self-doubt, self-questioning, or outrage, racial micro-aggressions create a condition where racist discourse avoids detection within common legal statutes of discrimination. They are the gentler, kinder forms of racism that affect the academic performance of students of color because unlike White children, who face challenges, minorities have the added burden of race. Their White counterparts share other educational problems, but Whiteness is not one of them.

Framing race in order to accomplish certain ends speaks to the rhetorical strategies that favor or disfavor racial groups within social contestation and within an existing structure. Feagin's (2009) concept of the "White racial frame" argues that the master race deploys discourse in such a way as to minimize the pervasive nature of racism as well as to exonerate its own culpability in the process. Sociocultural on one hand and cognitive on the other, White racial framing combines affective and mental states (not to be confused with mindsets), which articulate with larger structures of race. Attempting to theorize racial feeling and thinking, Feagin advances our understanding of race discourse as an assemblage of cognitive and bodily, conscious and unconscious, and rational and emotional responses. Harkening back to Williams's (1977) notion of the "structure of feeling," the White racial frame also reminds us of Foucault's (1977) biopolitics or political anatomy insofar as race language becomes a form of *somapolitics* (see also Goldberg, 1990).

Foucault's intervention strikes a blow to the racial *cogito* as hopelessly mental, devoid of embodiment and affective investment (see Leonardo & Zembylas, 2013). His explanation is a clear example of the power of discourse to link with structure, or the cultural politics of racial economy. It problematizes attempts to name injuries without an appropriate link to broader structures, such as the discourse of White male victimization, which lacks any empirical basis (Winant, 1997). The White racial frame is bogus not simply because its effects are as real as racism. It showcases the ability for feeling to graduate to the level of emotion, the first arguably related to the senses, which is then made intelligible, even if distorted, through discourse. It speaks to the power of discourse to drive understanding, which depends on selecting details while ignoring others, and creating conditions for racially motivated actions.

Discourses of Limitations. In education and social science generally, there is no paucity of discourses that penalize and punish students of color for their perceived limitations. Known popularly as culture of poverty arguments, these discourses position Black and Latino students as damaged and damaging to the educational enterprise (see Glazer & Moynihan, 1970; O. Lewis, 1968). However, disparaging remarks, or what Parker (2011) calls "discourses of derision," have been around for many decades, predating the 1960s poverty scholarship that discursively shifted later in the 1990s to the underclass debates (see Kelley, 1998), without necessarily changing the pathologizing gaze that disciplines students of color.

Brown (2011) documents the changing discourses since the 1930s regarding the construction of the "Black male" by social scientists. Using Popkewitz's (1998) concept of "populational reasoning" and Pride's (2002) "conceptual narrative," Brown finds that the work of discourse, with slight variations, consistently portrays Black males through the commonsense construction as a "problem." The alternative discourse comes in the 1970s when insurgent scholars dared to frame Black male behavior as adaptations to an otherwise hostile racist social condition. With Black nationalism thrown in, Black males are renarrated as possessing survival and linguistic skills that a predominantly White teacher population woefully misunderstands. Their overcompensated masculinity, which "cool pose theory" deems is a result of their emasculation by Black women, is reinterpreted as a consequence of and protection against "failure threat" (cf. Steele's stereotype threat, 2004; see Chapter 3).

Despite these and other attempts to speak to larger structural determinants that create the construction we know as the "Black male" (see Brown & Donnor, 2011; Ferguson, 2001), the discourse of Black male pathology, irresponsibility, and anti-achievement orientation continues. Reaching a near-crisis moment of representation, the issue is so serious that the University of Pennsylvania Graduate School of Education, under the leadership of Professor Shaun Harper and the support of Dean Andrew Porter, has developed an initiative devoted specifically to understanding and raising the achievement of Black males. As the related brochure makes clear, this begins with high-lighting a different model of Blackness, one imbued with images of success. It also has spawned an academic journal at UPenn dedicated to research around Black male education.

As Brown notes, the crisis confirms Ian Hacking's (1995) Foucauldian-inspired notion of "human kind," or the penchant for classifying, tabulating, and sorting human populations, which has characterized the human and so-cial sciences. Students of color do not sit idly and internalize the discourses that target, even victimize, them. Minority students also summon discourses of resistance to abate their victimization (Yosso, 2006), but when they are interpellated by perspectives that frame them as problems, these discourses accomplish what they set out to do. The conclusion is not that people of color are weak and somehow lacking resilience, but to combat representa-tions they had little power in creating requires power they do not necessarily wield. Paradoxically, Whites who believe in these deficit-based discourses—that is, find it hard to resist them—are rarely depicted as lacking the resilience necessary to refute them. Whites are not taken to the same task when they believe in the problematic representations of people of color. It seems there is a double standard at work.

Appropriation of Meaning. Discourses are not only about controlling lan-guage without the appropriate apparatuses to support them. Without control of the means of signification, racial ideologies do not stick. As an ideology, race hegemony is flimsy, always requiring rejuvenation and re-adhesion. In order to stick, race discourses require repetition (Butler, 1990) and recruiting "*common sense narratives*" (Brown, 2011, p. 2071; emphasis in original) to do their work. Race power is not only the ability to exercise control over the division of labor; it also wields control over the division of meaning.

For example, because Black and other minority artists do not dominate the discursive and representational apparatuses, their cultural productions are often representative (Julien & Mercer, 1996). By this, Julien and Mercer mean that, as a dominant racial group, Whites control the means of com-munication, such as media and the arts, and therefore produce more varied discourses to depict White life. By comparison, moviemakers of color, even relatively powerful figures like Spike Lee, feel the weight of having to capture the entirety of Black life in their films. Of course, they are destined to fail at this. In addition, it does not speak of White artists' own problematic produc-tion of Blackness in their work. As a result of the one-shot opportunities for representation for many cultural producers of color, they choose more essen-tialist depictions of minority life, attempting to signify it *in toto.* Essentialist as they may be, these works say less about their authors and more about the conditions under which they work and the limitations placed on them.

Challenges for Critical Race Discourse. As an assemblage of ideological representations, race discourse is less about accurate renditions of "reality" than about what it enables or forecloses. Although subordinate races may possess more reliable knowledge about the nature of racism in that they are not invested in distorting its real basis, their discourses are judged for what they reveal rather than their claim to truth. Stuart Hall (1996b) is clear when he promotes a cultural politics without guarantees. By this he means that unlike modernism's promises of transparency between language and reality as long as reason is able to triumph, discourse is defined by a certain will to represent. That is, when racial minorities counter White discourses with alternative accounts of history, there is nothing to prevent them from revealing one story while covering another. This is why "intersectional analyses" (Crenshaw, 1991) of the "matrix of domination" (P. H. Collins, 2000) open up possibilities of what Hall (1996a), inspired by Laclau (1977), calls a theory of articulation.

Articulation theory can build race discourses that are attuned to gendered, sexualized, and classed histories insofar as they create an entanglement that makes it impossible to disaggregate at the level of politics even if they can be differentiated conceptually. As a discursive ensemble, co-formations speak to the power package of race, class, and gender during important events in history, such as colonization (see Grosfoguel, 2007). Quijano's (2000) discourse of "coloniality of power" fills a racial void left by Wallerstein's (1987) world systems theory by adding the history of race and colonization to world economic development. Arguing that colonialism was the mode that capitalism took in order to Europeanize the world economy, Quijano reveals what Wallerstein's Marxism's leaves out. Not to be outdone, Lugones (2007) takes Quijano to task for covering up the gendered consequences of colonialism, which introduced not only Eurocentric structures into indigenous lands but a patriarchal rule that made gender an accomplishment of men.

These agonistic race discourses are not easy to promote in education where the bottom line of test scores and other outputs are the ruling ideas. Flanked by the discourse of neoliberalism, neopositivist pedagogy limits students' understanding of race structures within the logic of market options and personal choices (see Sandler & Apple, 2010). This all but leaves students with the impression that a structural explanation of racism is inconvenient if not also undesirable. Neoliberalism limits discourse about race to the machinations of the "free" market, the sovereign decisions of atomized individuals, and labels failure as the sign of a certain inability to maximize one's chances within a presumed-to-be-fair competition (see Giroux, 2010).

It is not that neoliberalism fails to recognize the fact of racism. It does not go that far. However, it reduces otherwise citizen subjects to abstract consuming subjects so that the problem of racism is displaced onto the plane of individual acts within a race-neutral system. After only several decades of race-conscious policies, like affirmative action, and structure-sensitive analysis of racism starting with the Civil Rights era (see Perlstein, 2004), neoliberal discourse and its educational cognates of No Child Left Behind and Race to the Top find the answer to racism in a decisively race-blind solution. The unbridled belief in free-market ideology is ironic in light of the real lessons about failure that the business world has made accessible for education policymakers (Dimitriadis, 2010).

In a color-blind era, the challenges to critical race discourse run the gamut. For example, public race dialogue is driven by the logic of the apparently race-neutral market. Every discourse about race is not just a way to frame the issues in order to compel people to act in particular ways, but it is a way to define the "human" within racialized understandings. Humanism shows its "inability to effectively counter such inhumanities . . . motivated by a particular definition of what it means to be human" (Biesta, 2006, p. 5). Neoliberalism reduces learning to the calculable outcomes of choice, whereas, as Biesta reminds us, learning is precisely the ability to prepare for the incalculable and the risks this education takes, such as those that educators face when they confront race.

APPRAISAL OF CULTURAL STUDIES, RACE, AND EDUCATION

A Cultural Studies framework on race is one of the most effective ways to teach students, even at the youngest ages, the importance of the symbolic aspect of race. Reduced to neither a speculative idea nor material fact, race's effectivity as a cultural relation confirms its representational power. Although Cultural Studies perspectives favor the symbolic over the material, it is more a matter of emphasis within the theoretical edifice.

For instance, White productions of controlling images of Blackness affect how Blacks are understood in the public imagination, often through the prism of a negation or fundamental lack. This would have been enough, but this deployment of power also influences how people of color see themselves, sometimes internalizing the negative images. Indicative of a symbolic relation, race power is the ability to convince subordinate races, through subtle force and equally through social consent, that images reflect a pre-existing reality (Volosinov, 2006). Moreover, the work that goes into representation is obfuscated by the master race's claims to objectivity in order to mask its group interests. Naïve but certainly not innocent, this move is betrayed by what Volosinov (2006) calls the natural "multiaccentuality" of meaning or what Bakhtin (1981) refers to as "heteroglossia." The master race reduces the play of meaning, such as the field of culture, into the pretenses of a cultural arbitrary disguised as a universal (Bourdieu & Passeron, 1977/1990).

The turn to representation in critical studies of race marks the ascendance of culture as a material, rather than idealist, relation. Du Bois's (1904/1989) intervention is a key moment when, through his use of symbols, like the "veil" and "twoness," he unleashes a powerful explanation of the imposition and imposing presence of Whiteness in the lives of Blacks. Likewise, Fanon (1952/1967) uses the concept of "mask" to explain the inauthenticity of Blackness as a f/pigment of the White imagination, from which the pathological representation of Blackness stems. These advances in race theory represent extensions of materialist frameworks, inherited from Marx and his disciples, to create a tributary that, while avoiding a form of reductive economic materialism, goes by the label of "corporeal" theories of race. A somatic relation metaphorized through associations between skin color and human worth, the meaning of race is accomplished through the regulation of bodies.

Here, representation makes it possible to romanticize people of color and demonize them at the same time. Tiger Woods discovered this when he committed his transgressions and crossed from the multiracial darling of American sports to its dark angel. After all the bouts in the media regarding his ambiguous identity, signified by his childhood label of "Caublinasian" (a combination of Caucasian-Black-Indian-Asian), his sexual escapades confirm in the White imagination that he is Black after all.

Minorities do not have the luxury of ambiguity within the U.S. racial formation. Either you are the solution, as in Asians (see Prashad, 2000), or you are the problem, as in Blacks (see Du Bois, 1904/1989). How it feels to be one or the other is ultimately not the point, Du Bois's insight notwithstanding. Both are not presentable therefore represented for, within the prerogatives of Whiteness. Fitting nicely into Foucault's (1977) concept of "political anatomy," race subjectivation takes on special significance. Here "subject" takes on the double meaning of (1) becoming a subject of race and (2) being subjected to it.

A quarter-century before Foucault, Fanon (1952/1967) uncovered the power of representation to distort both Black self-understanding as well as Whites' public, social understanding of Blackness. Obscured by a proverbial "mask," Blackness is haunted by a fundamental distortion created by Whiteness. On one level, Blackness is nothing but a representation, a creation for the sole purpose of being negated in the White imaginary. Blackness is a representation for the assertion of Whiteness and rarely for the benefit of Blackness, a mirror created in order for Whiteness to know itself. Blacks may be able to learn Whiteness, but in the end they are betrayed by the fact of their own corporeal Blackness.

For example, the ability to speak French enables Blacks to put on a White mask, to put on the White world (cf. Fordham & Ogbu, 1986). However, because race is a somatic relation, the essence of Blackness under the mask betrays them. In schools, teachers may teach Black children White ways, even promote Whiteness as their destiny. But it remains to be said that, like the blood on Lady Macbeth's hands that will not wash off, the Black student cannot rub off the Blackness.

The Tyranny of Representation:
From Social Facts to Social Constructions

The turn to representation in race studies requires the radical decentering of the subject at the same time that it argues for the centrality of subjectivity. To some, this is a source of confusion as Cultural Studies seems bent on announcing the death of the subject while relying on it for subject formation. It can be cleared up by recalling that the "death of the subject" is the eulogy for a certain liberal, autonomous subject (see Biesta, 2006). The modernist myth that projected a rational, thinking agent is called into question, here redefined as the intersubjective product of multiple discourses fighting to define, and therefore regulate, his or her self-understanding. As such, representational politics achieves great power not only by influencing our actions, but precisely by driving them, by providing the constraints under which possible interventions and intelligibilities may emerge. Few discursive systems are more powerful than race, especially within a U.S. context, in accomplishing this task. It has the ability to explain the alpha and omega of schooling and why it takes its current shape and appearance.

For instance, it may be argued that children of color in schools are treated in disparaging ways because of their representations in books, public racetalk, and images. In particular, dropout and incarceration rates of Black and Latino students result from a regime of narratives, which write them into history in pathological ways and produce consequences that disempower them (see Brown, 2011). Taken to its logical conclusion, race-as-representation projects a problem as well as a solution. For if the positioning of people of color within the symbolic is their main source of struggle, it follows that counter-representations would go a long way in alleviating the problem. No reasonable educator would argue against this logic, understanding the power of the image to influence young minds.

However, this section examines where the line between social facts and social constructions begins because no reasonable educator would argue that, despite their power, representations determine students' fate. It is more complicated than that. Without insisting on the sovereign subject, representations may produce how students are understood, but they do not determine them either.

Link Between Culture and Structure. People's inner world is a dialectical counterpart to their objective conditions. Volosinov (2006) is clear about the inextricable link between culture and structure when he says that "*the forms of signs are conditioned above all by the social organization of the participants involved and also by the immediate conditions of their interaction.* When these forms change, so does sign" (p. 21; emphasis in original). Furthermore:

1. Ideology may not be divorced from the material reality of signs.
2. The sign may not be divorced from the concrete forms of social intercourse.
3. Communication and the forms of communication may not be divorced from the material basis. (p. 21)

With respect to race ideology, representations provide the ligament or connective tissue between objective conditions and subjective life. Representations depend on objective conditions to provide the raw materials that ideology converts into culture. Freire (1970/1993) seems to agree when he claims that the ideological process of education turns nature into culture through mediation.

Representation happens in the domain of signs where language does its work to transform matter into meaningful units of understanding. Without subjective appropriation of the material world, the world means nothing, and a world without meaning is not a human world. Conversely, a world without an objective condition does not supply objects of knowledge that could be turned into forms of self- and social understanding. All this suggests that representation achieves little in the way of becoming autonomous from objective conditions that provide its basic material, without which there would be nothing to symbolize. Furthermore, social relations like race are represented with the support of institutions, without which racial ideology would not stick. With institutions to buoy them, race representations do not just do their work, but they accomplish certain ends.

Cultural Politics of Representation. Here I would like to discuss Coloma's (2006) description of homelessness. In a series of helpful passages, Coloma performs the necessary connection between language and material existence. Longing for a home that never was and arguably never will be, Coloma (2006) reflects during his research in the Philippines:

My desires to identify as a Filipino and claim the Philippines as home were tempered by others who saw me as someone who had been "gone for so long" and could no longer belong. My research travel to the Philippines and my subsequent return to the USA confirmed what I had felt deep down: the Philippines is no longer my home, and the USA will never become one. (p. 23)

Although the material condition of homelessness should not be minimized, Coloma's nomadic description of diasporic existence provides the missing link within dominant frameworks of race theory. Rey Chow (1993) describes the migrant as a person in transit between cultures, for whom homelessness is the only home "state" (as cited by Coloma, 2006, p. 24), and reminds us that exilic existence is not to be mourned or celebrated but becomes a source of knowledge, of subjectivity. Whiteness conveniently forgets its own history of immigration from European lands and forgoes the knowledge that stems from such historical disjuncture. Instead, it uproots indigenous people all over the world in order to take root, calling other peoples' home its own and denies them the same right.

Ambivalence, about which I will have more to say in Chapter 5, allows Coloma (2006) to represent racialized existence, but he does so in a manner that testifies to its brutal fact without grieving it or reducing it to metaphor. He writes:

> The realization of homelessness elicited the ambivalent emotions of pain and pleasure. My pain derived from letting go of powerful "home" categories, such as Filipino and American, that are infused with essentialist discourses. I had to come to terms with the idea that the power of essentialism was simultaneously its allure and downfall: it offered both a badge of belonging and definition as well as a shackle of rigidity and constraint. My pain was rooted in knowing that there is no "home", as it was construed, for me to go to. (p. 24)

It strikes me that the cultural politics of representation, its tyranny as well as solace, allows Coloma to establish the necessary insight and distance from his direct experience. The pedagogical moment of doing the work of representation means that the risk of essentialism is taken in order for any worthwhile learning to take place, that reification, while certainly to be avoided, is a risk in critical work on race. That race representation is accompanied by reification goes without saying, but a committed race scholar understands it as a complementary part of genuine race work.

Representing Blackness vs. Reality. In another example, by analyzing Black representations in textbooks, Brown (2011) draws a link between social facts and the social constructions that fuel them. Representing Blackness has become an academic tradition, a national pastime, the production of which traditionally was controlled by White academics and intellectuals. Robin Kelley (1998) questions this tradition's racial politics when he documents the cultural and urban wars to which popular reports, like Moynihan's, give birth. With a little Foucault thrown in, we may argue that Kelley documents a regime of knowledge that disciplined an entire generation of scholars with respect to the problem of the color line. From the underachievement to the underclass debates, Black families and communities became the "favorite" problem that needed fixing. Brown joins this literature because education did not escape this logic as Black students became the center of the achievement gap discourse. From pathology to pathos, these narratives construct Blackness through emotion-filled descriptions of struggling students and how to explain their plight.

How much responsibility educators can attach to race representation with respect to racial trends is not straightforward. When social science literature represents Black males as violent or shiftless, these are not value-free descriptions and therefore deserve critical scrutiny. But when the same literature includes trends in Black communities, such as the higher rate of single-home families with missing fathers or male figures, it is not easily set aside as a social construction. Of course, the repetition, consistent emphasis, or stress that falls on certain facts over others is a discursive choice and becomes an issue within the economy of representation (Foucault, 1972). However, there are at least a couple issues to broach.

First, it is not fully compelling that representation better explains this predicament than the racio-political economy that produces community and family breakdown. The instability such dynamics produce when joblessness and poverty subvert decent living conditions becomes an overwhelming explanation for individual, family, and community (under)development. Despite the 1970s reframing of Black males' ability to cope creatively with their lived conditions, those same conditions seem more responsible for their coping strategies. Second, even if it is reasonable to hold these social constructions as blameworthy, they do not remain social constructions for long and graduate to social facts. The rate of single-parent Black homes is an empirical reality, even if it is exacerbated by problematic representations, and thus requires a materialist analysis. Contrary representations, as launched by "The Cosby Show" in the 1980s, are equally problematic for they do not reflect Black families in general, despite their appeal to a counter-script regarding the crisis in Black representation. Notwithstanding its popularity among Blacks and Whites alike, to some Cosby was simply out of sync with Black reality.

Representations are, after all, not to be taken as a stand-in for reality but a corner slice of it. They bear resemblance to the real as an elephant's tail is an organic part of the animal. Early in their education, children learn the useful skill of distinguishing the real from fiction. As young children, they are frightened by scary movies, and an adult's response is inevitably, "It's only a movie. It's not real." This example oversimplifies the point, but the ability to tell the real from the real-like, while not radically separable, is an important skill. In fact, it is part of the development of people of color to dissociate crude representations of their experience from their actual, lived experience. To do otherwise is to anoint representations with more power than they have, which gives them tyranny over our lives. For as much as hip hop, for example, and rap in particular, values "realness," it is performative, which does not suggest it is any less effective or convincing.

As an artifice, rap's claim to realness is not "real" as such but is itself a form of representation, one that resonates with experience but equally so with social taste and the senses. It is part and parcel of racial politics, in which people of color partake, that rap or hip hop lays claim to speaking for the real. Representations may inspire action, which may recommend them, but their effect is defined more by a sense of revelation than truth. Representations and counter-representations are valued for their effect rather than their ability to project an accurate rendition of reality.

Connecting Representation and Racial Outcomes. The ligature that connects representation and racial outcomes is arguably the social policies to which information dissemination, such as media constructions and social science research, gives birth. When Moynihan (1965) and others made certain choices to represent, in their truncated form, Black families, these representations jived with the White imaginary's understanding of the "Negro problem." Even Oscar Lewis's (1968) liberal sensibilities are no match for Whiteness, and his structural explanations for Black poverty were overshadowed by the second half of his argument, which described the coping strategies that poor Blacks developed as a response to their economic marginalization. These cultural strategies were recast as autonomous from larger structural relations. From William Julius Wilson (1978) to Massey and Denton (1993), Black cultural decay is evident. The point of contention is not the accuracy of these claims or their cultural-genetic (i.e., culturally essentialist) excesses, but their apprehension of a causal mechanism between structure and culture.

Marxist science was guilty of a certain scientism that reached its logic in Althusser's (1971) appropriation of Bachelard's (1985) concept of the "epistemological rupture," later rebadged by Althusser as the "epistemological break" (p. 38). Through this trope, Althusser affirms the forging of a new problematic, one that is ever more scientific in its threshold crossing between new knowledge and a new theory of society. For Bachelard's student, that science was Marxism. However, in the same move, Althusser gives ideology a shot in the arm, which energizes it as a relation not hopelessly stuck in chimerical representations of the world. In short, representations take on a new life of their own. Captured in the concept of "overdetermination," ideology's role is elevated to a perpetual, autonomous status, no longer relegated as the redheaded stepchild of materialism. For example, in the 2012 Summer Olympics, the ideology of royalty was in full splendor, even centuries after the dissolution of the material structure of monarchy. The Queen may not produce the show, but she still functions as a director, becoming the cultural symbol of *Great* Britain.

The uptake of representations is where the real damage plays out when we consider that the culture of poverty scholarship drove the formation of U.S. social policies for several decades, from the War on Poverty to the War on Drugs. This seems to be Derrick Bell's (2005a) point when he takes Orlando Patterson to task when Bell's former Harvard colleague rails against Black cultural pathology as the internal explanation for Black poverty absent external causes, such as White racism. Because representations become public fodder for policymaking, Bell warns against words that wound a community already injured. Although Bell admits to the compounding effects of Black cultural limitations, the former founder of CRT is better known for his criticisms of White hypocrisies.

After many decades of representing the apparent "uneducability" of children of color, U.S. education decided that enough was enough, and the tough-love measure of No Child Left Behind was conceived. What could be dubbed as the "War on Schools" (Leonardo, 2007), NCLB located the problem in two main culprits of Black underachievement. After reconfirming the "Negro child problem," NCLB proceeded to hold accountable failing schools and their teachers. Because enduring and dominant representations in the White imaginary vacillated between genetic and cultural inferiorities of families of color, it is no surprise that NCLB, as the policy embodiment of Whiteness, does not indict structural racism, perennial segregation, and economic exploitation as more reasonable suspects for the crimes against students of color and their families. Although success would not have been guaranteed had a federal initiative represented the problem in these terms, eschewing them signaled its predictable defeat. President Obama is forced to clean up the "educational spill," like the oil that floated in the Gulf during the early years of his first term. But Obama's Race to the Top, a policy that has many of the trappings of neoliberalism, leaves the same critics of NCLB uneasy.

Thus, to do their work, representations require the help of social policies in order to stick. When taken out of historical context, narratives of Black male absence in the household fuel the creation of myths surrounding their moral promiscuousness, irresponsibility, and the like, as Brown rightly argues. But it remains to be said whether such myths, while certainly unhelpful and ultimately nefarious, are better explanations than, say, the high rate of Black male incarceration that leads to their absence in the family. Even the myth of the Black criminal fails to explain the disproportionate number of young Black men in the juvenile system—not simply a myth anymore—without the powerful explanation of Black poverty and social isolation. Young Black men may even, on some level, believe they are criminal within the regime of racial images, but the policy-industrial complex that produced the 3-Strikes Law under President Clinton is the document that turns images into deeds, or words into law. Latino children may invite the ire of someone like Samuel P. Huntington (1997) when he perceives them as contributors to America's cultural decay, but immigration laws that are pro-immigration while being anti-immigrant rights, such as a comprehensible education under the *Lau* v. *Nichols* statutes, provide the bullets for the guns of representation.

These policies crystallize the incipient, and sometimes not so subtle, ethos regarding the "problem" of people of color. None of this analysis is incompatible with or vitiated by a representational approach, but it is a matter of emphasis. Racist representations do their harm, but the policies to which they give rise perform the incision. Policies may be a regime of representations like others, but like Austin's (1962) perlocutionary speech acts, race policies are where representations accomplish their meanness as a material force. Policy is where language codifies race relations, where intellectual interpretations become enforced and all too real. In the next section, I will outline a materialist, although not necessarily Marxist, understanding of race.

Race Matterism vs. Race Materialism: Linguistic Determinism and Sign Fetishism

Notwithstanding the appeal of postmodern theory, which is a staple of Cultural Studies, modernist philosophies and materialist theories have responded aggressively to the current crisis in social and educational theory. Indeed, there has been a shift in the cultural field through electronic communication, cyber identities, and mediatized subjectivities. We understand that Foucault and fatness are surveilled by discourses of thin; Baudrillard's bawdy narratives bring us some needed bounce in social theory; Lyotard's language games are laudable for exposing the limitations of Western meta-narratives as universal for all societies. But to suggest that we are beyond the age of material relations as an objective force is surely to perpetuate another myth in the name of social fiction: social because it is still social theory; fiction because it projects a futuristic present out of sync with current, real processes. The dialectical tension between discourse and materialist theories of race is productive, but the "end of the real" thesis is unsustainable and, at worst, complicit with relations of exploitation. Ludic postmodernists succeeded in dodging Scylla only to strengthen Charybdis. It is the difference between what Ebert (1996) calls materialist theory and "matterism."

Identity Politics. There is something to suggest that the new identity politics, or the politics of difference, and materialist politics are compatible. For the very notion of identity is traceable to the material flow of life and how, for example, the Black body is commodified as a hypersexualized subject. In other words, a materialist-identity politics is part of an overall and more complete transformation of objective life insofar as it leaves its stamp on our subjectivity. One of these markings is the important role that space plays in identity formation. As Ricky Lee Allen (1999) suggests, identity does not take shape in empty places but is saturated with discourses of space. He goes on to say:

> No event can take place without space. No memory is without spatial essence, nor can a space be read without memories of a spatial context. To remember a time is also to remember a place. To have a thought is to have a place for that thought. One of the first acts of human life is to occupy a space. Moving, communicating, sensing, and behaving are all spatial. Sex and sexuality are spatial as well. *Nothing humans can do escapes space; life cannot be lived nor imagined without it.* (p. 253; emphasis in original)

Allen's brand of "radical identity politics" considers the spatiality of identity in both the real and imagined sense. Identity is real and part of the productive process because students gain an identity through their place in practical activity (Nasir, 2012).

To the extent that identity is abstract, it is imagined. It is very much like the sort of thing that Levi-Strauss described as a "virtual center (*foyer virtuel*) to which we must refer to explain certain things, but without it ever having a real existence" (cited in Brubaker & Cooper, 2000, p. 9). Like identity, race has real and nonreal dimensions, invented as well as lived elements. Reducing race to one or the other forgets that it lives through ideological manipulation, but its effectivity requires material institutions and resource investment, such as schools and the media. Naturalizing race, as uncritical work is predisposed to do, or minimizing it, of which orthodox Marxism is guilty, does not testify to the social fact of race contestation.

Differential Play of Silence. With deconstruction, we understand that Western metaphysics has functioned under the sign of logocentrism, or the privileging of the "metaphysics of presence," as Derrida (1976) defines it. In this, Western philosophy is guilty of neglecting the differential play of silence in the sign's apparent self-presence, a silence that both "supplements" and subverts the metaphysics of presence. For example, the signifier "White" exists only in relation to its silent, and disparaged, other internal to it, or "non-White." Fanon (1952/1967) said as much when he claimed, "For not only must the Black man be Black; he must be Black in relation to the White man" (p. 110). In another instance, the signifier "rational" (read: men) exists only in supplementarity with "emotional" (read: women). It is this silence that compromises the security of the sign in our attempt to fix the play of meaning.

In fact, Baudrillard (1994) explains that speech (as opposed to language) is the central difference between humans and animals. He writes:

> They, the animals, do not speak. In a universe of increasing speech, of the constraint to confess and to speak, only they remain mute, and for this reason they seem to retreat far from us, behind the horizon of truth. But it is what makes us intimate with them. It is not the ecological problem of their survival that is important, but still and always that of their silence. In a world bent on doing nothing but making one speak, in a world assembled under the hegemony of signs and discourse, their silence weighs more and more heavily on our organization of meaning. (p. 137)

It is not rationality, civilization, or labor that distinguishes humans from animals, but our capacity and their failure to speak. Although speaking creates poetry and beauty, it also institutes racial violence through discursive castration and linguistic lynching.

Tracing violence through silence is innovative if this means that silence does not signify emptiness. It represents a subjective field of experience that is never completely severed from its other; that is, silence is intimate with presence. It is not a stretch to relate this description to the discursive formation of Whiteness, which is parasitic on the discourses about people of color. In the act of speaking, White discourse recalls its relationship with its radical other, indeed depends on it.

Limited Power of Discourse over Objective Conditions. Even though there are, as deconstruction correctly suggests, differences *within* signs—like class, gender, and race—there exist important differences *between* them. That is, races and classes have both discursive and nondiscursive aspects to them, but discourse does not determine the objective conditions around an exploited, alienated student of color. Moreover, regardless of how a sweatshop worker constructs the meaning around her work or the joy she may receive fraternizing with her co-workers (if this is even allowed), her labor is still exploited and alienated. Regardless of how she may conceptualize her working conditions as somehow better than the objective conditions of being workless, her work still satisfies someone else's search for profit. Although resignification may assist the project of social transformation, it alone cannot feed the hungry and house the homeless. For the exploited have needs that are more immediate than their desire to be constructed in particular ways, although we may appreciate that they are in dire straits because of the way they are perceived as undeserving in the first place. In profound ways, if we provided the hungry with food, they might care less about how they were inserted into discourse!

Anti-intellectualism aside, discourses define human subjects and rationalize social organization in ways that make it possible for racial oppression to exist. This fact notwithstanding, Ebert (1996) claims that despite the realness of language, this does not mean that the real is made up of language. If race theorists make everything real, then nothing is real. The corpo*reality* of race, while not only material, is reduced to a trope or signification. As a social category and analytical tool, the real no longer serves any heuristic value for revolutionary understanding. It melts into thin air. There has to be a point wherein distinctions, as opposed to differences, have to be made with respect to the production or signification of race. Against idealism, Marx once discouraged fighting phrases with phrases. If we substitute, according to Scatamburlo-D'Annibale and McLaren (2004), "signification" for "phrases," the same limitation arises. Not a heck of a lot of difference.

For example, although discourse may affect the real through regimes of meaning and truth, discourse alone results in an amputated praxis because it denies the fact that signs have power not only from within but also from without. Defining power as diffuse, as Foucault (1978) advocates, forgets that power not only works through subjects as conduits and terminals, but is also the power to oppress, as Freire never tired of reminding us. Foucault (1986) attempts to make power *available* for the "care of the self," or those strategies, following Deleuze and Guattari's (1983) "body without organs" (i.e., without organization), to improve upon the self beyond humanistic regimes of truth. This has much to recommend it.

But regimes of truth gain their privilege largely through their relationship with institutional power: in other words, through the real. Racist signifiers "work" the way they do because their targets are institutionally disempowered to begin with. There is hardly an existing White subject whose material life is threatened by the signifier "honkey," which does not come with institutional power to keep down Whites. On the other hand, epithets are oppressive to racialized minorities because of their place in the racial formation, as well as because of how these signifiers have been used to break down their psyche and self-confidence, all of which have material consequences. No amount of reclaiming the word will succeed in substantially changing the racist landscape without a simultaneous transformation of material relations.

Discourse as a Representation of the Real. That said, language and discourse cannot be materialized away. That is, discourse's constitutive power to construct the real, without actually producing it, cannot be explained away but instead is linked to the material, as argued by Volosinov (2006) or John Frow (1994). The real is understood through signs that influence the construction of the real. If we understand this process in a dialectical manner, then the superstructure and base produce overdeterminations (Althusser, 1969), or that culture produces effects onto the economy. In this, Althusser accomplishes what J. M. Fritzman (1998) calls a version of "poststructural materialism." Althusser's specter invokes the transformation within orthodox Marxism to explain the role of discourse in creating subjects for the reproduction of the conditions of production. That is, in response to Lukács's humanist or Hegelian Marxism, Althusser's anti-humanist brand of Marxism opts for a theory of subjectivity. Foucault's studies take Althusser's ideas to their logical conclusion. Althusser's problematic starts with the ideological interpellation of humans as subjects of ideology, in this case, of race.

As mentioned in the first part of this chapter, discourse interpellates, or inserts, humans into subject positions within language practice. Attempting to understand how ideology "works," Althusser explains that it is through discourse that subjects for production are secured by capital. Elsewhere, I have taken Althusser's basic framework to argue for race subjectivation. Ideological apparatuses, like schools, induct students into their places within production and race relations by first inserting them into discourse. As far as Althusser emphasizes the base as the first cause, he is materialist, and as far as he eternalizes ideology, he is poststructural. Through discursive practices, racial subjects (mis)recognize their imaginary relations to the real for their real relations. *In other words, discourse is a form of representation of the real and not the real itself.*

In his response to postmodern theory, Terry Eagleton (1996) affirms real, historical language. He writes, "The linguistic animal has the edge over its fellow creatures in all kinds of ways. . . . Only a linguistic animal could have history, as opposed to what one imagines for a slug is just the same damn thing over again" (p. 73). To Eagleton, the capacity for language truly represents a human accomplishment. But Eagleton's difference from postmodernists hinges on language not as a given but as a way to transform our sensuous life. It is true enough that humans have a language sensitive to the nuances of everyday life, and snails do not. The critical difference between the two is the former's ability to change the objective basis of life through language rather than exist as its object. When language, as discourse, gives form to the world, then the form it assumes must be assessed as well.

For example, a materialist framework on race may construct the world as a material, even economic, process, but this also leads it into certain praxiological commitments about addressing social relations. It may be a discourse just like any other, but it embodies a set of interventions that stem from its discursive structure: for example, class struggle, race discrimination, and revolutionary praxis. Just as modernism cannot materialize away language, neither can postmodernism signify away the real.

Media Representations. A critical education requires that students understand how material relations currently work, how the commodity form assumes its shape, and how reification naturalizes the real in what Ernest Mandel (1976) calls the "gigantic enterprise of dehumanization" (p. 65). Unfortunately, race is one of its central nodes. For example, critical race education insists that practical intellectuals deconstruct discourses for the purposes of arriving at silences that betray their racio-economic interests. In analyzing media representations, Herman and Chomsky (2002) propose the strategy of disaggregating representations that manufacture the public's consent under the guise of professional journalism.

In Guy Debord's (1994) terms, a revolutionary analysis of the media must arrive at its spectacular structure. That is, capital's new technological form as "spectacle" provides ideological distractions that divert the public's attention from a fuller understanding of the production of real life. As Debord (1994) puts it, "The SPECTACLE IS *capital* accumulated to the point where it becomes image" (p. 24; emphasis in original) and the media uses "police methods to transform *perception*" (p. 74; emphasis in original). As long as the media produces race spectacles and propaganda in which the masses invest affectively, then it becomes more difficult to arrive at the political economy of mass media, an industry worth billions of U.S. dollars through advertisements, all of which are part and parcel of the productive system and its exploitation of labor, racial commodification of the image, and search for profit.

Take this example from the early 1990s. A *Canon* camera television ad features the world-ranked tennis player Andre Agassi smacking paint-soaked tennis balls into a wall. Known as a rebel in professional tennis (Agassi refused to attend the Wimbledon Championships in London because he disdained wearing white), Agassi takes on the image of an unorthodox sportsman for *Canon's* new model, "the EOS Rebel." The camera has nothing to do whatsoever with tennis or rebellion, that is, the image value has little to do with the product's use value. The message–"Image Is Everything"–works through the commodification of viewers' desire to associate with the image of a sexy sportsman: Agassi. The bottom line is to generate purchases of the camera, and as long as the capitalist can tap into the buyers' desires, then relations of production become unquestioned. Purchasing becomes a form of enfleshing the spectacle and fulfilling desire through vicarious associations.

Taking its cue from this ad, the maker of *Sprite* inverts the *Canon* message by portraying playground athletes and flashing the message–"Image is nothing. Thirst is everything. Obey your thirst." Hence, even the apparent attempt at negation shows a recuperative logic. Obeying your thirst is clearly an image that suggests an atavistic notion of humans as animals. Furthermore, when we keep in mind *Sprite's* hip-hop campaign in the early 1990s (a rather "successful" one), then we understand that the company targets young African Americans through racist overtures of the sexed-up, virile

Black body. One might suggest that *Sprite*'s large increase in revenue since its hip-hop campaign implies that it "works" and that *Sprite*'s products satisfy buyers' needs. In addition, intellectuals may suggest that the innocent public is not being duped by the clever ad campaigns, but that the masses are acting on their own desires. It is not the empirical case that the masses have avoided spectacles, but rather that they want more spectacles! The concern here is less with frustrations over contradictions (and yes, they can be frustrating) and more with explaining them.

The corporate media manipulates images into spectacles, and this is not a haphazard event. Advertisement designers decide on their target audience, brainstorm on common desires presumed to thrive in this segment of society (a social construction), and then combine suggestive images to prey on their audience's affective profile. If *Sprite*'s campaign works, then it results from the discursive manipulation of desire, not its fulfillment. *Sprite* summons the strongest myths surrounding boys and men, particularly young African Americans as animalistic, and exploits them for profit within a racialized class relation.

Resistance against this arrangement involves discursive interventions into the racialized organization of class relations, coupled with an understanding that the circle of praxis is completed when schools and society are materially reorganized. Said another way, images are first made intelligible at the level of discourse, then transformed as knowledge through the subject's understanding of real relations. As the real and hyperreal become more difficult to distinguish, the causes of racial strife and their accompanying misery become harder to decipher.

CHAPTER 5

Race Ambivalence and a Multidimensional Theory of Racism and Education

On November 4, 2008, the United States entered a new era of race relations when the nation elected its first Black president, Barack Obama. Whether intellectuals want to brand the event as a new day of post-racial proportions or a new stage for a continuing race politics, or whether it ultimately signifies racial progress or a reconfiguration of White hegemony, *something significant happened.* For some, Obama's election confirmed a prediction that the United States was over the racial hump from which it has been running away for centuries, like a dog escaping its own tail. That said, we also hear objections to the idea that Obama is a "real" African American man, casting aspersions over his authenticity by virtue of the fact that he is mixed-race with White, and part of the educated and political elite, among other things.

Perhaps ironic and germane to this discussion, doubts about Obama's Blackness are also a blow to the one-drop rule, or hypodescent, which transforms any part-Black person to fully Black in the United States. Questions surrounding Obama's identity paradoxically signal a dismantling of the one-drop rule because they compromise the notion of pure races, a staple of U.S. racialization. All that said, it is more likely that Obama is a mixed-race Black man, and a brilliant politician at that. His mixed-race heritage is a topic he did not eschew during his campaign, embracing the fact that he had a Kenyan father, while his mother was White and hailed from Kansas. He did not evade race as much as he skillfully managed it. Much has been made of the idea that Obama represents the poster child of "post-race" identity, indeed the symbol of a new race era.

What was unimaginable not long ago to many U.S. citizens has now become a reality. The deceased rapper, Tupac Shakur, in a track titled "Changes," once opined that the United States was not likely to have a Black president. To some, surely this moment is indicative of the United States approaching a post-race condition. This would overstate the case in light of the fact that Obama's campaign against Senator Hillary Clinton was highly racialized, not to mention the lynch-mob mentality of the protestors who stormed the Capitol ostensibly to display their dissatisfaction with Obama's health reform. The irony is not lost when one considers that his health reform would likely help the modest White American protestors. At stake here is precisely Whites' long-term interests of racial supremacy even as they are willing to forego short-term benefits by adopting the new health plan. We are tempted to interpret the situation as an expression of deep White *resentment,* coupled with frustration at being unable to express these feelings directly.

Acknowledging White retrenchment in the face of a Black man in the White House, Obama's ascendancy also signals another trend in the form of ambivalence with respect to otherwise entrenched notions of race, such as the rule of hypodescent. Whether a sea change is about to happen, these are interesting times to study race relations. The noted ambivalence may represent an opportunity for a discussion on the merits of a post-race analysis rather than the more usual suspicion that it is another limp attempt at color-blindness, a moment that progressive educators can utilize.

With the Obama moment setting the tone, this chapter considers the insights of post-race writings within the general field of race theory. It is necessary, at least concerning the United States, to begin with Obama, who has sparked interest in the debates around post-race thinking. To some, it represents *the* signature example of post-race possibilities. First, I introduce the main contours of post-race thinking as a form of *aspiration* rather than a description of society as it exists. That is, whereas conservative thought uses post-raciality as a *fait accompli,* progressives have the opportunity to consider it as a future goal and in effect wrestle the concept away from its common-sense use. As Omi and Winant (1994) argue, the racial project comprises material and cultural projects along the color line. The task at hand is to ask questions about the possibility of a "post-racial project."

Second, I analyze the theoretical space of race ambivalence as a source of possible insights when race theory becomes aware of and reflective about its own conceptual apparatus. Here, I favor the concept of ambivalence over the usual and helpful construct of racial contradictions because the former allows educators to establish some distance from the naturalness of race, its seeming permanence, which is the first step in making its familiarity appear strange. Third, I present post-race thinking, defined as a form of ambivalence, as precisely the opportunity that affords educators the space to move race pedagogy into a different direction. Finally, I end this chapter and book by imagining the long-term implications for hope in a post-race society that counters the short-term optimism of Whiteness.

THE STUBBORN SIGNIFICANCE OF RACE AND RACISM

In terms of a material organization of U.S. society, there is nothing to suggest that race is on the wane when the racial wealth gap (Oliver & Shapiro, 1997) is still a force, yet talks of reparations receive less attention than Paris Hilton's latest exploits. The language of race is still part of everyday life in the United States, and Obama's case is not an example of transcending race altogether and rather highlights the ambivalent share of it. But suggesting that U.S. society is still organized around the language of skin color says nothing about our preference that it discontinue in this vein. This is the third space of post-race discussion, which exists uncomfortably alongside the first space of race-in-perpetuity and second space of color-blindness. One might suggest that we live in an *era of race ambivalence.*

The condition of ambivalence does not prevent most scholars from engaging the question and study of race; in fact, I argue we must. But it is becoming increasingly difficult to rely on the stability of race thought. Brett St. Louis (2002) explains this ambivalence:

> As the intellectual descendants of Du Bois we inhabit, for the most part, a scholarly age wise to the scientific myths, spurious rationality and dubious facticity of "race." We have long been aware that "race" has no sustainable biological foundation and, convinced of its socially constructed basis, we instead recognize the *racialization* of different "groups" that are culturally, socially and historically constituted. We also largely agree that socially recognizable "races" demonstrate significant degrees of *internal* as well as *external* differentiation. It is clear therefore at least for much of the academy, that the inviolable sanctity of race is under fire, it is under erasure. (pp. 652–653; emphasis in original)

Race scholars carry on as usual, but we do so with an increasing sense of doubt and doom about the very nature of our topic. It is possible that racial organization has always been under the threat of erasure or obliteration, and the latest set of challenges speaks to its continuing evolution. The intellectual's livelihood also may be under erasure, but something more important than this remains: our search for racial emancipation. When Gilroy (1998) announces that "race ends here," he points to the conceptual flimsiness of racial organization that may create as many problems as it purports to solve. It leads St. Louis (2002) to propose a nominalist or "weak" form of race thinking that claims that "race is a contributory, not determining or principal, local existential element within human existence" (p. 670), in order to observe its social materiality without further reifying its fallacious ideality.

Race is not declining as a structuring principle of U.S. society. Moreover, the United States is not alone, as demonstrated by experiences from Canada and Australia (Graham, 2011; Ibrahim, 2011). There may be signs for the prognosis of race's decline, as Gilroy (2000) clearly provokes, but they are inconclusive at best and mistaken at worst. This fact notwithstanding, the current moment or "crisis" presents an opportunity to ask new questions, to search for new understandings. It may be the case that two apparently opposite trends of color-blindness and racial progress are occurring. Gilroy's argument does not depend primarily on its empirical veracity but on its logical conclusions. That is, scholars cannot wish away race, but we can recommend its impeachment. Contrary to the declining significance of race, we can make a good case that race relations pulsate as strongly as ever, perhaps even more significantly than in previous eras. It is possible that both phenomena are happening simultaneously: race entrenchment and ambivalence. As Mills (1997) asserts, there is no transracial class solidarity and therefore the reality of race, at least for the moment, remains self-evident.

Post-Race Thought vs. Color-Blindness

A society does not reach a post-race situation by downplaying race and the reality of racial contestation, as in policies that turn a color-blind eye to race and education in a desperate attempt *to make the States united again* (if they ever were). Downplaying race struggle will ensure that it continues at the level of social practice, as both race and racism have "gone underground" (Chesler, Peet, & Sevig, 2003, p. 219). Of course, racism may be overt and above ground, and receive insufficient attention as denial becomes the easier route. Suggesting that race does not matter, does not necessarily make it so, as Gotanda (1995) clearly shows in his debunking of the apparent color-blindness of the U.S. constitution. Lopez's (2006) study displays in full splendor the awkward way that the courts have used both scientific and commonsense arguments to legalize the construct of Whiteness.

This chapter's argument goes against the notion that the best way to rid society of racial discrimination is to stop making distinctions based on race, which is more of a slogan than a sign of a genuine engagement of racism (A. Lewis, 2003). However, that race matters does not suggest that society should continue existing in a racial form—that race should keep mattering. That is, insofar as the United States is racially structured, skin-color stratified, and somatically signified, this does not automatically recommend their perpetuity. So the task is not only to promote anti-racism but to consider the post-race position, which is to say, the *politics of being anti-race*, or the dispreference for the continuation of a racially organized society. To be clear, this is a race-conscious, as opposed to a race-neutral, proposition. It not only requires acknowledging the fact of race, but also necessitates entering the field of racial contestation in order to end, rather than to perpetuate, it.

The prognostication of race's future asks neither the question of race's current significance nor its real past, but more important, its projected destiny. It draws from Nayak's (2006) assertion that "post-race ideas offer an opportunity to experiment, to re-imagine and to think outside that category of race" (p. 427). To be more precise, post-race ruminations allow educators to recast race, even work against it, as Gilroy suggests, but this move cannot be accomplished with the pretense of thinking *outside* the category of race. As I (2005b, 2009a) argue elsewhere, in a racialized formation, *race has no outside.* As Graham and Slee (2008) note, following Deleuze, assuming an outside maintains an illusory interiority, thus reproducing the original problems associated with margins and centers (see also Lather, 2003).

At this point, in advanced Western societies like the United States, there is no way to deal with race from a position outside of race relations. We are caught up in racemaking at every turn, and presuming access to its outside comes with dangerous implications, usually complicit with color-blindness. Rather, it suggests the possibility of *undoing race from within instead of from without,* of coming to full disclosure about what race has made of us to which we no longer consent. If race has no outside, is it possible to talk of its *elsewhere?* If color-blindness does not work as policy, is it supportable as a utopic aspiration? Is there a foreseeable end to the language of race? In this sense, the unmaking of race interests the oppressed races more than the master race, which arguably is more invested in its continuation (see also Ibrahim, 2011). Therefore, the analysis does not proceed from the audacious pronouncement that this move is plausible but asks whether or not it is possible and, more important, preferable.

Problematizing the Vague Uses of Race

Given the bogus beginnings of race, dismantling race from the inside seems warranted and within the realm of possibilities. The language of race and the racial dimensions of language are a source of much symbolic violence (Bourdieu & Passeron, 1977/1990), beginning with the moment that human differences were reduced to skin differences. Although racialized minorities, as skin collectives, may mobilize around the concept of race and find strength (indeed a source of pride) in their survival from and resilience against White supremacy, skin ontologies are not sustainable ways to organize society, even after the demise of racism. What would it mean to dismantle racism but not disband social groups based on skin color? It is possible to discredit race at this level of analysis. However, given race's omnipresence, in U.S. society in particular, the task seems impossible in the Derridean sense. Although race arguably has a 500-year pedigree, ideologically it feels eternal, just like the unconscious (Althusser, 1971).

This chapter occupies a space wedged between the possible and the impossible, between the precept of and a preference for race. It requires not only a language of possibility (Giroux, 1988), but equally a language of impossibility (Biesta, 1998; Cho, 2012). Post-racial analysis is ethically justifiable despite the independent issue of and slim chances for success because Whites show such low levels of investment in critical race work (McPhail, 2003). But as I argue later, alongside McPhail, the hope in ending racism trumps the despair in Whiteness.

The concept of race and utility of race analysis have been staples of social theory and education for quite some time. One can hardly read or write about the challenges of education without confronting the "problem of race." In fact, as I have pointed out earlier, the ubiquitous language of the "achievement gap" is inherently a racial gap. That said, the future of the race concept has been left relatively untouched—for example, in its leading discourses of multiculturalism, Critical Race Theory, and anti-racism. *As a relation*, race is seldom deemed problematic. Questioning race becomes tantamount to interrogating the very existence of racial groups, risking the very self we have come to know. Or worse, sometimes race is elided and dangles as a proxy for the vague identity of "social group," at times conflated with ethnicity, at times sliding into nationality. No doubt these concepts are interrelated, but they are by no means synonymous, at least not without some loss in clarity. For example, it is not uncommon to read treatises on race in education, which comfortably analogize it with ethnicity and leave the educator unsure of how culture achieves a color in the process.

Racism then becomes a descriptor of any institutional arrangement where a group has suffered at the hands of another group because of race's currency in the U.S. imagination. However, there are other sources of injury, such as xenophobia and ethnocentrism, which are related to race but not reducible to it. *In the United States, a group's grievance is not recognized until it becomes racialized.* In a literal sense, oppression is not understood before it is expressed in a racial language, tied to racial terms, and it does not enter popular cognition until it enters racial reasoning. To repeat Derrida's point, no language, no racism; therefore, we must know language in order to know racism. This does not mean that recognition equates with resolution of the problem, and 150 years since the fall of slavery, the United States is no closer to granting African Americans 40 acres and a mule. The upshot is that until the point of insertion into race, a claim to historical reparations meets with only glancing interest. In the case of African American reparations, even insertion into race does not signal success.

In the United States, race has become common sense and sometimes loses both its specificity and edge. Our attempts to intervene into racism come with difficulties when the language of intelligibility contained in race is not held up to be problematic. The language of race has saturated U.S. society to the point that it loses its strangeness as a bogus social relation, even if it retains effectivity. Schools are part of how race is maintained through race's educative function. In other words, educators daily teach young people the naturalized status of race, its foreverness. Educators may question racism, but they rarely interrogate the status of race. The color-blind teacher is perhaps most guilty of this crime as he or she enacts race while denying its reality, but the color-blind teacher is not the only one who takes race for granted. In general, racism has to end, as the saying goes, but race has a different destiny; it should stay. It acquires a privileged place in history and utopia, an explanation of where we have been but also an apparently inextricable part of our future. Here, I want to recognize that the possibility of race's disappearance does not mean that culture *in toto* goes with it.

The Permanence of Race

To the extent that Black culture exists, it is possible that an African American ethnicity endures. A Black or Brown aesthetics may continue, but within the context of race one cannot be sure that it is not, in some manner, a form of protection against White racism: aesthetics of color as a kind of weapon. Paul Taylor (2008) argues that within a racial formation, no theory of race is divorced from a theory of aesthetics, and no notion of beauty is free from racialization. Such was the case with "Black is beautiful" during the 1960s and 1970s, when African Americans pushed back against the demeaning images of Blackness in U.S. society. This establishes the fact that Blackness or otherness may be a source of positivity when it fights against its dehumanization within race relations. The same cannot be said for a White American ethnicity insofar as this is the secret cousin of White raciality, which, as Roediger (1994) and other abolitionists remind us, is nothing but false and oppressive (see Chapter 3).

Whiteness must go. Dumas (2009) seems to agree when he admits that he has learned to love and trust certain Whites, whereas Whiteness is never to be trusted. Here we may notice that as a subfield of race theory, Whiteness Studies exhibits a tendency to recenter Whiteness, even a sense of White fetishism. The Left's derogation of Whiteness differs from its valorization from the Right, but both recenter it. Whiteness Studies disturbs the balance in its insistence on centering Whiteness in order ultimately to dislodge it from its seeming permanence. In *A Black Theology of Liberation*, Cone (1990) goes further by arguing that Whites can destroy their Whiteness only by joining racially oppressed communities, whereby their White being passes into Black being. This choice does not follow the usual election of Blackness for Whites who vicariously experience its benefits without its burdens. To be critical, it must be a simultaneous disidentification with Whiteness and identification with otherness. In the end, they become neither White nor Black, but free.

Regarding racism and the status of race, even Bell's (1992) insurrectionary injunction of the "permanence of racism" does not suggest that he *prefers* the continuation of racial inequality, but in his deployment of racial realism, he admits to its stubborn reality. Here he is right as there is more evidence to point to racism's perpetual status than to its eventual demise, as White America has proven time and again its fundamental sheepishness toward racial equality. But with respect to race as a future organizing principle for society, Bell is more quiet and, one assumes, more accepting. Race appears permanent as well, and this time without the added irony given to the permanence of racism. What does it mean to clutch onto race but purge racism?

The permanence-of-race-as-skin-color thesis has received some criticism. Loic Wacquant (1997, 2002) interrogates not only the utility of this move, but also the questionable, folk-knowledge status of race that passes as scientific or analytical. Or worse, Wacquant fears that with the reality of U.S. imperialism enacted at the level of theory, "American" race analysis is exported as a general world analysis rather than a particular set of assumptions. Take the example of the Hutus and Tutsis, where an apparent race war is waged between the slender-constructed Tutsis and the Hutus (Freedman, Weinstein, Murphy, & Longman, 2008). Although one recalls the traditional skin-based racialization introduced by the Belgian colonizers into Rwanda, this relation has mutated to a complex architecture of non–skin-color-driven racial distinction today. Slenderness is racialized and associated with Europeanness and therefore represents a higher aesthetics, but it is nominally associated with skin color since both Hutus and Tutsis are practically indistinguishable on this index.

On the Brazilian front, a well-known phenomenon goes by the phrase of "money Whitens." That is, a higher class status affords (pun intended) people of color the power to purchase Whiteness, which speaks to the intimate connection between race and capital. For now, I will not make more of these events than necessary since alternative forms of racialization are outweighed by the more pervasive skin-based racism circulating globally, accelerating through the globalization of racialized beauty industries, such as cosmetic surgery and skin Whitening creams (see Hunter, 2005).

With respect to the suggestion of a racial condition absent racism, Hirschman (2004) observes that this anachronism belies the fact that race has always existed alongside racism. No race, no racism. To be clear on this point, racialization is not the mere recognition of skin-color differences *qua* differences but an entire social system founded on a value system designed to elevate lightness (as a sign of godliness, among other things; see Dyer, 1997) and denigration of darkness as sign of an equally dark soul. When the Taina/o people of Puerto Rico regarded as beautiful the Spaniards' armor, they were not expressing a preference for racial organization as much as they were enamored by a new form of difference; this event also challenges the otherwise naturalized assumption that human societies inherently fear and desire to control difference.

The preference for lightness predates colonization of the Americas when we note that the Bible reminds us, "There was light and it was good." Race enters the room precisely when it becomes a justificatory discourse for an entire society. So it is less important to ask whether or not Jesus Christ is White (after all, Whites did not exist then) than to ascertain the consequences of racializing Jesus and justice, of projecting race back into a raceless past because of a raced present, even to the point of distorting and Whitening Christ's racial marking (arguably brown-toned) within current understanding.

As understood here with respect to race and racism, to continue the former while arguing to dismantle the latter is a bit like a Marxist imagining capitalism without exploitation. To the Marxist, no amount of restructuring capital rids it of labor exploitation. Likewise, no amount of resignification will rescue race (Gilroy, 2000). Decoupling race from racism to argue that racial hierarchy, and not racial difference, is the problem is a bit like suggesting that tracking practices that are hierarchical in schools can be reimagined *sans* the stratification. If that were to happen, it simply would not be called tracking anymore.

By definition, tracking *is* hierarchical (Oakes, 2005). We are tempted to imagine tracking as the lynchpin of racial oppression in schools, but Oakes, Joseph, and Muir (2004) remind educators of a more pervasive differential access to high-status knowledge that, while exacerbated by tracking practices, recalls the near-complete racial segregation of society, with the United States as an exemplar. Supported by Massey and Denton's (1993) *American Apartheid*, segregation studies explain the simple fact that in a racialized social system most Blacks attend school with other Black children, tracked with respect to one another rather than with Whites. In the same vein, race without racism simply would not be race as we know it. In all likelihood, it would be a society without race. With the arrival of post-race studies, new opportunities for analysis, insights, and recent ambivalence have made it possible to ask fundamental questions about the status of race.

RACE AMBIVALENCE

Admittedly, a post-race analysis is not a simple task and is liable to make one an intellectual punching bag of critics from left to right. Currently, few spaces in the academy exist where a progressive discussion of a society beyond the color line can attract a sympathetic ear because it has been associated with color-blind pundits, like Dinesh D-Souza; reactionary politicians, like Ward Connerly; or conservative intellectuals, like Shelby Steele. Or, it attracts the wrong attention and becomes co-opted. In fact, one may be able to cite post-race tendencies in Martin Luther King, Jr., just before he was assassinated or in Frantz Fanon (see Gilroy, 2000; Nayak, 2006), but there is always the real and public fear that their message will be interpreted without its spirit. For example, Ward Connerly, a former University of California Regent, attempted to appropriate King's platform in order to launch the "Racial Privacy Act." Had it not been convincingly defeated in California, it would have outlawed any public institution's ability to gather racial data. It would have made it difficult—nearly impossible—to track racial discrimination in education, the health industry, and labor market. One treads on soft ground when it comes to engaging a post-race language.

But it is important to consider the implications of post-race in order to continually re-examine long-held beliefs about race and whether the ultimate existential choice of disappearing is warranted in order to reappear as something else we would prefer. But as Graham (in press) has noted elsewhere, in terms of identity this involves the risk of death in order to become a recognizable subject, of giving up certain identities to become something else. For subjects who have very little power to fall back on, it is understandable to desire holding onto current, but problematic, identities in light of an unknown (and perhaps not better) option. Race sits strategically at a crossroads that demands scholarship that is attentive not only to its declining or rising significance but to its very future as a system of intelligibility.

Race Theory Becomes Aware of Itself: The Case for Abolition

Race scholarship that forsakes a conceptual engagement of its own premises takes for granted the naturalized status of race. Questioning its solidity now seems unreal, caught up in unnecessary solipsistic arguments about the ostensible and unquestionable fact of race. After all, race groups exist, and race history is indisputable. Race is real. End of story.

There are several limitations to accepting race uncritically and unconditionally. Race was an invention, and its matter-of-fact existence today should not be confused with its objective reality without the daily dose of reification.

It is worthwhile intellectually to debate the conceptual status of race if racism significantly depends on the continuation of a *racialized mindset.* This is perhaps what James Baldwin was referring to when he claimed that as long as White people think they are White, there is no hope for them (cited by Roediger, 1994, p. 13). After all, it is difficult to imagine White racism without the prior category of race that is responsible for White *perception* concerning which groups deserve a blessed or banished life. The challenge for Whites is to unthink their Whiteness because race trouble arrived at the scene precisely at the moment when White bodies began thinking they were White people.

The birth of White people allows for the first premise of racism: that Whites are better than people of color. This is a simplified reduction of a rather complex process, but it captures the basic operation of racial superordination and subordination. If a group is simply better than another group, then the former in religious terms is saved, in epistemological terms represents the true knower, in aesthetic terms constitutes the beautiful, and in ontological terms plainly exists. This is not just the genesis of Whiteness, but of the very domain we know as race. Whiteness and race are the large and small arms of a clock that began over 500 years ago. But if I am correct in announcing the coming of *late Whiteness,* their hours are numbered.

The abolitionist opposes encouraging an overt racial language and discourages greater awareness on the part of Whites so common to racial pedagogy. Instead Whites are asked to forget their racial rootedness. The caveat is that it is a form of White privilege to even ponder "giving up" one's racialization, a luxury that people of color simply do not possess. That established, it does not contradict the idea that this is the preferred collective path that abolitionists believe we should follow. The abolitionist assumption is that Whites already know intimately their Whiteness, which is different from suggesting that they understand their Whiteness. Whiteness is the default position of the human, and it is unnecessary to qualify one with the other. A White person need not describe his or her Whiteness because it goes without saying. Toni Morrison (1993) says as much when she asserts that characters in novels are assumed to be White until the text explicitly writes them into the story as people of color.

Writing "White" into narratives actually can be jarring for Whites whose self-identification with an unnamed Whiteness exposes their racial investment. Increasing racial recognition is built on the faulty premise that Whites are ignorant of their racial world, when in fact it does not take much of a threat to Whiteness for Whites to erect barriers around what Cheryl Harris (1995) calls "Whiteness as property." In short, Whites know they are White and do not need to be made aware of this first fact. More important, they know from whom they are set apart: people of color. Therefore, the common suggestion in education that teacher education programs ought to teach White preservice teachers a heightened awareness of their Whiteness misses the target. Becoming aware of one's Whiteness is one thing, but acknowledging how one's Whiteness translates into political and social structures responsible for racial domination is quite another.

Or worse, education programs construct Whites as passive observers of race, who must be taught to recognize their raciality. To the abolitionist, this move further embeds their Whiteness. Every day, U.S. educators teach White children that they are White: from curriculum selection that prioritizes Western epistemology, to cultural classroom practices that bridge the home-to-school divide for Whites and maintain the distance for students of color, to apparently race-neutral policies like No Child Left Behind, which make a casual, rather than causal, pass at race. Opposite racial awareness, Whites must now forgo their Whiteness, disowning it before they even own up to it. Although the abolition movement faces grim prospects about success, its proponents are correct to challenge this oft-unquestioned premise of White ignorance. Said another way, post-race is intimate with post-White discourses. The abolition of Whiteness is at the same time the abolition of White people, an invention that must now be forgotten. This move is not without ironies, and waiting for Whites to forgo their Whiteness is like waiting for Godot (see also Ibrahim, 2011), which necessitates the critical participation of people of color (see Chapter 4).

Conceptualizing race is intimately tied to performing it. Perceiving race as real then is tied to acting on it. The upshot is that taking up the race concept asks the primary question, "What is race?" without which race analysis proceeds commonsensically rather than critically. For example, the question of which collectivities constitute a racial group is still unsettled in the United States. Is race a Black–White skin phenomenon that *implicates* other groups, like Asians and Latinos, which are quasi-races? If this is true, then it seems racial progress in the United States will result only when the modern contradiction between Whites and Blacks is resolved. One could call this model the modernist racial discourse of race-as-skin-color, a binary spectrum with Whites and Blacks at two poles and other races incorporated ambiguously along the continuum. Or are there multiple racial projects, each articulating itself in specific ways for different groups?

For instance, in the United States race has affected each group differently, such as the significant history of citizenship status for Asians, sovereignty and land rights for Native Americans, documented immigration for Latinos, and enslavement for African Americans. If this is true, then it necessitates a postmodern racial perspective (not always synonymous with a post-race philosophy) that decenters skin color from the focus of racial analysis and places it alongside other physical markers (as distinct from culture), such as Eastern eyes and Latino looks. In all, the obviousness of race is becoming increasingly strange.

Big Bang Race Theory vs. Steady State: Setting the Parameters

As a social relation, racism maintains its distinction from cultural imperialism by emphasizing somatic relations as proxies for deciding human worth. Race is a relation of bodies, and culture enters the process only when it is recruited, as in the case of "new racism," which replaced the biological basis of racism with its cultural cognate (Barker, 1990). In this transformation, people of color are inferior to Whites based on the difference in their cultural, rather than genetic, make-up. Moreover, in both the biological and cultural understanding of race, the post-race imagination is mobilized as a mode of possibility after the glow of race relations. Although still surrounding us like the primordial warmth of the Big Bang, the heat of racialization will reach its end point, and the possibility of a Big Squeeze ultimately will develop, causing an eventual implosion.

In contrast to a Steady State theory of race, which provides a portrait of racialization as changing but ultimately eternal as a social relation, a Big Bang theory posits a definite beginning and possible end of race as we know it. But this implosion, as in the field of physics, not only is catastrophic, but provides the elements necessary for life. Just as we are composites of the iron and other heavier atoms left over from supernovas, future generations will comprise debris gathered from the ashes of a racial involution. Like planets and stars, which result from gravity's ability to collapse material into a sphere, post-race society will represent the gradual accretion of race material from a time when race used to matter. Life does not start anew *per se,* but a new history begins.

Without broaching these definitional debates and directional issues about the destiny of race, critical race analysis ceases to have a future because it cannot imagine a situation that makes it obsolete. For if, as an intervention into racist formations, race analysis is to realize its goal, it eventually may have to disappear as a condition of its own success. Marx predicted as much when it came to class and capitalism, which sowed their own seeds of destruction. This is different from the desire to organize around skin politics in order to end it altogether. A post-race perspective is not the attempt to elide and evade race in order to imagine its disappearance. Quite the opposite. Post-race discourse makes race visible, maps its operations, and enters its interpellations. It is ambivalent not about these commitments but on the issue that racial distinctions should be an endless ride without a destination. *If all good things come to an end, surely bad ones ought to.* One may be tempted to brand the inability to deal critically with the future of race as evidence of a certain anti-intellectual tendency. But that would be inflammatory and in the end does more harm than good. For a post-race project is not only an intellectual project but equally political, conceptual on one hand but actional on the other (see Fanon, 1952/1967).

Reducing the problem of racism to the conceptual status of race comes with its own difficulties, as if racism were caused by a concept rather than racially motivated actions, such as educational segregation and labor discrimination. For Guillaumin (1995), nothing short of dismantling the race concept can rescue us from racism. The focus should be on the concept of race, not White supremacist institutions, like slavery. Not the attempt to exterminate Native Americans, the limiting of Asian American mobility by curtailing their citizenship rights, or the constant attacks on Latino autonomy in the United States. Not the forced removal of "half caste" Aboriginal children from their families and communities to "breed out" the indigenous peoples of Australia. Not the social engineering called "Whitening" in Brazil through selective immigration from Europe in the early decades of the 1900s. Not the South African social incarceration of Blacks. We could go on but it seems apparent that racism is not ultimately the problem of people who think there are races "out there" but the materially coordinated set of institutions that results from people's actions. Certainly these actions have their root in the concept of race, but a whip in the hand seems as responsible for racism as an idea in the head.

POST-RACE AS AN OPPORTUNITY

Instigated by cultural studies, post-race discourses, as distinct from Marxist orthodoxy, provide an opportunity to ask new questions about race made possible by studies in the politics of representation, language being one of its privileged mechanisms. According to Gilroy (2000), post-race discussions signal an opportunity rather than something to be feared insofar as race understanding may be advanced in order that race may not remain standing. Like Marxism in the current conjuncture, post-race analysis is a politics that proceeds without guarantees, with race under possible erasure (see Hall on Marxism, 1996b). It is, as Gilroy (2000) punctuates, a politics of race abolition. It is a "crisis of raciology," enabled by "the idea that 'race' has lost much of its common-sense credibility because the elaborate cultural and ideological work that goes into producing and reproducing it" takes more than it gives; that race "has been stripped of its moral and intellectual integrity"; that "there is a chance to prevent its rehabilitation"; and that race "has become vulnerable to the claims of a much more elaborate, less deterministic biology" (pp. 28–29).

Earlier, Gilroy (1993) argued for a Black Atlantic perspective that would link historical continuities among the four continents of Africa, Europe, and South and North America to counter the bombastic claims of European enlightenment. Since then, it appears that Gilroy's ambivalence toward race thinking, or raciology, has increased, leading him to pronounce his position "against race." Gilroy finds that the amount of race work that goes into antiracism fails ultimately to provide a positive alternative beyond the negation of racism. At the end of our travels, absent the fight against racism, race becomes an empty vessel. In effect, Gilroy transitions from a trans-Atlantic racial argument to a trans-racial Atlantic argument.

Signifying the "Post" in Post-Race Theory

As Paul Taylor (2008) has suggested, the innovation of post-race analysis does not signal the end of race as we know it. Rather, like the "post" in post-analytic philosophy, the "post" in post-race analysis signals an opening made possible by a conceptual ambivalence, not the closing of race scholarship. It allows new questions, as products of intellectual and material development, to surface. Like the "post" in many schools of thought among extant theories, post-race is the ability of race theory to become self-aware and critically conscious of its own precepts. It signals the beginning of the end of race theory proper, which becomes near impossible to continue in the same vein. A race theory that becomes self-aware of its own constitutive activity enters the next stage of development in a dialectical movement of the thought process. Race theory becomes post-race precisely for the same reasons that modern thought is compromised by postmodern theory. Modern theory still exists but only after it reckons with the postmodern (Lyotard, 1984). Likewise, race theory emerges as something different, if not new, through the filter of post-race. It alters the politics of race scholarship.

I believe Taylor is right to frame the discussion in this manner. It avoids the otherwise vulgar suggestion that we are "beyond race" or have "transcended race" for usually unsubstantiated reasons. It acknowledges the debt owed to race analysis proper but propels it forward without jettisoning it. What do we make of society as we remake race in a daily way? Like one might ask about modern theories after the postmodern moment, what does race analysis look like after the arrival of post-race thought? For all of Baudrillard's ranting against modern teleologies and determinisms, he did not succeed, before his death, in making them irrelevant. However, he forced a response from modernist thinkers. As a carbuncle on their theories, Baudrillard and other postmodernists pushed social theory and their intellectual adversaries into different directions, if not forward. Post-race analysis accomplishes a similar move, forcing a hard and sometimes difficult look at race theory.

Race understanding has arrived at the uncomfortable street corner where our bodies meet their socially constructed racial identity and where we leave the same intersection unsure of what we have just become as a result of race. Gilroy (2000) writes, "We always agree that 'race' is invented but are then required to defer to its embeddedness in the world" (p. 52). Nayak (2006) laments, "The problem that race writers encounter, then, is how do we discuss race in a way that does not reify the very categories we are seeking to abolish?" (p. 415). What is to be done about race?

If race was a f/pigment of the Occidental imagination, it is one of life's deepest ironies that people of color hang on dearly to a concept created in order to oppress them. Many centuries later, U.S. minorities find it hard to imagine a post-race society, either because they suspect that color-blind Whiteness is up to its old tricks again or they are invested in a hard-fought sense of an oppositional identity, the giving up of which means a fundamental loss of meaning. Of course, it goes without saying that many Whites cannot imagine a post-race society either. As Nayak (2006) observes, "For minority ethnic groups the erasure of race may equate with the obliteration of an identity and shared way of life. . . . The concept of race, however tarnished it may appear, has provided an important meeting place for political mobilization, inclusion and social change" (p. 422). Although Nayak commits the usual slide between ethnicity and raciality—something he misrecognizes when he asserts that "Whiteness is not homogeneous but fractured by the myriad ethnic practices" (p. 417)—he is correct to note that race (not only racism) is a source of the problem as well as a resource of meaning for racially despised groups. Yet he misses an opportunity.

Whiteness is precisely homogenizing, wiping out ethnic differences in favor of racial solidarity. This is Whiteness' *modus operandi* and emphasizing myriad (White) ethnic practices misrecognizes White raciality. This does not suggest that ethnic differences are not relevant for Whites, as the Irish–English, German–Jewish, or Turk–Greek Cypriot relations make plain (see Zembylas, 2008). This fact notwithstanding, in places as diverse as the United States and Australia, White ethnic differences play second fiddle to Whiteness inasmuch as White ethnicity is a demotion whereas White raciality becomes a promotion because the former makes Whites concrete while the latter keeps them abstract. For people of color, race is a condition of their being, and to dispute its centrality in their lives violates their perceived right to be, and usually without the profitable returns that White ethnics gain as they shed their identity to ascend to White raciality.

As a result, race takes away from, more than it gives to, people of color. It certainly benefits Whites more than non-Whites, even as Whites give up their ethnic language, customs, and identity (see Ignatiev, 1995). The upshot is that these losses are well worth giving up for Whiteness. In fact, hanging on to ethnicity, which makes Whites visible and concrete, decreases their ability to guard the invisibility and abstraction called Whiteness. This does not mean that Whites are eager to give up race, but there is less of an ironic return for them.

This point extends Nayak's (2006) claim that "it is precisely because Whiteness is seen as an unmarked racial category that the loss of race for White theoreticians can appear inconsequential" (p. 422). We might distinguish between Whiteness' discursive sleight-of-hand to conjure up a post-race reality and Whites' general unwillingness to relinquish race privilege. Giving up race is consequential for Whites, for it is responsible for the lightness of their being, a sense of existential lack of tethers. Their sense of freedom and mobility is a direct and negative correlation with the restrictions people of color face. Whites' post-race attitude is belied by their racial behavior.

A post-race situation is a threat to Whites' very existence and can come only at a great loss for them, which may be greater than the loss of meaning for racial minorities. Racial recollections for minorities do not vanish with a post-race reorganizing, such as the South African case, but White domination and privilege may be eradicated structurally, which does not suggest that Whiteness does not continue in the form of ideology. Arguably, race memory serves as the constant reminder against the return of White supremacy, just as Jewish remembering of the Holocaust represents vigilance against its repetition. Race comes with advantages for Whites, and it is precisely the lack of guarantees that accompanies post-race analysis that threatens White privilege for it unsettles expectations on which many Whites have counted. To the White race abolitionist, the antidote includes acting against Whiteness as if it were an affront to one's own humanity (see Ignatiev & Garvey, 1996b).

To be sure, people of color have relied on race as a stable system of meaning on which to base their self-understandings, but this process occurs as a response to the first fact of White domination. Without White domination, there is little need to assert Black, Brown, Red, or Yellow self-love, whose history is a defense against the imposition of White power. Race ambivalence is intended to challenge White supremacy before it is designed to threaten its victims. Although post-race scholars do not underestimate this loss of meaning, they consider it worth the risk for it is a system of meaning that creates more problems than promises. This loss, as Nayak suggests, can be turned into a gain.

Making Sense of the Crisis in Raciology

To dispel further any notions that this model mystifies the inner workings of race, education under post-race assumptions makes it clear that it is made possible precisely by testifying to the inhuman tendencies of a racialized humanism. Gilroy (2000) contends that his "[planetary] humanism is conceived explicitly as a response to the sufferings that raciology has wrought" (p. 18), not its obfuscation. To Gilroy, the crisis in raciology represents less a crisis of identity and more the uncertain status and preferable (rather than inevitable) demise of race, not only at the level of signification but also at the level of social organization.

Sweeping global changes in the economy and diasporic movement complicate and compromise racial worldmaking, stripping it of previous guarantees and predictive value as an autonomous relation. New events in history disturb our race-as-skin-color expectations, such as the apparent racial contest undetermined by skin color but mediated by somatic politics between Hutus and Tutsis in Rwanda. In Australia, one may look White but identify as indigenous, and Aboriginals with Black features are not accepted as authentically indigenous. Of course, in the United States there is a long tradition within communities of color regarding the colorism that affects their lives (Hunter, 2005). Although the Rwandan case should not be overinterpreted as proof of the waning effect of skin-color difference, for which we have more worldwide evidence, the Rwandan situation brings new insights to race analysis by introducing the reinterpretation of bodily differentiation through primary markers besides skin color. Even the multiracialization of beauty images, which includes increasingly more Black and Brown faces, signals new anxieties about race, but this time by disturbing clear lines of racial demarcation rather than their enforcement.

Whereas race thought was revolutionary in its own right, this new stage of development represents a revolution of the revolution, or the dynamic continuation of that transformation. To the extent that raciology introduced White subversion of the humanity inhered in people of color, post-race represents the attempt to subvert the subversion, to negate the negation. Race changed some subjects into people of color; it may be time to change again. This does not suggest that racism or racialization fails to exert its dominant imprint on social processes, subject formation, and State-sponsored policies. However, it means that both race struggle and raciology may begin the day but in no way end it, giving way to the era of racial ambivalence.

I have no desire to overstate the case. Made clear by the stubborn standard of Whiteness—from Tyra Banks, Halle Berry to Beyoncé Knowles, to Jennifer Lopez and Selma Hayek—light skin still, according to Hunter (2005), approximates White beauty standards. But as colonized peoples challenge White supremacy across the globe and gain access to networks of power monopolized by Whites, counting on race stratification becomes ironically ambiguous and upsets racial expectations. This is a condition not to be deplored ultimately as a sense of loss, at least not in the manner that one grieves the passing of a seemingly endless war that has given this life much meaning.

Putting race to peace may open up possibilities for other ways of being, other ways of knowing that heretofore have been limited or closed, particularly for people of color. The loss should not be minimized but should be countered by a sense of clarity concerning the neuroses of race about which Fanon (1952/1967) spoke so forcefully and that Gilroy calls the "rational absurdity of 'race'" (p. 14). But like the absurdity of life as we know it, to which existentialists and phenomenologists alike were attuned, we can avoid racial dread by fully committing to our choices. Gilroy taps a certain post-racial tendency in Fanon, whose attempts to restore Blacks in their proper human place represent Black analytics, or negritude, in order then for Blackness to vanish under its own weight (see also Nayak, 2006). Just how the problems of humanism fold into the refashioning of the human in a post-race condition remains contested, opening the door for Gilroy's pragmatic, planetary, and postanthropological humanism. Blackness, for example, may remain a culture yet disappear as a racial category. Gilroy clarifies, "There will be individual variation, but that is not 'race'" (p. 42). Gilroy is quite clear that race does not equate with "group," and his goal is not to deride human difference. This last point is worth elaborating.

Human differences continue, but whether or not skin-color variation should form the basis for social organization is the question. As a modern principle, race is a particular grouping of individuals into social groups. As embodied collectivities, these social groups could very well continue intact as we enter a post-race society, but they will no longer be considered skin groups once the race principle has been discredited. The bodies remain, but they will be conceptualized differently as post-racial subjects. African Americans may continue as an ethnic group so Blackness as a form of cultural practice may thrive in the absence of race where "skin, bone, and even blood are no longer the primary referents of racial discourse" (Gilroy, 2000, p. 48). African Americans will neither sever completely their relation with Blackness as a racial experience, which is historical, nor be reduced to it. Racial solidarity will be liberated from the "cheapest pseudo-solidarities: forms of connection that are imagined to arise effortlessly from shared phenotypes, cultures, and bio-nationalities" (Gilroy, 2000, p. 41). Of course, Gilroy is speaking of both non-Whites and Whites who desperately cling to identity as a visual confirmation of their politics.

On one hand, it is Whites who, in their fetish of color, clearly profit from racial politics as a form of interest consolidation more than people of color who mobilize identity movements as a form of defense against White supremacy (see Lipsitz, 1998). On the other hand, although clearly necessary at this juncture, race-based identity politics brings with it essentialized forms of belonging that may be secondary concerns to the problem of White supremacy but smacks of what Appiah (1990) calls intrinsic racism, or the reproduction of raciology through assumptions about family resemblance.

As much as race politics may bring people of color together in a common struggle against White supremacy, it also becomes a source of division when it comes to that elusive grail of authenticity in one instance and the assumption of sameness that denies people of color their uniqueness in the other. They are literally thrown into some situations where the only possible commonality they have with others is the fact that they are people of color. These cheap forms of "pseudo-solidarities" among minorities, of which Gilroy speaks, are tyrannies that remain even after we write the obituary of racism, where race continues to encourage "ready-to-wear racial identities" (St. Louis, 2002) or what Pollock (2004) calls "lump sum" identities. It is hardly conducive to progressive politics. In the end, race creates emotional investments that lead to what Cheng (2001) calls "melancholy," a sense of loss, for both Whites and people of color.

TOWARD A NEW DAY IN RACE RELATIONS:
A COMMENTARY ON HOPE AND OPTIMISM

As race relations enters its late phase of development, its contradictions become more ripe and obvious. Its logics hang desperately onto a worldview that becomes more anachronistic. This does not mean that race struggle becomes obsolete. On the contrary, post-race condition is reached precisely by exposing the myths held up for so long by a pigmentocracy that is Whiteness, which people of color both love and hate because they have been taught for so long to admire the White and hate the Black. Self-love in this instance is always uncertain for it is bound up with self-doubt. The possibility of ending race is the task of bringing back clarity to a situation that for so long has been clouded with the miseducation of racialized humans. This is the challenge of post-race thinking.

We live in a time when race is under intense questioning. Color-blind race discourse challenges the invocation of race analysis even in its most mainstream versions. However, progressive scholarship has taken this situation and reversed people's normal expectations. Like Judo, post-race analysis takes the otherwise reactionary implications of color-blindness and uses its momentum against itself. For color-blindness is often the performance of feigning indifference to race while enforcing its practice. In a complicated dance with hegemony, post-race scholars strike a compromise that upsets the head-to-head confrontation that usually results in racial antagonism. There is something subversive in this move. Post-race proponents argue for the moribund status of race, but do not rehabilitate race. Where they differ from color-blind pretenders is their ability to go *through* race instead of *around* it. They are able to speak to race rather than about it.

Ultimately, a post-race perspective enables educators to distinguish between hope and optimism. Whereas color-blindness is usually associated with a White mindset or lived experience, post-race is a theory of color, which does not mean that scholars of color are always its authors. A bright student of mine once suggested that "hope is White" (Rachel Lissy, personal communication, 2009). By this she meant that Whites exhibit an abundance of hope concerning racial progress when compared with a rather pessimistic Black prognosis of the same problem. I took this remark to mean that even hope is racial and subject to its rationality. It struck me as insightful, and I am grateful for her comment that provoked me to think critically about the distinctions between hope and optimism.

I would refine the insight this way: While Whites are optimistic about race, they are not hopeful, whereas people of color are precisely the opposite, hopeful but pessimistic. When it comes to race progress, Whites show much optimism because small increments of improvement are taken as signs of White tolerance. It produces the psychological advantage of focusing on "how far we have come" instead of the more loaded "how far we still have to go." For if Whites compare present inequalities with past cruelties, not only do Black lives look that much better but White tolerance looks that much greater.

Whereas Gramsci (1971), borrowing from Rolland, once distinguished between the "pessimism of the intelligence, optimism of the will" (p. 175), *Whites show an optimism of the intellect and pessimism of the will.* In short, we cannot equate White optimism with real hope, which takes a certain will that Whites have shown themselves to lack. They are prone to exaggerate racial progress because focusing on the continuing significance of racism indicts their collective inability to end the problem once and for all. They feel good without necessarily having to make good. For all the optimism they express toward racial progress, they lack hope in its actional sense. For Whites, hope is abstract. This is hardly post-racial.

In contrast, if people of color have represented anything in the history of race relations, it is hope. It is one of the few "advantages" that people of color have over Whites. Hope is built into the experience of people of color as an ontological part of their being (see Freire, 1970/1993). How else does one explain their ability to withstand centuries of racial oppression? It is premised on the hope that one day it will end despite the fact that they are disappointed by Whites' ability to converge racial progress with their own interests (Bell, 1992). It is a way of carving out some happiness within conditions of grief. Time and time again, people of color cling to hope as the force that prevents them from despair and resignation. It is historical and allows them to see setbacks as opportunities for defiance. In fact, they project hope onto Whites more than they sometimes deserve, a surplus hopefulness that Whites underappreciate because they would rather emphasize the animosity of people of color over their grace.

We have seen that Barack Obama's 2008 presidential campaign for his first term was built on the audacity of hope, and Reverend Jesse Jackson's battle cry was "keep hope alive." Even Derrick Bell's apparent bleakness is contradicted by his early endorsement of Obama in a 2008 AERA address. Hope is what propelled Bell to support change. As a concrete possibility, peace will be approached by people of color through a critical, honest appraisal of racialization. Their hope attenuates the otherwise realistic pessimism they feel about race relations, which may keep them bitter. A language of hope is concrete for people of color because it is not just a future ideal but a way to exist in the present. It is a dream, not a fantasy. It is not an abstract feeling but a concrete emotion or, better yet, an emotional praxis (Chubbuck & Zembylas, 2008).

Post-race thought is ultimately hopeful. It may be a form of surplus hopefulness in light of the formidable presence of race and the fact of racism, but people of color have always relied on a certain distortion of reality as someday better than itself, also called utopia. As part of emotional praxis, post-race perspectives allow racially oppressed minorities to recognize anger as part of history without its cementing into a form of indignation (Hattam & Zembylas, 2010). Like post-indignation, post-race analysis does not allow race to cement more than necessary. It recognizes race thinking as historical, and, like anger, is a natural consequence within a condition of racialization without graduating to the victimhood that can result from both indignation and raciology. In effect, post-race analysis is the sublimation of racial anger into a form of hope because "investing in anger cannot form a particularly skillful political/pedagogical strategy for responding to colonization, racism or nationalism" (Hattam & Zembylas, 2010, p. 25). Post-race analysis is the recognition that the language of race has been necessary in order to understand what we have made of race and what it has made of us. But race is ultimately insufficient and shows its weakening grip over us. Post-race opens up ambivalence in our search for a more humanizing language and a humane material condition. This is an education worth the name.

References

Aanerud, R. (1999). Now more than ever: James Baldwin and the critique of White liberalism. In D. McBride (Ed.), *James Baldwin now* (pp. 56–73). New York: New York University Press.

Adorno, T. (1991). *The culture industry* (J. Bernstein, Ed.). New York: Routledge.

Ahmed, S. (2004). Declarations of Whiteness: The non-performativity of anti-racism. *Borderlands E-journal*, *3*(2), 1–22. Available at www.borderlands.net.au /vol3no2_2004/ahmed_declarations.htm

Akom, A. (2008). Ameritocracy and infra-racial racism: Racializing social and cultural reproduction theory in the twenty-first century. *Race, Ethnicity & Education*, *11*(3), 205–230.

Alcoff, L. (1998). What should White people do? *Hypatia*, *13*(3). Available at www.msu .edu/-hypatia/White?People.htm

Alim, H. S., Ibrahim, A., & Pennycook, A. (Eds.). (2009). *Global linguistic flows*. New York: Routledge.

Allen, R. L. (1999). The socio-spatial making and marking of "us": Toward a critical postmodern spatial theory of difference and community. *Social Identities*, *5*(3), 249–277.

Allen, R. L. (2002a). The globalization of White supremacy: Toward a critical discourse on the racialization of the world. *Educational Theory*, *51*(4), 467–485.

Allen, R. L. (2002b). *Whiteness as territoriality: An analysis of White identity politics in society, education, and theory* (Unpublished doctoral dissertation). University of California, Los Angeles.

Allen, R. L. (2005). Whiteness and critical pedagogy. In Z. Leonardo (Ed.), *Critical pedagogy and race* (pp. 53–68). Malden, MA: Blackwell.

Allen, R. L. (2009). "What about poor White people?" In W. Ayers, T. Quinn, & D. Stovall (Eds.), *Handbook of social justice in education* (pp. 209–230). New York: Routledge.

Althusser, L. (1969). *For Marx* (B. Brewster, Trans.). New York: Verso.

Althusser, L. (1971). *Lenin and philosophy* (B. Brewster, Trans.). New York: Monthly Review Press.

Althusser, L. (1976). *Essays in self-criticism* (G. Lock, Trans.). London: Humanities Press.

Andersen, M. (2003). Whitewashing race: A critical perspective on Whiteness. In A. Doane & E. Bonilla-Silva (Eds.), *White out* (pp. 21–34). New York: Routledge.

Anyon, J. (1980). School class and the hidden curriculum of work. *Journal of Education,*
    162(1), 67–92.
Anyon, J. (1997). *Ghetto schooling: A political economy of urban educational reform.* New
    York: Teachers College Press.
Anyon, J. (2009). Introduction: Critical social theory educational research, and intel-
    lectual agency. In J. Anyon (Ed.), *Theory and educational research* (pp. 1–23). New
    York: Routledge.
Anyon, J. (2011). *Marx and education.* New York: Routledge.
Appiah, K. (1990). Racisms. In D. T. Goldberg (Ed.), *Anatomy of racism* (pp. 3–17).
    Minneapolis: University of Minnesota Press.
Apple, M. (2000). *Official knowledge: Democratic education in a conservative age* (2nd ed.).
    New York: Routledge and Kegan Paul. (Original work published 1979)
Apple, M. (2003). Freire and the politics of race in education. *International Journal of*
    Leadership in Education, 6(2), 107–118.
Apple, M. (2004). *Ideology and curriculum* (3rd ed.). New York: RoutledgeFalmer.
Apple, M. (2006). *Educating the "right" way* (2nd ed.). New York: Routledge.
Apple, M. (2012). *Can education change society?* New York: Routledge.
Aristotle (1970). Poetics. In H. Adams (Ed.), *Critical theory since Plato* (pp. 48–66). San
    Diego: Harcourt Brace Jovanovich.
Aronowitz, S., & Giroux, H. (1985). *Education under siege.* Westport, CT: Bergin &
    Garvey.
Aronson, J. (2004). The threat of stereotype. *Educational Leadership, 62*(3), 14–19.
Artiles, A. (2008). Special education's changing identity: Paradoxes and dilemmas in
    views of culture and space. *Harvard Educational Review, 73*(2), 164–202.
Au, W. (2009). *Unequal by design.* New York: Routledge.
Austin, J. L. (1962). *How to do things with words.* Oxford: Oxford University Press.
Bachelard, G. (1985). *The new scientific spirit* (A. Goldhammer, Trans.). London:
    Beacon.
Bakhtin, M. (1981). *The dialogic imagination* (C. Emerson & M. Holquist, Trans.). Aus-
    tin: University of Texas Press.
Baldwin, J. (1985). A talk to teachers. In J. Baldwin (Ed.), *The price of the ticket: Collected*
    nonfiction 1948–1985 (pp. 325–332). New York: St. Martin's Press.
Baldwin, J. (1991). *The fire next time.* New York: Vintage Books.
Bales, K. (1999). *Disposable people.* Berkeley: University of California Press.
Balibar, E., & Wallerstein, I. (1991). *Race, nation, class.* London: Verso.
Banks, C. M. (2004). Intercultural and intergroup education, 1929–1959: Linking
    schools and communities. In J. Banks & C. Banks (Eds.), *Handbook of research on*
    multicultural education (2nd ed., pp. 753–769). San Francisco: Jossey-Bass.
Banks, J. (1993). Multicultural literacy and curriculum reform. In J. Noll (Ed.), *Taking*
    sides (7th ed., pp. 219–226). Guilford, CT: Dushkin Publishing Group.
Banks, J. (2005). Multicultural education: Characteristics and goals. In J. Banks & C.
    Banks (Eds.), *Multicultural education: Issues and perspectives* (5th ed., pp. 3–30). New
    York: Wiley.
Banks, J. (2006). *Race, culture, and education.* New York: Routledge.

Banks, J. (2008). *Teaching strategies for ethnic studies* (8th ed.). Boston: Allyn & Bacon.

Barker, M. (1990). Biology and the new racism. In D. T. Goldberg (Ed.), *Anatomy of racism* (pp. 18–37). Minneapolis: University of Minnesota Press.

Bataille, G. (1985). *Visions of excess: Selected writings 1927–1939* (A. Stoekl, Trans.). Manchester, UK: Manchester University Press.

Baudrillard, J. (1981). *For a critique of the political economy of the sign.* St. Louis, MO: Telos Press.

Baudrillard, J. (1994). *Simulacra and simulations.* Ann Arbor: University of Michigan Press.

Bedolla, L. G., & Rodriguez, R. (2011). *Classifying California's English learners: Is the CELDT too blunt an instrument?* Berkeley, CA: Center for Latino Policy Research.

Bell, D. (1992). *Faces at the bottom of the well: The permanence of racism.* New York: Basic Books.

Bell, D. (1995). Brown v. Board of Education and the interest convergence dilemma. In K. Crenshaw, N. Gotanda, G. Peller, & K. Thomas (Eds.), *Critical race theory* (pp. 20–29). New York: New Press.

Bell, D. (2005a). The Black sedition papers. In R. Delgado & J. Stefancic (Eds.), *The Derrick Bell reader* (pp. 320–327). New York: New York University Press.

Bell, D. (2005b). Meanness as racial ideology: The Port Chicago mutiny. In R. Delgado & J. Stefancic (Eds.), *The Derrick Bell reader* (pp. 339–344). New York: New York University Press.

Bell, D. (2005c). The role of fortuity in racial policy-making: Blacks as fortuitous beneficiaries of racial policies. In R. Delgado & J. Stefancic (Eds.), *The Derrick Bell reader* (pp. 40–45). New York: New York University Press.

Bell, D. (2005d). Wanted: A White leader able to free Whites of racism. In R. Delgado & J. Stefancic (Eds.), *The Derrick Bell reader* (pp. 328–336). New York: New York University Press.

Bernal, D. D. (1998). Using a Chicana feminist epistemology in education research. *Harvard Educational Review, 68*(4), 555–581.

Bernal, D. D., & Villalpando, O. (2005). An apartheid of knowledge in academia: The struggle over the "legitimate" knowledge of faculty of color. In Z. Leonardo (Ed.), *Critical pedagogy and race* (pp. 185–204). Malden, MA: Blackwell.

Bernstein, B. (1977a). Class pedagogies: Visible and invisible. In J. Karabel & A. H. Halsey (Eds.), *Power and ideology in education* (pp. 511–534). Oxford: Oxford University Press.

Bernstein, B. (1977b). Social class, language and socialization. In J. Karabel & A. H. Halsey (Eds.), *Power and ideology in education* (pp. 473–486). Oxford: Oxford University Press.

Best, S. (1995). The commodification of reality and the reality of commodification: Baudrillard, Debord, and postmodern theory. In D. Kellner (Ed.), *Baudrillard: A critical reader* (pp. 41–67). Stanford, CA: Stanford University Press.

Beyer, L., & Apple, M. (1988). Values and politics in the curriculum. In L. Beyer & M. Apple (Eds.), *The curriculum* (pp. 3–16). Albany: State University of New York Press.

Biesta, G. (1998). Say you want a revolution . . . Suggestions for the impossible future of critical pedagogy. *Educational Theory, 48*(4), 499–510.

Biesta, G. (2006). *Beyond learning.* London: Paradigm.

Blumenbach, J. F. (2000). On the natural variety of mankind. In R. Bernasconi & T. Lott (Eds.), *The idea of race* (pp. 27–37). Indianapolis: Hackett.

Bobo, L., & Smith, R. (1998). From Jim Crow racism to laissez-faire racism: The transformation of racial attitudes. In W. Katkin, N. Landsman, & A. Tyree (Eds.), *Beyond pluralism: The conception of groups and group identities in America* (pp. 182–220). Urbana: University of Illinois Press.

Bonacich, E. (1972). A theory of ethnic antagonism: The split labor market. *American Sociological Review, 37*(5), 547–559.

Bonilla-Silva, E. (1997). Rethinking racism: Toward a structural interpretation. *American Sociological Review, 62*(3), 465–480.

Bonilla-Silva, E. (2001). *White supremacy and racism in the post-civil rights era.* Boulder, CO: Lynne Rienner.

Bonilla-Silva, E. (2003). *Racism without racists: Color-blind racism and the persistence of racial inequality in the United States.* Lanham, MD: Rowman & Littlefield.

Bonilla-Silva, E. (2005). Introduction–"Racism" and "new racism": The contours of racial dynamics in contemporary America. In Z. Leonardo (Ed.), *Critical pedagogy and race* (pp. 1–36). Malden, MA: Blackwell.

Bonilla-Silva, E. (2011). Beyond Obama's historical symbolism: The heavy weight of being Black/Brown in a racist society. In P. Orelus (Ed.), *Race, class, language, and gender: A dialogue with Noam Chomsky and other leading scholars* (pp. 147–160). Lanham, MD: Rowman & Littlefield.

Bourdieu, P. (1977a). Cultural reproduction and social reproduction. In J. Karabel & A. H. Halsey (Eds.), *Power and ideology in education* (pp. 487–511). Oxford: Oxford University Press.

Bourdieu, P. (1977b). *Outline of a theory of practice* (R. Nice, Trans.). Cambridge: Cambridge University Press.

Bourdieu, P., & Passeron, J. (1990). *Reproduction in education, society, and culture.* Thousand Oaks, CA: Sage. (Original work published 1977)

Bourdieu, P., & Wacquant, L. (1992). *An invitation to reflexive sociology.* Chicago: University of Chicago Press.

Bowles, S., & Gintis, H. (1976). *Schooling in capitalist America.* New York: Basic Books.

Brayboy, B. (2005). Toward a tribal critical race theory in education. *The Urban Review, 37*(5), 425–446.

Brown, A. (2011). "Same old stories": The Black male in social science and educational literature, 1930s to the present. *Teachers College Record, 113*(9), 2047–2079.

Brown, A., & Brown, K. (2010). Strange fruit indeed: Interrogating contemporary textbook representations of racial violence toward African Americans. *Teachers College Record, 112*(1), 31–67.

Brown, A., & De Lissovoy, N. (2011). Economies of racism: Grounding education policy research in the complex dialectic of race, class, and capitalism. *Journal of Education Policy, 26*(5), 595–619.

Brown, A., & Donnor, J. (Eds.). (2011). The education of Black males in a "post-racial" world [Special issue]. *Race, Ethnicity & Education, 14*(1).

Brubaker, R., & Cooper, F. (2000). Beyond "identity." *Theory and Society, 29*(1), 1–47.

Buras, K. (2008). *Rightist multiculturalism.* New York: Routledge.

Buras, K. (2010). Education, cultural politics, and the new hegemony. In Z. Leonardo (Ed.), *Handbook of cultural politics and education* (pp. 341–371). Rotterdam, The Netherlands: Sense Publishers.

Bush, M. (2005). *Breaking the code of good intentions: Everyday forms of Whiteness.* Lanham, MD: Rowman & Littlefield.

Butler, J. (1990). *Gender trouble.* New York: Routledge.

Butler, J. (2004). *Undoing gender.* New York: Routledge.

Callinicos, A. (1976). *Althusser's Marxism.* London: Pluto Press.

Carter, P. (2003). "Black" cultural capital, status positioning, and schooling conflicts for low-income African American youth. *Social Problems, 50*(1), 136–155.

Chang, J. (2005). *Can't stop won't stop.* New York: Picador.

Chapman, T. (2005). Peddling backwards: Reflections of Plessy and Brown in the Rockford public schools de jure desegregation efforts. *Race, Ethnicity & Education, 8*(1), 29–44.

Cheng, A. (2001). *The melancholy of race.* Oxford: Oxford University Press.

Chesler, M., Peet, M., & Sevig, T. (2003). Blinded by Whiteness: The development of White college students' racial awareness. In A. Doane & E. Bonilla-Silva (Eds.), *White out* (pp. 215–230). New York: Routledge.

Cho, S. (2012). *Critical pedagogy and social change.* New York: Routledge.

Chow, R. (1993). *Writing diaspora: Tactics of intervention in contemporary cultural studies.* Bloomington: Indiana University Press.

Chubb, J., & Moe, T. (1990). *Politics, markets, and America's schools.* Washington, DC: The Brookings Institution.

Chubbuck, S. (2004). Whiteness enacted, Whiteness disrupted: The complexity of personal congruence. *American Educational Research Journal, 4*(2), 301–303.

Chubbuck, S., & Zembylas, M. (2008). The emotional ambivalence of socially just teaching: A case study of a novice urban school teacher. *American Educational Research Journal, 45*(2), 274–318.

Churchill, W. (1995). *Since predator came.* Oakland, CA: AK Press.

Cole, M. (2012). Critical race theory in education, Marxism and abstract racial domination. *British Journal of Sociology of Education, 33*(2), 167–183.

Cole, M., & Maisuria, A. (2007). "Shut the f*** up", "you have no rights here": Critical race theory and racialisation in post-7/7 racist Britain. *Journal for Critical Education Policy Studies, 5*(1). Available at www.jceps.com/?pageID=article&articleID=85

Coleman, J. (1966). *Equality of educational opportunity.* Washington, DC: U.S. Department of Health, Education, and Welfare.

Coleman, J. (1988). Social capital in the creation of human capital. *American Journal of Sociology, 94*(Suppl.), 95–120.

Collins, P. H. (2000). *Black feminist thought: Knowledge, consciousness, and the politics of empowerment* (2nd ed.). New York: Routledge.

Collins, P. (2004). *Black sexual politics.* New York: Routledge.

Collins, R. (1979). *The credential society.* New York: Academic Press.

Coloma, R. (2006). Border crossing subjectivities and research: Through the prism of feminists of color. *Race, Ethnicity & Education, 11*(1), 11–27.

Cone, J. (1990). *A Black theology of liberation.* MaryKnoll, NY: Orbis Books.

Cox, O. (1970). *Caste, class, and race.* New York: Monthly Review Press.

Craib, I. (1992). *Anthony Giddens.* New York: Routledge.

Crenshaw, K. (1991). Mapping the margins: Intersectionality, identity politics, and the violence against women of color. *Stanford Law Review, 43*(6), 1241–1299.

Crenshaw, K., Gotanda, N., Peller, G., & Thomas, K. (1995). Introduction. In K. Crenshaw, N. Gotanda, G. Peller, & K. Thomas (Eds.), *Critical race theory* (pp. xiii–xxxii). New York: New Press.

Cross, W. E., Jr. (1978). Models of psychological nigresence. *Journal of Black Psychology, 5*(1), 13–31.

Darder, A., & Torres, R. (2004). *After race.* New York: New York University Press.

Darling-Hammond, L. (2010). *The flat world and education.* New York: Teachers College Press.

Debord, G. (1994). *The society of the spectacle* (D. Nicholson-Smith, Trans.). New York: Zone Books.

Deleuze, G., & Guattari, F. (1983). *Anti-Oedipus: Capitalism and schizophrenia* (R. Hurley, M. Seem, & H. Lane, Trans.). Minneapolis: University of Minnesota Press.

Delgado, R. (2011). Unveiling majoritarian myths and tales about race and racism. In P. Orelus (Ed.), *Race, class, language, and gender: A dialogue with Noam Chomsky and other leading scholars* (pp. 7–15). Lanham, MD: Rowman & Littlefield.

De Lissovoy, N. (2010). A global standpoint? Reification, globalization, and contemporary praxis. In Z. Leonardo (Ed.), *Handbook of cultural politics and education* (pp. 141–160). Rotterdam, The Netherlands: Sense Publishers.

Delpit, L. (1995). *Other people's children.* New York: New Press.

Derrida, J. (1976). *Of grammatology* (G. Spivak, Trans.). Baltimore: Johns Hopkins University Press.

Derrida, J. (1985). Racism's last word. *Critical Inquiry, 12*(1), 290–299.

Dewey, J. (1938). *Experience and education.* New York: Macmillan.

DiAngelo, R. (2006). White fragility: I'm leaving. In D. Armstrong & B. McMahon (Eds.), *Inclusion in urban educational environments* (pp. 213–240). Charlotte, NC: Information Age Publishing.

DiAngelo, R. (2012). *What does it mean to be White?* New York: Peter Lang.

DiMaggio, P. (1979). Review essay: On Pierre Bourdieu. *American Journal of Sociology, 84*(6), 1460–1472.

Dimitriadis, G. (2010). Lessons learned from Enron: What the business world really has to teach us. In Z. Leonardo (Ed.), *Handbook of cultural politics and education* (pp. 71–86). Rotterdam, The Netherlands: Sense Publishers.

Dimitriadis, G. (2012). Hip hop: From live performance to mediated narrative. In M. Forman & M. A. Neal (Eds.), *That's the joint: The hip hop studies reader* (pp. 579–594). New York: Routledge.

Dixson, A., & Rousseau, C. (2005). And we are still not saved: Critical race theory in education ten years later. *Race, Ethnicity & Education, 8*(1), 7–27.

Donnor, J., & Brown, A. (2011). Editorial: The education of Black males in a "post-racial" world. *Race, Ethnicity & Education, 14*(1), 1–5.

Dreeben, R. (1968). *On what is learned in school.* Reading, MA: Addison-Wesley.

Du Bois, W. E. B. (1984). *Dusk of dawn.* Edison, NJ: Transaction Publishers. (Original work published 1940)

Du Bois, W. E. B. (1989). *The souls of Black folk.* New York: Penguin Books. (Original work published 1904)

Du Bois, W. E. B. (1998). *Black reconstruction in America, 1860–1880.* New York: Free Press. (Original work published 1935)

Dumas, M. (2009). Theorizing redistribution and recognition in urban education research: "How do we get dictionaries at Cleveland?" In J. Anyon with M. Dumas (Eds.), *Theory and educational research: Toward critical social explanation* (pp. 81–108). New York: Routledge.

Durkheim, E. (1933). *The division of labor in society* (G. Simpson, Trans.). New York: Free Press.

Durkheim, E. (1956). *Education and sociology.* Glencoe, IL: Free Press.

Dyer, R. (1997). *White.* London: Routledge.

Dyson, M. E. (with Chennault, R.). (1998). Giving Whiteness a Black eye: An interview with Michael Eric Dyson. In J. Kincheloe, S. Steinberg, N. Rodriguez, & R. Chennault (Eds.), *White reign* (pp. 299–328). New York: St. Martin's Griffin.

Eagleton, T. (1996). *Postmodernism and its illusions.* Oxford: Blackwell.

Ebert, T. (1996). *Ludic feminism and after.* Ann Arbor: University of Michigan Press.

Ellison, R. (1995). *Invisible man.* New York: Vintage. (Original work published 1952)

Ellsworth, E. (1997). Double binds of Whiteness. In M. Fine, L. Weis, L. Powell, & L. Wong (Eds.), *Off White* (pp. 259–269). New York: Routledge.

Espiritu, Y. L. (1993). *Asian American panethnicity.* Philadelphia: Temple University Press.

Espiritu, Y. L. (2003). *Home bound: Filipino lives across cultures, communities, and countries.* Berkeley: University of California Press.

Essed, P., & Trienekens, S. (2007). "Who wants to feel White?" Race, Dutch culture and contested identities. *Ethnic and Racial Studies, 31*(1), 52–72. doi: 10.1080/01419870701538885

Fanon, F. (1967). *Black skin, White masks* (C. Markmann, Trans.). New York: Grove Press. (Original work published 1952)

Feagin, J. (2009). *The White racial frame.* New York: Routledge.

Ferguson, A. (2001). *Bad boys.* Ann Arbor: University of Michigan Press.

Fields, B. (1990, May–June). Slavery, race and ideology in the United States of America. *New Left Review, I*(181), 95–118.

Fields, B. (2003). Of rogues and geldings. *The American Historical Review, 108*(5). Available at www.historycooperative.org/journals/ahr/108.5/fields.html

Fordham, S. (1988). Racelessness as a factor in Black students' school success: Pragmatic strategy or pyrrhic victory? *Harvard Educational Review, 58*(1), 54–84.

Fordham, S., & Ogbu, J. (1986). Black students' school success: Coping with the "burden of 'acting White.'" *Urban Review, 18*(3), 176–206.

Foucault, M. (1972). *The archaeology of knowledge* (A. M. Smith, Trans.). New York: Pantheon Books.

Foucault, M. (1977). *Discipline and punish.* (A. Sheridan, Trans.). New York: Vintage Books.

Foucault, M. (1978). *The history of sexuality* (Vol. I; R. Hurley, Trans.). New York: Vintage Books.

Foucault, M. (1980). *Power/knowledge* (C. Gordon, Ed.). New York: Pantheon Books.

Foucault, M. (1982). The subject and power. In H. Dreyfus & P. Rabinow (Eds.), *Michel Foucault: Beyond hermeneutics and structuralism* (pp. 208–226). Brighton, UK: Harvester.

Foucault, M. (1986). *The care of the self* (R. Hurley, Trans.). New York: Vintage Books.

Frankenberg, R. (1993). *White women, race matters: The social construction of Whiteness.* Minneapolis: University of Minnesota Press.

Frankenberg, R. (2001). The mirage of an unmarked Whiteness. In B. Rasmussen, E. Klinenberg, I. Nexica, & M. Wray (Eds.), *The making and unmaking of Whiteness* (pp. 72–96). Durham, NC: Duke University Press.

Fraser, N. (1997). *Justice interruptus.* New York: Routledge.

Freedman, S. W., Weinstein, H., Murphy, K., & Longman, T. (2008). Teaching history after identity-based conflicts: The Rwanda experience. *Comparative Education Review, 52*(4), 663–690.

Freire, P. (1993). *Pedagogy of the oppressed* (M. Ramos, Trans.). New York: Continuum. (Original work published 1970)

Freire, P., & Macedo, D. (1995). A dialogue: Culture, language, and race. *Harvard Educational Review, 65*(3), 377–402.

Fritzman, J. M. (1998). Louis Althusser: Poststructural materialist. In M. Peters (Ed.), *Naming the multiple: Poststructuralism and education* (pp. 49–64). Westport, CT: Bergin & Garvey.

Frow, J. (1994). Marxism and literary history. In T. Eagleton (Ed.), *Ideology* (pp. 295–302). London: Longman.

Gates, H. L., Jr., & Steele, C. (2009). A conversation with Claude Steele: Stereotype threat and Black achievement. *Du Bois Review, 6*(2), 251–271.

Giddens, A. (1986). *The constitution of society.* Berkeley: University of California Press.

Gillborn, D. (2005). Education as an act of White supremacy: Whiteness, critical race theory and education reform. *Journal of Education Policy, 20*(4), 485–505.

Gillborn, D. (2006a). Critical race theory and education: Racism and anti-racism in educational theory and praxis. *Discourse, 27*(1), 11–32.

Gillborn, D. (2006b). Public interest and the interests of White people are not the same: Assessment, education policy, and racism. In G. Ladson-Billings & W. Tate (Eds.), *Education research in the public interest: Social justice, action, and policy* (pp. 173–195). New York: Teachers College Press.

Gillborn, D. (2008). *Racism and education: Coincidence or conspiracy?* New York: Routledge.

Gillborn, D. (2011). The fight against racism and classism. In P. Orelus (Ed.), *Race, class, language, and gender: A dialogue with Noam Chomsky and other leading scholars* (pp. 17–30). Lanham, MD: Rowman & Littlefield.

Gillborn, D., Rollock, N., Vincent, C., & Ball, S. (2012). "You got a pass, what more do you want?": Race, class and gender intersections in the educational experiences of the Black middle class. *Race, Ethnicity & Education, 15*(1), 120–139.

Gilligan, C. (1993). *In a different voice: Psychological theory and women's development.* Boston: Harvard University Press.

Gilroy, P. (1993). *The Black Atlantic.* Cambridge, MA: Harvard University Press.

Gilroy, P. (1998). Race ends here. *Racial and Ethnic Studies, 21*(5), 838–847.

Gilroy, P. (2000). *Against race.* Cambridge, MA: Belknap Press of Harvard University.

Giroux, H. (1988). *Teachers as intellectuals.* Westport, CT: Bergin & Garvey.

Giroux, H. (1992). *Border crossings.* New York: Routledge.

Giroux, H. (1995a). Language, difference, and curriculum theory: Beyond the politics of clarity. In P. McLaren & J. Giarelli (Eds.), *Critical theory and educational research* (pp. 22–38). Albany: State University of New York Press.

Giroux, H. (1995b). Teachers, public life, and curriculum reform. In A. Ornstein & L. Behar (Eds.), *Contemporary issues in curriculum* (pp. 41–49). Boston: Allyn & Bacon.

Giroux, H. (1997a). Racial politics and the pedagogy of Whiteness. In M. Hill (Ed.), *Whiteness: A critical reader* (pp. 294–315). New York: New York University Press.

Giroux, H. (1997b). Rewriting the discourse of racial identity: Towards a pedagogy and politics of Whiteness. *Harvard Educational Review, 67*(2), 285–320.

Giroux, H. (1999). Rethinking cultural politics and radical pedagogy in the work of Antonio Gramsci. *Educational Theory, 49*(1), 1–19.

Giroux, H. (2010). Neoliberalism, pedagogy, and cultural politics: Beyond the theatre of cruelty. In Z. Leonardo (Ed.), *Handbook of cultural politics and education* (pp. 49–70). Rotterdam, The Netherlands: Sense Publishers.

Glazer, N. (1997). *We are all multiculturalists now.* Cambridge, MA: Harvard University Press.

Glazer, N., & Moynihan, P. (1970). *Beyond the melting pot* (2nd ed.). Cambridge, MA: MIT Press.

Goldberg, D. T. (1990). Introduction. In D. T. Goldberg (Ed.), *Anatomy of racism* (pp. xi–xxiii). Minneapolis: University of Minnesota Press.

Goldberg, D. T., & Essed, P. (2002). Introduction: From racial demarcations to multiple identifications. In P. Essed, & D. T. Goldberg (Eds.), *Race critical theories* (pp. 1–11). Malden, MA: Blackwell.

Gotanda, N. (1995). A critique of "Our constitution is color-blind." In K. Crenshaw, N. Gotanda, G. Peller, & K. Thomas (Eds.), *Critical race theory* (pp. 257–275). New York: New Press.

Gottesman, I. (2010). Sitting in the waiting room: Paulo Freire and the critical turn in the field of education. *Educational Studies, 46*(4), 376–399.

Graham, L. J. (2011). The product of text and "other" statements: Discourse analysis and the critical use of Foucault. *Educational Philosophy and Theory, 43*(6), 663–674.

Graham, L. J. (in press). The cost of opportunity. In J. Marshall & L. Stone (Eds.), *The poststructuralism in education handbook*. Rotterdam, The Netherlands: Sense Publishers.

Graham, L. J., & Slee, R. (2008). An illusory interiority: Interrogating the discourse/s of inclusion. *Educational Philosophy and Theory, 40*(2), 277–293.

Gramsci, A. (1971). *Selections from prison notebooks* (Q. Hoare & G. Smith, Eds. & Trans.). New York: International Publishers.

Grande, S. (2004). *Red pedagogy*. Lanham, MD: Rowman & Littlefield.

Grosfoguel, R. (2007). The epistemic decolonial turn: Beyond political-economy paradigms. *Cultural Studies, 21*(2), 211–223.

Guillaumin, C. (1995). *Racism, sexism, power and ideology*. London: Routledge.

Gulson, K. (2011). *Education policy, space and the city: Markets and the (in)visibility of race*. New York: Routledge.

Hacking, I. (1995). The looping effect of human kinds. In D. Sperber, D. Premack, & A. J. Premack (Eds.), *Causal cognition: A multidisciplinary approach* (pp. 351–394). Oxford: Oxford University Press.

Hall, S. (1980). Race, articulation, and societies structured in dominance. In *Sociological theories: Race and colonialism* (pp. 305–345). Paris: UNESCO.

Hall, S. (1996a). On postmodernism and articulation: An interview with Stuart Hall. In D. Morley & K. Chen (Eds.), *Stuart Hall* (pp. 131–150). London: Routledge.

Hall, S. (1996b). The problem of ideology: Marxism without guarantees. In D. Morley & K. Chen (Eds.), *Stuart Hall* (pp. 25–46). London: Routledge.

Hall, S. (1997). Introduction. In S. Hall (Ed.), *Representation: Cultural representations and signifying practices* (pp. 1–11). Thousand Oaks, CA: Sage.

Harding, S. (1991). *Whose science? Whose knowledge?* Ithaca, NY: Cornell University Press.

Harris, A. (2008). From color line to color chart: Racism and colorism in the new century. *Berkeley Journal of African-American Law & Policy, 10*(1), 52–69.

Harris, C. (1995). Whiteness as property. In K. Crenshaw, N. Gotanda, G. Peller, & K. Thomas (Eds.), *Critical race theory* (pp. 276–291). New York: New Press.

Hartmann, D., Gerteis, J., & Croll, P. (2009). An empirical assessment of Whiteness theory: Hidden from how many? *Social Problems, 56*(3), 403–424.

Hartsock, N. (1987). Rethinking modernism: Minority vs. majority theories. *Cultural Critique, 7*(Fall), 187–206.

Hattam, R., & Zembylas, M. (2010). What's anger got to do with it? Towards a post-indignation pedagogy for communities in conflict. *Social Identities, 16*(1), 23–40.

Helms, J. (Ed.). (1991). *Black and White racial identity*. Westport, CT: Greenwood Press.

Herman, E., & Chomsky, N. (2002). *Manufacturing consent: The political economy of the mass media*. New York: Pantheon Books.

Hill, J. (2008). *The everyday language of White racism*. Malden, MA: Wiley-Blackwell.

Hill, M. L. (2009). *Beats, rhymes, and classroom life*. New York: Teachers College Press.

Hirschman, C. (2004). The origins and demise of the concept of race. *Population and Development Review, 30*(3), 385–415.

hooks, b. (1984). *Feminist theory: From margin to center*. Boston: South End Press.

hooks, b. (1992). *Black looks.* Boston: South End Press.

hooks, b. (1996). *Killing rage.* New York: Holt Paperbacks.

hooks, b. (1997). Representing Whiteness in the Black imagination. In R. Frankenberg (Ed.), *Displacing Whiteness* (pp. 165–179). Durham, NC: Duke University Press.

Howard, G. (1999). *We can't teach what we don't know: White teachers, multiracial schools.* New York: Teachers College Press.

Howard, G. (2000). Reflections on the "White movement" in multicultural education. *Educational Researcher, 29*(9), 21–23.

Howard, T. (2010). *Why race and culture matter in schools.* New York: Teachers College Press.

Hughes, S., & North, C. (2012). Beyond popular cultural and structural arguments: Imagining a compass to guide burgeoning urban achievement gap scholars. *Education and Urban Society, 44*(3), 274–293.

Hunter, M. (2005). *Race, gender, and the politics of skin tone.* New York: Routledge.

Huntington, S. P. (1997). *The clash of civilizations and the remaking of world order.* New York: Touchstone.

Ibrahim, A. (2011). Will they ever speak with authority? Race, post-coloniality and the symbolic violence of language. *Educational Philosophy and Theory, 43*(6), 619–635.

Ignatiev, N. (1995). *How the Irish became White.* New York: Routledge.

Ignatiev, N. (1997). *The point is not to interpret Whiteness but to abolish it.* Talk given at the Conference on the Making and Unmaking of Whiteness, University of California, Berkeley. Available at http://racetraitor.org/abolishthepoint.html

Ignatiev, N., & Garvey, J. (1996a). Abolish the White race: By any means necessary. In N. Ignatiev & J. Garvey (Eds.), *Race traitor* (pp. 9–14). New York: Routledge.

Ignatiev, N., & Garvey, J. (1996b). Editorial: When does the unreasonable act make sense? In N. Ignatiev & J. Garvey (Eds.), *Race traitor* (pp. 35–37). New York: Routledge.

Ingram, D. (2005). Toward a cleaner White(ness): New racial identities. *The Philosophical Forum, XXXVI*(3), 243–277.

Jaggar, A., & Rothenberg, P. (Eds.). (1993). *Feminist frameworks* (3rd ed.). Boston: McGraw Hill.

Jameson, F. (1993). Postmodernism and the consumer society. In E. A. Kaplan (Ed.), *Postmodernism and its discontents* (pp. 13–29). New York: Verso.

Jhally, S. (Director & Producer). (1997). bell hooks: Cultural criticism and transformation [Video]. Northampton, MA: Media Education Foundation.

Jocson, K. (2008). *Kuwento* as multicultural pedagogy in high school ethnic studies. *Pedagogies, 3,* 241–253.

Julien, I., & Mercer, K. (1996). De margin and de centre. In D. Morley & K. Chen (Eds.), *Stuart Hall* (pp. 450–464). London: Routledge.

Katz, J. (2006). *The macho paradox.* Naperville, IL: Sourcebooks.

Katz, J. (2010). It's the masculinity, stupid: A cultural studies analysis of media, the presidency and pedagogy. In Z. Leonardo (Ed.), *Handbook of cultural politics and education* (pp. 477–507). Rotterdam, The Netherlands: Sense Publishers.

Kelley, R. (1998). *Yo' Mama's disfunktional! Fighting the culture wars in urban America*. Boston: Beacon Press.

Kincheloe, J. (1993). *Toward a critical politics of teacher training*. Westport, CT: Bergin & Garvey.

Kincheloe, J., & Steinberg, S. (1998). Addressing the crisis of Whiteness: Reconfiguring White identity in a pedagogy of Whiteness. In J. Kincheloe, S. Steinberg, N. Rodriguez, & R. Chennault (Eds.), *White reign* (pp. 3–29). New York: St. Martin's Griffin.

Kincheloe, J., Steinberg, S., Rodriguez, N., & Chennault, R. (Eds.). (1998). *White reign*. New York: St. Martin's Griffin.

King, D. (1993). Multiple jeopardy: The context of a Black feminist ideology. In A. Jaggar & P. Rothenberg (Eds.), *Feminist frameworks* (3rd ed., pp. 220–236). Boston: McGraw Hill.

Kirkland, D. (2010). "Black skin, White masks": Normalizing Whiteness and the trouble with the achievement gap. *Teachers College Record.* Available at www.tcrecord .org/PrintContent.asp?ContentID=16116

Kliebard, H. (1995). *The struggle for the American curriculum, 1893–1958* (2nd ed.). New York: Routledge & Kegan Paul.

Kohli, R., & Solórzano, D. (2012). Teachers, please learn our names! Racial microaggressions and the K–12 classroom. *Race, Ethnicity & Education, 15*(4), 441–462.

Kuhn, T. (1970). *The structure of scientific revolutions.* Chicago: University of Chicago Press.

Laclau, E. (1977). *Politics and ideology in Marxist theory.* London: New Left Books.

Laclau, E., & Mouffe, C. (2001). *Hegemony and socialist strategy.* London: Verso.

Ladson-Billings, G. (1998). From Soweto to the South Bronx: African Americans and colonial education in the United States. In C. Torres & T. Mitchell (Eds.), *Sociology of education: Emerging perspectives* (pp. 247–264). Albany: State University of New York Press.

Ladson-Billings, G. (2004a). Just what is critical race theory and what's it doing in a *nice* field like education. In G. Ladson-Billings & D. Gillborn (Eds.), *The Routledge-Falmer reader in multicultural education* (pp. 49–67). New York: RoutledgeFalmer.

Ladson-Billings (2004b). New directions in multicultural education: Complexities, boundaries, and critical race theory. In J. Banks & C. Banks (Eds.), *Handbook of research on multicultural education* (2nd ed., pp. 50–65). San Francisco: Jossey-Bass.

Ladson-Billings, G. (2005). The evolving role of critical race theory in educational scholarship. *Race, Ethnicity & Education, 8*(1), 115–119.

Ladson-Billings, G. (2007). From the achievement gap to the education debt: Understanding achievement in U.S. schools. *Educational Researcher, 35*(7), 3–12.

Ladson-Billings, G., & Tate, W. F., IV. (1995). Toward a critical race theory of education. *Teachers College Record, 97*(1), 47–68.

Lareau, A. (2000). *Home advantage.* Lanham, MD: Rowman & Littlefield.

Lareau, A. (2003). *Unequal childhoods.* Berkeley: University of California Press.

Lather, P. (2003). Applied Derrida: (Mis)reading the work of mourning in educational research. *Educational Philosophy and Theory, 35*(3), 257–270.

Lave, J., & Wenger, E. (1991). *Situated learning.* Cambridge: Cambridge University Press.

Lee, S. (2005). *Up against Whiteness.* New York: Teachers College Press.

Lenin, V. I. (1963). *What is to be done?* Oxford: Oxford University Press.

Leonardo, Z. (2002). The souls of White folk: Critical pedagogy, Whiteness studies, and globalization discourse. *Race, Ethnicity & Education, 5*(1), 29–50.

Leonardo, Z. (2003). Interpretation and the problem of domination: Paul Ricoeur's hermeneutics. *Studies in Philosophy and Education, 22*(5), 329–350.

Leonardo, Z. (2004a). The color of supremacy: Anti-racist education and White domination. *Educational Philosophy and Theory, 36*(2), 137–152.

Leonardo, Z. (2004b). Critical social theory and transformative knowledge: The functions of criticism in quality education. *Educational Researcher, 33*(6), 11–18.

Leonardo, Z. (2004c). The unhappy marriage between Marxism and race critique: Political economy and the production of racialized knowledge. *Policy Futures in Education, 2*(3&4), 483–493.

Leonardo, Z. (Ed.). (2005a). *Critical pedagogy and race.* Malden, MA: Blackwell.

Leonardo, Z. (2005b). Through the multicultural glass: Althusser, ideology, and race relations in post-civil rights America. *Policy Futures in Education, 3*(4), 400–412.

Leonardo, Z. (2007). The war on schools: NCLB, nation creation, and the educational construction of Whiteness. *Race, Ethnicity & Education, 10*(3), 261–278.

Leonardo, Z. (2009a). Pale/ontology: The status of Whiteness in education. In M. Apple, W. Au, & L. Gandin (Eds.), *Routledge international handbook of critical education* (pp. 123–136). New York: Routledge.

Leonardo, Z. (2009b). *Race, Whiteness, and education.* New York: Routledge.

Leonardo, Z. (2010). Affirming ambivalence: Introduction to cultural politics and education. In Z. Leonardo (Ed.), *Handbook of cultural politics and education* (pp. 1–45). Rotterdam, The Netherlands: Sense Publishers.

Leonardo, Z., & Porter, R. K. (2010). Pedagogy of fear: Toward a Fanonian theory of "safety" in race dialogue. *Race, Ethnicity & Education, 13*(2), 139–157.

Leonardo, Z., & Zembylas, M. (2013). Whiteness as technology of affect: Implications for educational praxis. *Equity & Excellence in Education, 46*(1), 150–165.

Lewis, A. (2003). Some are more equal than others: Lessons on Whiteness from school. In A. Doane & E. Bonilla-Silva (Eds.), *White out* (pp. 159–172). New York: Routledge.

Lewis, O. (1968). The culture of poverty. In D. P. Moynihan (Ed.), *On understanding poverty: Perspectives from the social sciences* (pp. 187–220). New York: Basic Books.

Lipman, P. (2004). *High stakes education: Inequality, globalization, and urban school reform.* New York: RoutledgeFalmer.

Lipsitz, G. (1998). *The possessive investment in Whiteness.* Philadelphia: Temple University Press.

Loewen, J. (1995). *Lies my teacher told me.* New York: New Press.

Lopez, I. H. (2006). *White by law.* New York: New York University Press.

Lorde, A. G. (1984). *Sister outsider.* Freedom, CA: Crossing Press.

Lubienski, S. (2003). Celebrating diversity and denying disparities: A critical assessment. *Educational Researcher, 32*(8), 30–38.

Lugones, M. (2007). Heterosexualism and the colonial/modern gender system. *Hypatia, 22*(1), 186–209.

Lukács, G. (1971). *History and class consciousness* (R. Livingstone, Trans.). Cambridge, MA: MIT Press.

Lynn, M. (1999). Toward a critical race pedagogy: A research note. *Urban Education, 33*(5), 606–626.

Lynn, M., & Dixson, A. (Eds.). (2013). *The handbook of critical race theory in education.* New York: Routledge.

Lynn, M., & Jennings, M. (2009). Power, politics, and critical race pedagogy: A critical race analysis of Black male teachers' pedagogy. *Race, Ethnicity & Education, 12*(2), 173–196.

Lyotard, J. (1984). *The postmodern condition* (G. Bennington & B. Massumi, Trans.). Minneapolis: University of Minnesota Press.

Macedo, D. (2000a). The colonialism of the English-only movement. *Educational Researcher, 29*(3), 15–24.

Macedo, D. (2000b). Introduction to *Pedagogy of the oppressed.* New York: Continuum.

MacLeod, J. (1987). *Ain't no makin' it.* Boulder, CO: Westview Press.

MacSwan, J. (2005). Codeswitching and generative grammar: A critique of the MLF model and some remarks about modified minimalism. *Bilingualism: Language and Cognition, 8*(1), 1–22.

Maldonado-Torres, N. (2007). On the coloniality of being: Contributions to the development of a concept. *Cultural Studies, 21*(2-3), 240–270.

Mandel, E. (1976). Introduction. In K. Marx, *Capital* (Vol. I, pp. 11–86). London: Penguin Books.

Martin, E. (1992). Body narratives, body boundaries. In L. Grossberg, C. Nelson, & P. Treichler (Eds.), *Cultural studies* (pp. 409–423). New York: Routledge.

Marx, K., & Engels, F. (1964). *The communist manifesto.* New York: Washington Square Press.

Marx, K., & Engels, F. (1970). *The German ideology.* New York: International Publishers.

Massey, D., & Denton, N. (1993). *American apartheid.* Cambridge, MA: Harvard University Press.

Matias, C. (2012). Who you callin' White?! A critical counterstory on colouring White identity. *Race, Ethnicity & Education.* doi: 10.1080/13613324.2012.674027

McCarthy, C., & Logue, J. (2010). Re-reading class, re-reading cultural studies, re-reading tradition: Neo-Marxist nostalgia and the remorselessly vanishing pasts. In Z. Leonardo (Ed.), *Handbook of cultural politics and education* (pp. 269–288). Rotterdam, The Netherlands: Sense Publishers.

McGrew, K. (2011). A review of class-based theories of student resistance in education: Mapping the origins and influence of *Learning to labor* by Paul Willis. *Review of Educational Research, 81*(2), 234–266.

McIntosh, P. (1992). White privilege and male privilege: A personal account of coming to see correspondences through work in women's studies. In M. Andersen & P. H. Collins (Eds.), *Race, class, and gender: An anthology* (pp. 70–81). Belmont, CA: Wadsworth.

McIntyre, A. (1997). *Making meaning of Whiteness.* Albany: State University of New York Press.

McIntyre, A. (2000). A response to Rosa Hernandez Sheets. *Educational Researcher, 29*(9), 26–27.

McLaren, P. (1995). *Critical pedagogy and predatory culture: Oppositional politics in a postmodern era.* New York: Routledge.

McLaren, P. (1997). *Revolutionary multiculturalism: Pedagogies of dissent for a new millennium.* Boulder, CO: Westview Press.

McLaren, P. (1998). Whiteness is . . . the struggle for postcolonial hybridity. In J. Kincheloe, S. Steinberg, N. Rodriguez, & R. Chennault (Eds.), *White reign* (pp. 63–75). New York: St. Martin's Griffin.

McLaren, P., Carrillo-Rowe, A., Clark, R., & Craft, P. (2001). Labeling Whiteness: Decentering strategies of White racial domination. In G. Hudak & P. Kihn (Eds.), *Labeling: Pedagogy and politics* (pp. 203–224). New York: Falmer Press.

McLaren, P., Fischman, G., Serra, S., & Antelo, E. (2002). The specter of Gramsci: Revolutionary praxis and the committed intellectual. In C. Borg, J. Buttigieg, & P. Mayo (Eds.), *Gramsci and education* (pp. 147–178). Lanham, MD: Rowman & Littlefield.

McLaren, P., & Torres, R. (1999). Racism and multicultural education: Rethinking "race" and "Whiteness" in late capitalism. In S. May (Ed.), *Critical multiculturalism: Rethinking multicultural and antiracist education* (pp. 42–76). Philadelphia: Falmer Press.

McPeck, J. (1992). Thoughts on subject specificity. In S. Norris (Ed.), *The generalizability of critical thinking* (pp. 198–205). New York: Teachers College Press.

McPhail, M. L. (2003). Race and the (im)possibility of dialogue. In R. Anderson, L. Baxter, & K. Cissna (Eds.), *Dialogue: Theorizing difference in communication studies* (pp. 209–224). Thousand Oaks, CA: Sage.

Memmi, A. (1965). *The colonizer and the colonized.* Boston: Beacon Press.

Miles, R. (2000). Apropos the idea of "race" . . . again. In L. Back & J. Solomon (Eds.), *Theories of race and racism* (pp. 125–143). New York: Routledge.

Mills, C. (1997). *The racial contract.* Ithaca, NY: Cornell University Press.

Mills, C. (1998). *Blackness visible: Essays on philosophy and race.* Ithaca, NY: Cornell University Press.

Mills, C. (2003a). *From class to race: Essays in White Marxism and Black radicalism.* Lanham, MD: Rowman & Littlefield.

Mills, C. (2003b). White supremacy as sociopolitical system: A philosophical perspective. In A. Doane & E. Bonilla-Silva (Eds.), *White out* (pp. 35–48). New York: Routledge.

Milner, H. R., IV. (2010). *Start where you are, but don't stay there.* Cambridge, MA: Harvard University Press.

Mirza, H. (Ed.). (1997). *Black British feminism: A reader.* London: Routledge.

Mirza, H. (2009). Plotting a history: Black and postcolonial feminisms in "new times." *Race, Ethnicity & Education, 12*(1), 1–10.

Moll, L., & Gonzaiez, N. (2004). Engaging life: A funds-of-knowledge approach to multicultural education. In J. Banks & C. Banks (Eds.), *Handbook of research on multicultural education* (2nd ed., pp. 699–715). San Francisco: Jossey-Bass.

Morley, D., & Chen, K. (Eds.). (1996). *Stuart Hall.* London: Routledge.

Morrison, T. (1993). *Playing in the dark: Whiteness in the literary imagination.* New York: Vintage Books.

Moynihan, D. P. (1965). *The Negro family: The case for national action.* Washington, DC: Office of Policy Planning and Research, U.S. Department of Labor.

Nasir, N. (2012). *Racialized identities.* Stanford, CA: Stanford University Press.

Nasir, N. S., & Shah, N. (2011). On defense: African American males making sense of racialized narratives in mathematics education. *Journal of African American Males in Education, 2*(1), 24–45.

Nayak, A. (2006). After race: Ethnography, race and post-race theory. *Ethnic and Racial Studies, 29*(3), 411–430.

Nieto, S. (2003). *Affirming diversity* (4th ed.). New York: Longman.

Noguera, P. (1996). Confronting the urban in urban school reform. *The Urban Review, 28*(1), 1–19.

Noguera, P. (2003). *City schools and the American dream.* New York: Teachers College Press.

North, C. (2006). More than words? Delving into the substantive meaning(s) of "social justice" in education. *Review of Educational Research, 76*(4), 507–535.

Oakes, J. (2005). *Keeping track* (2nd ed.). New Haven. Yale University Press.

Oakes, J., Joseph, R., & Muir, K. (2004). Access and achievement in mathematics and science: Inequalities that endure and change. In J. Banks & C. Banks (Eds.), *Handbook of research on multicultural education* (pp. 69–90). San Francisco: Jossey-Bass.

Oliver, M., & Shapiro, T. (1997). *Black wealth, White wealth: A new perspective on racial inequality.* New York: Routledge.

Omi, M., & Winant, H. (1994). *Racial formation in the United States: From the 1960s to the 1990s* (2nd ed.). New York: Routledge.

Orelus, P. (2011a). *Courageous voices of immigrants and transnationals.* New York: Peter Lang.

Orelus, P. (2011b). Mapping and engaging the debate on race, racism, and other "isms." In P. Orelus (Ed.), *Race, class, language, and gender: A dialogue with Noam Chomsky and other leading scholars* (pp. 1–5). Lanham, MD: Rowman & Littlefield.

Osayande, E. (2010). Word to the wise: Unpacking the White privilege of Tim Wise. Available at www.peopleofcolororganize.com/analysis/word-wise-unpacking -White-privilege-tim-wise/

Park, J., & Park, E. (2005). *Probationary Americans.* New York: Routledge.

Parker, L., & Stovall, D. (2005). Actions following words: Critical race theory connects to critical pedagogy. In Z. Leonardo (Ed.), *Critical pedagogy and race* (pp. 159–174). Malden, MA: Blackwell.

Parker, W. (2011). Constructing public schooling today: Derision, multiculturalism, nationalism. *Educational Theory, 61*(4), 413–432.

Parsons, T. (1959). The school class as a social system: Some of its functions in American society. *Harvard Educational Review, 29*(4), 297–318.

Pedroni, T. (2007). *Market movements: African American involvement in school voucher reform*. New York: Routledge.

Perlstein, D. (2004). *Justice, justice*. New York: Peter Lang.

Peters, M. (2012). *Education, philosophy, and politics*. New York: Routledge.

Pollock, M. (2004). *Colormute*. Princeton, NJ: Princeton University Press.

Popkewitz, T. (1998). *Struggling for the soul: The politics of schooling and the construction of the teacher*. New York: Teachers College Press.

Porter, R. (2012). *Contested humanity: Blackness and the educative remaking of the human in the twentieth century* (Unpublished doctoral dissertation). University of California, Berkeley.

Portes, A., & Rumbaut, R. (2001). *Legacies*. Berkeley: University of California Press.

Prashad, V. (2000). *The karma of brown folk*. Minneapolis: University of Minnesota Press.

Preston, J. (2009). *Whiteness and class in education*. Rotterdam, The Netherlands: Springer.

Preston, J. (2010). Concrete and abstract racial domination. *Power and Education, 2*(2), 115–125.

Pride, R. (2002). *The political use of racial narratives*. Urbana: University of Illinois Press.

Quijano, A. (2000). Coloniality of power, Eurocentrism, and Latin America. *Nepantla, 1*(3), 533–580.

Rains, F. (1997). Is the benign really harmless? Deconstructing some "benign" manifestations of operationalized White privilege. In J. Kincheloe, S. Steinberg, N. Rodriguez, & R. Chennault (Eds.), *White reign* (pp. 77–101). New York: St. Martin's Griffin.

Rich, A. (1993). Compulsory heterosexuality and lesbian existence. In A. Jaggar & P. Rothenberg (Eds.), *Feminist frameworks* (3rd ed., pp. 489–491). Boston: McGraw Hill.

Richardson, M. (1994). *Georges Bataille*. New York: Routledge.

Richardson, T., & Villenas, S. (2000). "Other" encounters: Dances with Whiteness in multicultural education. *Educational Theory, 50*(2), 255–273.

Ricoeur, P. (1986). *Lectures on ideology and utopia* (G. Taylor, Ed.). New York: Columbia University Press.

Rimonte, N. (1997). Colonialism's legacy: The inferiorizing of the Filipino. In M. Root (Ed.), *Filipino Americans* (pp. 39–61). Thousand Oaks, CA: Sage.

Robinson, C. (1993). The production of Black violence in Chicago. In D. Greenberg (Ed.), *Crime and capitalism* (pp. 279–333). Philadelphia: Temple University Press.

Rodriguez, N., & Villaverde, L. (Eds.). (2000). *Dismantling White privilege*. New York: Peter Lang.

Roediger, D. (1991). *The wages of Whiteness*. New York: Verso.

Roediger, D. (1994). *Toward the abolition of Whiteness*. New York: Verso.

Rondilla, J., & Spickard, P. (2007). *Is lighter better? Skin-tone discrimination among Asian Americans*. Lanham, MD: Rowman & Littlefield.

Rose, T. (1994). *Black noise: Rap music and Black culture in contemporary America*. Hanover, NH: Wesleyan University Press.

Rose, T. (2008). *The hip hop wars*. New York: Basic Civitas Books.

Rothenberg, P. (Ed.). (2002). *White privilege: Essential readings on the other side of racism.* New York: Worth Publishers.

Rumbaut, R. (1996). Prologue. In S. Pedraza & R. Rumbaut (Eds.), *Origins and destinies: Immigration, race, and ethnicity in America* (pp. xvi–xix). Belmont, CA: Wadsworth.

Said, E. (1979). *Orientalism.* New York: Random House.

Said, E. (2000). *Reflections on exile.* Cambridge, MA: Harvard University Press.

Sandler, J., & Apple, M. (2010). A culture of evidence, a politics of objectivity: The evidence-based practices movement in educational policy. In Z. Leonardo (Ed.), *Handbook of cultural politics and education* (pp. 325–340). Rotterdam, The Netherlands: Sense Publishers.

San Juan, E., Jr. (1994). Problematizing multiculturalism and the "common culture." *MELUS, 19*(2), 59–84.

San Juan, E., Jr. (2005). From race to class struggle: Marxism and critical race theory. *Nature, Society, and Thought, 18*(3), 333–381.

Scatamburlo-D'Anniballe, V., & McLaren, P. (2004). Class dismissed? Historical materialism and the politics of "difference." *Educational Philosophy and Theory, 36*(2), 183–199.

Shah, N. (2013). Racial discourse in mathematics and its impact on student learning, identity, and participation. Unpublished dissertation. University of California, Berkeley.

Shilling, C. (1992). Reconceptualizing structure and agency in the sociology of education: Structuration theory and schooling. *British Journal of Sociology of Education, 13*(1), 69–87.

Sivanandan, A. (1982). *A different hunger: Writings on Black resistance.* London: Pluto Press.

Sleeter, C. (1993). How White teachers construct race. In C. McCarthy & W. Crichlow (Eds.), *Race, identity, and representation in education* (pp. 157–171). New York: Routledge.

Sleeter, C. (1995). Reflections on my use of multicultural and critical pedagogy when students are White. In C. Sleeter & P. McLaren (Eds.), *Multicultural education, critical pedagogy, and the politics of difference* (pp. 415–437). Albany: State University of New York Press.

Sleeter, C. (2011). Becoming White: Reinterpreting a family story by putting race back into the picture. *Race, Ethnicity & Education, 14*(4), 421–433.

Sleeter, C., & Bernal, D. D. (2004). Critical pedagogy, critical race theory, and antiracist education: Implications for multicultural education. In J. Banks & C. Banks (Eds.), *Handbook of research on multicultural education* (2nd ed., pp. 240–258). San Francisco: Jossey-Bass.

Small, M., Harding, D., & Lamont, M. (2010). Introduction: Reconsidering culture and poverty. *The Annals of the American Academy of Political and Social Science, 629*(1), 6–27.

Smith, D. (1989). *The everyday world as problematic.* Boston: Northeastern University Press.

Smith, L. T. (1999). *Decolonizing methodologies.* London: Zed Books.

Solis, J., Kattan, S., & Baquedano-López, P. (2009). Socializing respect and knowledge in a racially integrated science classroom. *ScienceDirect, 20*(3), 273–290.

Solórzano, D. (1998). Critical race theory, racial and gender microaggressions, and the experiences of Chicana and Chicano scholars. *International Journal of Qualitative Studies in Education, 11*(1), 121–136.

Solórzano, D., & Yosso, T. (2002). Critical race methodology: Counterstorytelling as an analytical framework for education research. *Qualitative Inquiry, 8*(1), 23–44.

Spivak, G. (1988). Can the subaltern speak? In C. Nelson & L. Grossberg (Eds.), *Marxism and the interpretation of culture* (pp. 271–313). Urbana: University of Illinois Press.

Spring, J. (1991). *American education* (5th ed.). New York: Longman.

St. Louis, B. (2002). Post-race/post-politics? Activist-intellectualism and the reification of race. *Ethnic and Racial Studies, 25*(4), 652–675.

Steele, C. (2004). A threat in the air: How stereotypes shape intellectual identity and performance. In J. Banks & C. Banks (Eds.), *Handbook of research on multicultural education* (pp. 682–698). San Francisco: Wiley.

Steinberg, S. (1998). The liberal retreat from race during the post-civil rights era. In W. Lubiano (Ed.), *The house that race built* (pp. 13–47). New York: Vintage Books.

Stovall, D. (2006). Forging community in race and class: Critical race theory, socialist critique, and the quest for social justice in education. *Race, Ethnicity & Education, 9*(3), 243–260.

Sue, S., & Okazaki, S. (1995). Asian American educational achievements: A phenomenon in search of an explanation. In D. Nakanishi & T. Nishida (Eds.), *The Asian American educational experience* (pp. 133–145). New York: Routledge.

Swartz, E. (1992). Emancipatory narratives: Rewriting the master script in the school curriculum. *Journal of Negro Education, 61*(3), 341–355.

Symcox, L. (2002). *Whose history? The struggle for national standards in American classrooms.* New York: Teachers College Press.

Tate, W. F., IV. (1997). Critical race theory and education: History, theory and implications. *Review of Research in Education, 22,* 191–243.

Tatum, B. D. (1997). *Why are all the Black kids sitting together in the cafeteria?* New York: Basic Books.

Taylor, E. (1998). A primer on critical race theory: Who are the critical race theorists and what are they saying? *Journal of Blacks in Higher Education, 19,* 122–124.

Taylor, P. (2008, April 26). *The racial stance: Pragmatism and post-analytic race theory.* Paper delivered at the New Perspectives on Race Theory Conference, University of San Francisco.

Thompson, A. (2003). Tiffany, friend of people of color: White investments in antiracism. *Qualitative Studies in Education, 16*(1), 7–29.

Thompson, J. (1984). *Studies in the theory of ideology.* Berkeley: University of California Press.

Twine, F. W., & Gallagher, C. (2008). The future of Whiteness: A map of the "third wave." *Ethnic and Racial Studies, 31*(1), 4–24.

Valdes, G. (2001). *Learning and not learning English.* New York: Teachers College Press.

Valenzuela, A. (1999). *Subtractive schooling: US-Mexican youth and the politics of caring.* Albany: State University of New York Press.

van den Berghe , P. (1978). *Race and racism* (2nd ed.). New York: Wiley.

Vaught, S. (2011). *Racism, public schooling, and the entrenchment of White supremacy.* Albany: State University of New York Press.

Veblen, T. (1994). *The theory of the leisure class.* New York: Dover.

Villenas, S. (2010). Thinking Latina(o) education with and from Chicana/Latina feminist cultural studies: Emerging pathways–decolonial possibilities. In Z. Leonardo (Ed.), *Handbook of cultural politics and education* (pp. 451–476). Rotterdam, The Netherlands: Sense Publishers.

Volosinov, V. (2006). *Marxism and the philosophy of language.* Cambridge, MA: Harvard University Press.

Vygotsky, L. (1978). *Mind in society* (4th ed). Cambridge, MA: Harvard University Press.

Wacquant, L. (1997). For an analytic of racial domination. *Political Power and Social Theory, 11,* 21–234.

Wacquant, L. (2002). From slavery to mass incarceration: Rethinking the "race question" in the United States. *New Left Review, 13,* 41–60.

Wallerstein, I. (1987). World-systems analysis. In A. Giddens & J. Turner (Eds.), *Social theory today* (pp. 309–324). Cambridge: Polity.

Warmington, P. (2009). Taking race out of scare quotes: Race-conscious social analysis in an ostensibly post-racial world. *Race Ethnicity & Education, 12*(3), 281–296.

Weber, M. (1978a). *Economy and society* (Vol. I; G. Roth & C. Wittich, Eds.; E. Fischoff, H. Gerth, A. M. Henderson, F. Kolegar, C. W. Mills, T. Parsons, M. Rheinstein, G. Roth, E. Shils, & C. Wittich, Trans.). Berkeley: University of California Press.

Weber, M. (1978b). *Economy and society* (Vol. II; G. Roth & C. Wittich, Eds.; E. Fischoff, H. Gerth, A. M. Henderson, F. Kolegar, C. W. Mills, T. Parsons, M. Rheinstein, G. Roth, E. Shils, & C. Wittich, Trans.). Berkeley: University of California Press.

Welner, K. (2006). K–12 race-conscious student assignment policies: Law, social science, and diversity. *Review of Educational Research, 76*(3), 349–382.

Williams, R. (1977). *Marxism and literature.* Oxford: Oxford University Press.

Willis, P. (1977). *Learning to labor.* New York: Columbia University Press.

Wilson, W. J. (1978). *The declining significance of race.* Chicago: University of Chicago Press.

Winant, H. (1997). Behind blue eyes. In M. Fine, L. Weis, L. Powell, & L. Wong (Eds.), *Off White* (pp. 40–53). New York: Routledge.

Winn, M. (2010). "Our side of the story": Moving incarcerated youth voices from margins to center. *Race, Ethnicity & Education, 13*(3), 313–325.

Wise, T. (2007). *White like me: Reflections on race from a privileged son.* New York: Soft Skull Press.

Woodson, C. (2000). *The mis-education of the Negro.* Chicago: African American Images.

Wright, H. (2003). An endarkened feminist epistemology? Identity, difference and the politics of representation in educational research. *Qualitative Studies in Education, 16*(2), 197–214.

Wu, F. (2002). *Yellow.* New York: Basic Books.

Yancey, G. (2003). *Who is White? Latinos, Asians, and the new Black/Nonblack divide.* Boulder, CO: Lynne Rienner.

Yancy, G. (2009). A professor tackles racism in the classroom. *The Chronicle of Higher Education, LVI*(8), B36–B37.

Yosso, T. (2005). Whose culture has capital? A critical race theory discussion of community cultural wealth. *Race Ethnicity & Education, 8*(1), 69–91.

Yosso, T. (2006). *Critical race counterstories along the Chicana/Chicano educational pipeline.* New York: Routledge.

Youdell, D. (2010). *School trouble: Identity, power and politics in education.* London: Routledge.

Young, R. (2006, Winter/Spring). Putting materialism back into race theory: Toward a transformative theory of race. *The Red Critique, 11.* Available at www.redcritique.org/WinterSpring2006/puttingmaterialismbackintoracetheory.htm

Zembylas, M. (2008). *The politics of trauma in education.* New York: Palgrave Macmillan.

Zinn, H. (2005). *A people's history of the United States.* New York: Harper Perennial.

Žižek, S. (1995). Multiculturalism, or, the cultural logic of multinational capitalism. In S. Žižek (Ed.), *Mapping ideology* (pp. 28–51). London: Verso.

Index

About the Author

Zeus Leonardo is associate professor of Education and affiliated faculty of the Critical Theory Designated Emphasis at the University of California, Berkeley. He has published numerous articles, books, and book chapters on critical social analysis of race, including *Race, Whiteness, and Education*; *Handbook of Cultural Politics and Education*; and, with W. Norton Grubb, *Education and Racism.* He has delivered dozens of invited talks, including AESA's endowed keynote, the R. Freeman Butts Lecture. Leonardo's current research interests involve the critical study of ideologies and discourses in education. Much of his work is interdisciplinary and draws insights from sociology, contemporary philosophy, and cultural studies. His research is informed by the premise that educational knowledge should promote the democratization of schools and society.